Second Edition

Cases and Experiential Exercises in Human Resource Management

Raymond L. Hilgert

John M. Olin School of Business
Washington University in St. Louis

Cyril C. Ling

Division of Business Administration and Economics
Illinois Wesleyan University in Bloomington

Recognizing the prior contributions of
Sterling H. Schoen, *Professor Emeritus*
Washington University in St. Louis

Prentice Hall, Upper Saddle River, New Jersey 07458

Library of Congress Cataloging-in-Publication Data

HILGERT, RAYMOND, L.
Cases and experiential execises in human resource management /
RAYMOND L. HILGERT, CYRIL C. LING—2nd ed.
   p. cm
Includes index.
ISBN 0-13-373267-3
1. Personnel management—Problems, exercises, etc.
2. Experiential learning—Problems, exercises, etc.   I. Ling, Cyril
C. (Cyril Curtis) II. Title
HF5549.15.H55   1996
658.3—dc20   95-19369

Acquisitions editor: *Natalie Anderson*
Project manager: *Edie Riker*
Marketing Manager: *Jo-Ann DeLuca*
Cover design: *Bruce Kenselaar*
Buyer: *Vincent Scelta*
Editorial assistant: *Nancy Proyect*

© 1996 by Prentice-Hall, Inc.
A Simon & Schuster Company
Upper Saddle River, New Jersey 07458

Printed in the United States of America

10 9 8 7 6 5 4 3 2 1

ISBN   0-13-373267-3

Prentice-Hall International (UK) Limited, *London*
Prentice-Hall of Australia Pty. Limited, *Sydney*
Prentice-Hall Canada Inc., *Toronto*
Prentice-Hall Hispanoamericana, S.A., *Mexico*
Prentice-Hall of India Private Limited, *New Delhi*
Prentice-Hall of Japan, Inc., *Tokyo*
Simon & Schuster Asia Pte. Ltd., *Singapore*
Editora Prentice-Hall do Brasil, Ltda., *Rio de Janeiro*

Contents

PART TWO
PEOPLE AT WORK

Cases

Experiential Exercises

PART THREE
MANAGING EMPLOYMENT AND PERFORMANCE

Cases

Experiential Exercises

PART FOUR
ISSUES IN MANAGING DIVERSITY

Cases

Experiential Exercises

PART FIVE
COMPENSATION MANAGEMENT

Cases

Experiential Exercises

PART SIX
EMPLOYEE REPRESENTATION AND LABOR RELATIONS   *245*

Cases

Experiential Exercises

Preface

Management has been defined as the process of getting results with and through the efforts of people. Regardless of the working environment or the technical specialties involved, most managers spend a major part of their time working with others and getting results through the efforts of others. This book focuses on problems, issues, policies, and practices related to managing people in working organizations. Its objective is to help the potential or practicing manager to develop the awareness, knowledge, and skills needed to solve human problems and to make appropriate organizational decisions.

Formal education and management training programs have utilized a variety of teaching and learning techniques: lectures, classroom discussions, internships, role playing, simulation, experiential exercises, and case studies. Case studies and experiential exercises have been among the most effective and popular approaches in developing the skills needed for human resource management. These techniques have the advantage of providing students with actual situations experienced by managers in various organizational settings. A case or exercise is usually interesting and challenging because the student is expected to reach a decision in a complex environment—just as though he or she were actually involved in the problem.

Cases and Experiential Exercises in Human Resource Management, Second Edition, presents text material, cases, and experiential exercises. The six-part arrangement of the book is for the convenience of its users, since the pervasiveness of human problems in organizations makes classifications difficult. The title, *Cases and Experiential Exercises in Human Resource Management,* suggests that human resources problems in organizations confront all managers, not only those in staff human resources (or personnel) departments.

Each part begins with brief introductory text material that surveys the topic area and cites laws, issues, and concepts that are prominently identified with that area. The identification of cases and experiential exercises is for the convenience of instructors and students. Each case is a written account of a situation that individuals have actually confronted. It may include not only the facts of the situation but also the feelings, opinions, and prejudices of the individuals involved in the situation, which influenced their actions. In studying a case, students do not read and discuss general theories; they study the facts, feelings, and opinions from which decisions must be made. This requires the study of a realistic situation, analysis of it, and arrival at logical decisions.

Experiential exercises, as we have identified them throughout the book, are sometimes similar to cases, except that they are usually written in a manner that places the reader directly into the problem situation as if he or she were experiencing it. Typically, experiential exercises are written using the second person ("you") or the exercise requires some type of role playing, simulation, project assignment, or problem solving in which the student becomes personally involved in analyzing and attempting to solve the problems at hand.

Fourteen cases and seven experiential exercises (or about 25 percent of the total) are new to this edition. The retained cases and exercises for the most part reflect issues and problems that are timeless in nature. Some have been edited, revised, or updated to maintain their viability and/or to reflect recent contemporary developments. A majority of the cases and exercises involve significant issues that are vital to the employee-employer relationship, such as problems of equal employment opportunity and managing diversity, employee representation, managing employment and work performance, and compensation. Further, the cases and exercises take place not only in business enterprises but also in governmental agencies, educational institutions, and hospitals in recognition of the significant role of the not-for-profit sector of our economy. The environments are varied in nature as well and include manufacturing plants, offices, retail settings, service businesses, and others.

We believe that the book has two primary areas of usefulness. First, it is a convenient and relatively inexpensive set of cases and exercises to supplement the concepts and theory found in most human resource/organizational management textbooks. At the college level, the book is most likely to be utilized as a companion or basic text in courses that emphasize human resources and problem solving. Second, the book can be used in management development seminars and supervisory training programs sponsored by universities and business firms.

Instructors will notice that the cases and exercises are presented without supplementary questions or study suggestions. Each instructor develops his or her own approaches for analysis and discussion. However, we have provided an extensive instructor's manual, which includes an overview of the case method, discussion materials, and suggested questions or approaches pertaining to each case or exercise. The instructor's manual also offers suggestions for role playing, arbitration case simulation, projects, and other unique instructional devices, as appropriate. Also in the instructor's manual are some additional cases that instructors may find useful for examinations and other purposes.

We recognize and appreciate the cooperation of various managers, colleagues, and students who assisted us in developing certain cases and exercises during our teaching and consulting activities. We acknowledge the prior contributions of our long-time colleague at Washington University, the late Dr. Joseph W. Towle, formerly Professor Emeritus of Management. Another former co-author, Dr. Sterling H. Schoen, is similarly recognized on the title page. We gratefully acknowledge the case writers and fellow professors who developed and contributed cases and experiential exercises for this book's collection. On the following pages, we list those (besides ourselves) who contributed cases and exercises.

Finally, we are grateful for the services of the administrative office staff of the John M. Olin School of Business of Washington University—particularly Karen Busch and Leslie Stroker—who word-processed the manuscripts for the book and instructor's manual.

Raymond L. Hilgert
Cyril C. Ling

Contributors

Ayres, Richard M. (FBI Academy): "Neglected Management"

Boyd, Charles W. (Southwest Missouri State University): "The MBO Game with One Player"; "Friction on the MIS Project"; "The Bonus Committee"

Carlson, Arthur E. (Washington University): "The Disabled Student"

Curran, A. Ranger (Keene State College): "The Smoke-Free Office Policy"; "See, We Were Right!"

Denton, D. Keith (Southwest Missouri State University): "The Bonus Committee"

Haimann, Theo (St. Louis University): "A Problem of Tardiness"

Hodgetts, James C. (University of Memphis): "Who Reports to Whom?"; "A Training and Development Problem at Sumerson Manufacturing"; "Atkins, Berry, and Jones vs. The John Rogers Corporation"; "Affirmative Action and Whom to Hire"; "Salary Inequities at Acme Manufacturing"

Hundley, John R. III (Indiana University–South Bend): "The Promotion of Melba Moore"

Hunger, J. David (Iowa State University): "Neglected Management"

Kidwell, Roland E. (Louisiana State University): "'Mentoring' the Sales Force, or Sexual Harassment?"

Kovach, Kenneth A. (George Mason University): "General Physical Condition as an Occupational Qualification"; "Unintentional Prejudice"; "Union Influence on Construction Company Hiring Practices"; "Management Persuasion of Potential Union Members"

PART ONE

Managing Human Resources in Organizations

CASES

EXPERIENTIAL EXERCISES

People working together produce most of the goods consumed in the world today. People working together provide most of the business and institutional services in our economy. The operation of our complex economy involves a multitude of enterprises—all of them based upon people working together.

Organization is the term used to describe groups of people working together to achieve common objectives. An organization may be as planned and formal as a large business corporation, or as informal as a picnic or fishing trip. Regardless of purpose or size, an association of individuals for the attainment of common goals is an organization.

Any organization will be more effective in pursuing its goals and objectives if the efforts of the people within the enterprise are properly directed and coordinated. In most business organizations, the direction and coordination of the efforts of others is a major component of the management's responsibilities. Every supervisor, foreman, or executive is a manager in the area of his or her responsibility. To a considerable degree, a manager's success depends on a capacity to understand how people work together and an ability to use this understanding to teach, coach, and guide the efforts of people to achieve desired objectives.

Some managers seem to be gifted with an ability to plan and organize work and to direct others without consciously knowing the "how" and "why" of their accomplishments. Other managers achieve such success only through careful and thorough study of organizational and human relationships. Nevertheless, most managers are able to improve their effectiveness by increasing their understanding of behavioral concepts of management and organization, such as the needs of people at work and how people can become more motivated to work together and to improve results.

Managerial job titles are not standardized and may have special meanings in certain organizations. In the broad sense, all supervisors, foremen, executives, and administrators are managers. Any individual is a manager when he or she has authority for the work of others and is responsible for their activities and the operations of an organization, company, or division.

THE NATURE OF HUMAN RESOURCE MANAGEMENT

Although managers are responsible for many resources, this book of cases and experiential exercises primarily concerns the management of people—that is, the *function* of *human resource management*. Some writers use the dual term *personnel/human resource management* to identify this managerial function, which focuses on planning, organizing, staffing, leading, controlling, and coordinating the activities of human resources (the personnel) in a working organization.

Although human resource management is recognized as a basic managerial responsibility that permeates virtually all management levels and activities, there are conflicting views concerning its scope and goals. Some authorities emphasize that human resource management should have as its primary objective the accomplishment of productive and profitable work, with a secondary concern for individual and group needs. Managers and writers who are mostly "bottom-line focused," "production-centered," and the like are usually associated with this view. However, other authorities believe that human resource management should include the recognition of individual worth and opportunities for the realization of individual potential within an organization. Much organizational behavior theory and research emphasizes the *human relations* approach, one that suggests that both the needs of individuals and those of employers can be met satisfactorily in organizational work environments.

Although it is difficult to define the exact scope of human resource management, we believe that *human resource management primarily consists of those management functions and activities related to the acquisition, development, and maintenance of human resources in a working organization. Further, successful human resource management implies that these functions and activities utilize the efforts of people with the other resources of an organization in such a manner that the objectives of the organization and the goals of individuals in the organization are attained to the highest degree compatible with the work situation.*

LOOKING INTO THE NEW MILLENNIA

For many companies and organizations, a return to policies and practices that are consistent with such a long-term human resource management philosophy is not imminent. Today's managers are under intense pressure to achieve economic and financial results, typically in a short-term time frame. Nevertheless, the management of people continues to be a demanding and challenging managerial responsibility. Managers must continually assess situations and events that reflect the dynamic nature of their operations as they are interrelated with those of an increasingly complex global business environment. The rate of change continues to accelerate. Firms throughout the country constantly seek ways to automate and improve production and other processes. Much clerical and administrative work is being done with computers and word processors. Expansion, acquisition, and disposal of facilities, buildings, and equipment are continually occurring events. New markets, new products, and changing processes place ever-increasing demands on organizations for the efficient utilization and sometimes reduction of human resources as well as physical and financial resources.

These and other dynamic developments compel human resource managers to ask and study such questions as: How can job satisfaction be provided for employees in the face of the rising expectations of people in a complex society? What motivational forces will be of primary concern to employees as societal values change and become less work-centered? Can drastic changes in production and operations be planned with sufficient sophistication to minimize serious harm to the workforce? Will work groups be developed that are flexible enough to permit reorganization and transfers within evolving organizational units? What long-range training and development programs will be required for the movement and upgrading of employees because of new demands for professional, technical, and managerial skills? What is management's responsibility for the welfare of workers who are displaced or adversely affected by change? Does management have responsibility beyond legal requirements in such areas as employee safety, health, welfare, pension benefits, and equal employment opportunity? To these complex questions can be added a growing list of increasingly specialized concerns such as freedom of speech in the workplace, privacy and confidentiality, and quality of the physical work environment.

The cases and experiential exercises of this first part of the book are representative of the many diverse issues and problems that confront managers of human resources, whether they are line managers or staff specialists in HR departments. The following Domain Statement of the Personnel/Human Resources Division of the Academy of Management also provides an overview of the multidimensional areas of the human resource management function that are reflected throughout all of the six parts of this book's collection of cases and exercises.

Domain Statement of the Personnel/Human Resources Division of the Academy of Management

The Personnel/Human Resources (P/HR) Division of the Academy of Management welcomes into its membership and activities scholars and practitioners who share an interest in human work organizations and the employment of human resources in these organizations for effective realization of social, economic, and individual goals. Comfortable within our ranks would be any and all persons whose studies and/or work activities are focused on one or more of the following:

1. The design of work organizations and their policies and procedures for effective economic utilization of human resources and the realization of human social goals.
2. The development, allocation, motivation, and performance of individuals as human resources in work organizations.
3. The administration and governance of work activities through such means as collective bargaining, industrial councils, and other forms of employee participation.

The Academy of Management is a professional organization of scholars and practitioners of management disciplines. The Personnel/Human Resources Division is one of the professional disciplines in the Academy.

4. The formulation, application, and evaluation of public policy intended to impact on the utilization of human resources in work organizations, including EEO.

A suggested, although evolving and thus by no means exhaustive, list of projects that would be of interest to P/HR Division members would include:

1. The role and experiences of personnel/human resources managers in work organizations, recognizing that all managers have P/HR responsibilities.
2. The methods by which personnel/human resource policies, programs, and procedures are decided upon, adopted, implemented, managed, and evaluated. Specific areas of concern here would include: human resource forecasting and planning; organization planning and design; task and team organization; staffing (recruiting, selection, internal allocations, and separations); training and development; career planning and development; compensation (including benefits and services); job analysis and job design; performance appraisal; EEO/AA; health and safety; human resource information systems; union-management relations.
3. The impact of P/HR activities, or changes in P/HR activities, on such individual and group outcomes as: productivity and/or performance, employee motivation, employee ability, attendance (or absenteeism), length of service (or turnover), occupational health and safety, job satisfaction, and organizational commitment.
4. The nature of legislative and related social developments relevant to the design and administration of P/HR policies, programs, and procedures and their impact. Included here would be such factors as labor legislation, EEO/AA legislation and guidelines, OSHA, ERISA, retirement legislation, and the like.

The study and practice of P/HR management draws on a number of basic disciplines, including psychology, sociology, economics, statistics and law, as well as related fields, most notably organizational behavior, which draw upon some of the same disciplines. Further, the field of P/HR cuts across several levels of analysis: the individual employee, work groups, the organization, and the environment. It is difficult, therefore, to differentiate the field from other, more basic areas from which it draws and to which it contributes concepts, methods, and methodologies. Perhaps our uniqueness, if indeed any such claim can be made, lies in our focus on human resources in employment settings, our interdisciplinary nature, and our concern for multiple levels of analysis.

Unfortunately, P/HR currently can lay claim to no unified, generally accepted theoretical framework. At present the field is an emerging blend of theory, research, and practice dedicated to the development of supportable generalizations which contribute to understanding, as well as influencing, and eventually solving the issues and problems inherent in the employer-employee relationship.

McCormic-McCann Company:
Changes under a Corporate Takeover

BACKGROUND

The McCormic-McCann Company, a Minnesota-based, family-owned maker of industrial controls, was recently acquired by American Electronics Corporation (AEC). The new corporate management quickly initiated a comprehensive review of its acquisition to evaluate managerial staff quality and performance. One focus of the review was McCormic-McCann's twelve-year-old assembly facility in Union Point, a town of about 5,000 people in southwest Minnesota. The small size of Union Point tended to make for generally low wage rates in the community. However, the McCormic-McCann Company had been paying wages that were about 25 to 30 percent higher than the "going wages" in maintaining its workforce of some 200 to 225 employees.

The new corporate strategy included appointing and developing a staff of managers that would be capable of meeting goals that American Electronics had set for its new subsidiary to improve its productivity and reduce its costs. Prior to the takeover, the managers at Union Point had been relatively comfortable in their positions, often failing to recognize areas that needed improvement. The new plant manager, Joe Simon, who was appointed by American Electronics, commented, "We need managers and supervisors who are constantly looking for ways to improve our profitability. If we stand still, we are actually losing ground."

RECRUITMENT AND TRAINING OF SUPERVISORS

In the past, McCormic-McCann had selected all of its supervisors from the hourly employees. However, the new plant manager decided to try something different. Jon Andrews, a college graduate, was transferred to supervision from engineering. Jon had a bachelor's degree and a master's degree in industrial technology as well as the "people skills" required in the supervisory position. He was well-accepted by the employees, and he was able to take some steps toward improving profitability. Because this transfer within the company worked out well, another college graduate was recruited to join the supervisory staff. After five interviews over a four-month period, Wendy Shaw, a business management major, was hired at the Union Point plant as a department supervisor.

All names are disguised.

Jon and Wendy were not the only college-trained supervisors at the plant. Joe Simon, the plant manager, had a B.S. in industrial technology. Patrick Scorn, the human resources manager, who came to Union Point with Joe Simon, had a B.A. in political science. Rick McDonald, a sectional supervisor, and George Rush, the plant engineer, had engineering degrees. The general manager, Stanley Carter, had a B.S.B.A. degree in finance. He worked primarily at the headquarters in Cascade but made occasional visits to Union Point.

The remainder of the managers and supervisors at Union Point were high school graduates. Jan Whitney and Tim Jones had been promoted to section manager positions from their assignments as first-line supervisors. Seven other first-line supervisors had been promoted from their hourly positions (see Exhibit C–1A).

EXHIBIT C–1A   Organizational Chart for McCormic–McCann Company (Union Point)

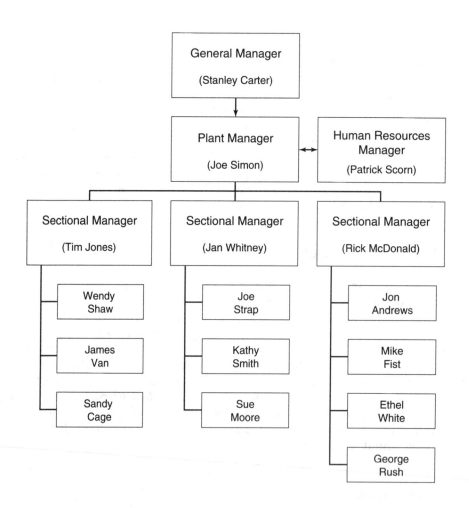

The first-line supervisors had received very little training before they began their jobs. When Jon Andrews was transferred to first-line supervision, he was given three days' notice of his new assignment. Although he welcomed the opportunity, Jon received his only training on the job. When Wendy Shaw began with the company two years ago, she was sent to a three-week "training program" at the company headquarters in Cascade. The program included discussions about "Dressing for Success" and "How to Give a Formal Presentation," and several technical product presentations were given by each of the company's divisions. However, this program did not include supervisory management training, because Wendy Shaw was the only person in a class of forty-eight who was in a supervisory position. The majority of the attendees were in engineering and sales. Jon Andrews was originally scheduled to attend the training program with Wendy, but he was forced to cancel at the last minute because of pressures from production requirements.

All of the remaining supervisors had received little training for their positions before they began. The previous plant manager had often said they received a "baptism by fire." As a result of this approach, some of the supervisors had difficulty making the transition from "hourly" to "management." However, when technical problems arose for the supervisors, they sometimes were sent to appropriate training programs—if the production schedule permitted their absence.

PERFORMANCE EVALUATION

The company's management had long operated under a type of "management by objectives" program. Each supervisor was to sit down annually with his or her manager and establish objectives. Among the items discussed were productivity improvements and cost-reduction goals.

The performance-appraisal system centered upon the objectives set at the beginning of the year. Depending on how well supervisors met their objectives, they would receive a rating of "unsatisfactory," "poor," "satisfactory," "good," "excellent," or "outstanding." The rating was the primary factor in determining a supervisor's merit increase. In the ten years prior to the takeover by American Electronics, no supervisor had received a rating of "outstanding," but virtually all of the supervisors received ratings of "excellent" or "good."

However, after the takeover by AEC, upper management began to be more demanding of the first-line supervisors at performance-appraisal time. As a result, a supervisor's rating could easily drop from "good" in one year to "poor" in the next year, even if the supervisor had maintained about the same level of performance. Several supervisors experienced this drastic change in evaluation, and all of the supervisors became increasingly insecure in their jobs. Two supervisors and several salaried staff persons were fired by management as a result of poor performance reviews. All of these individuals had been with the company for ten or more of the company's fifteen years of existence.

To add to the stress of the performance appraisals, sectional managers were typically late in performing the appraisal reviews. This waiting period made the first-line supervisors even more nervous because they feared that their reviews would be substandard. Several supervisors had to wait two to three months after the annual review date to receive their reviews.

Although the results of the reviews were not public knowledge, the "rumor mill" was very effective in communicating the "conclusion" that only college-educated and extremely dedicated supervisors would receive acceptable reviews from now on.

COMPENSATION

The compensation policy for first-line supervisors included a base salary plus compensation for overtime hours worked. "Overtime" was considered anything more than eight hours a day. However, overtime compensation for first-line supervisors was "straight time" rather than the "time and a half" for hourly workers.

The necessity of overtime in a department was determined by the supervisor. Because the plant was set up in a "job shop" format, it was difficult to judge exactly when overtime was required. As a result, a supervisor's decision to work overtime was rarely disputed by upper management. Although some situations did require overtime, a supervisor could reduce department overtime by scheduling work more efficiently or by implementing cost-reducing productivity improvements. Eager to make some changes in productivity, Jon Andrews and Wendy Shaw had worked diligently to make their departments run more efficiently. As a result, overtime in their departments was reduced, but this meant a reduction for their own paychecks as well.

Because of the obvious compensation advantage, employees exerted considerable pressure to work a substantial amount of overtime each week. Because the majority of supervisors had previously been hourly employees, they could easily relate to this attitude. In addition, there were no clear performance standards for hourly employees. Most employees knew the range of "acceptable performance" for their jobs, and some were known to work at the lower end of their range if they felt they were not receiving enough overtime.

Supervisors generally could make more money by working overtime than by receiving a superior performance review. If a supervisor performed well enough to keep his or her job, he or she was financially better off to maintain a steady overtime schedule. It was not uncommon for a supervisor to average ten to fifteen hours of overtime per week. Exhibits C–1B and C–1C outline two alternatives for a supervisor receiving a base salary of $31,200 (or $15.00 per hour).

EXHIBIT C–1B Merit Increase Alternative

RATING ON EVALUATION	ANNUAL PERCENTAGE INCREASE	ANNUAL DOLLAR EQUIVALENT	WEEKLY DOLLAR EQUIVALENT
Unsatisfactory	0	0	0
Poor	0	0	0
Satisfactory	2	624	12
Good	5	1,560	30
Excellent	7	2,184	42
Outstanding	10	3,120	60

EXHIBIT C–1C Overtime Premium Alternative

OVERTIME HOURS PER WEEK	ANNUAL DOLLAR EQUIVALENT	WEEKLY DOLLAR EQUIVALENT
2	1,560	30
5	3,900	75
10	7,800	150
12	9,360	180
15	11,700	225

RECENT DEVELOPMENTS

In the time since the company was acquired by American Electronics, McCormic-McCann had gone through numerous changes. Further, the company had not given an hourly wage increase to employees for two years in a row. Stanley Carter, the general manager, had left to work for one of McCormic-McCann's suppliers. Rick McDonald had requested to be transferred from his sectional manager position back to engineering; a manager from corporate headquarters was to replace him. Wendy Shaw decided to leave the company for other opportunities.

With all of the above in mind, Jon Andrews had become extremely frustrated with the inconsistency between management philosophy and management practices. Despite Jon's efforts at improving his department's productivity and efficiency, he had received only token salary increases since American Electronics had taken over the company. Andrews realized that he needed to make a personal decision soon. He had a wife and two small children to support, and he felt that his income at McCormic-McCann was far below his needs and expectations. Jon believed that he would have no difficulty in obtaining employment elsewhere at a higher salary, but he was reluctant to leave McCormic-McCann at this time. Jon Andrews decided that he would request a meeting with Patrick Scorn, the human resources manager, to discuss his own and the company's situations.

CASE-2

Turnover in the Bank

The Conservative State Savings Bank was a medium-sized bank located in a large southern city. A sizeable unit of the bank's operation was the check processing department. The employees in this department, who served as check-reader operators, were all women between the ages of eighteen and forty. The women fed checks into the check readers and manually input any "defective checks" into a computerized proofing system. The machines were the latest models and were spaced approximately 3 to 4 feet apart. There were about thirty check-reader operators; the other departmental employees were clerks and word and data processors who were connected with the check-collection process. In total, about forty women worked together in the same large room. There were four supervisors in the department, all of whom were women. These supervisors reported to Jennifer Szorba, a middle-level manager who had several other departments under her responsibility.

The bank had been experiencing an annual turnover rate in the check processing department of about 40 percent. This turnover rate had been steadily rising over the previous few years despite efforts by management to stem the trend. With turnover of this magnitude, efficiency had been greatly reduced.

IDENTIFYING THE PROBLEM

Juanita Nelson, a young staff employee in the human resources department, was assigned by Marvin Vanderber, Vice President for Operations of the bank, to investigate the situation. Top management hoped that Nelson might obtain better insights into the problems that existed in the check processing department and suggest ways of dealing with them.

As a first step, Juanita Nelson decided to choose a sample of former departmental employees who, for various reasons, had either left the bank voluntarily or who had been discharged within the preceding six months. She hoped to interview these ex-employees and to encourage them to speak objectively about their past jobs. Nelson selected a sample of ten former employees, but she was able to interview only six of them.[1] The remaining four had either changed addresses or were not available because of circumstances or personal reasons.

All names are disguised.
[1]See Exhibit C–2 for additional informtion concerning each former employee who was interviewed.

INTERVIEW INFORMATION

The types of questions Juanita Nelson asked during the interviews were meant to allow the former employees ample freedom to discuss their situations. By prearranged appointments, she interviewed these women either in their homes or at a nearby restaurant.

Jane Caldwell. According to bank personnel records, Jane Caldwell had resigned from her job "to remain at home." Caldwell stated that she had liked her job for the first two and one-half years of the three years of her employment. The thing she disliked most was that she had become totally bored with the routine of her job, and she felt that there was no hope of ever moving to a different department. On several occasions, she had mentioned to her supervisor her desire to get out of the check processing department, but Caldwell felt that her supervisor did not take her seriously. This was the major complaint she had concerning this supervisor.

According to Caldwell, one of her sources of difficulty had been that she was receiving a considerably higher salary than most of the employees in the department. Some of her co-workers knew about her higher salary and resented the fact that they were not paid as well. In fact, every time Caldwell received a raise, it seemed as if everyone knew about it before she was notified. Caldwell did not know how the others found out about her pay raises, but she alluded to the possibility that the departmental supervisors had let the information escape.

Pertaining to the bank's overall attitude toward its employees, Jane Caldwell believed that the bank regarded her as a number. She felt that the supervisors were too busy to help when problems came up. As a result, she felt that most of the employees in the department had very low morale and were concerned only with "putting in their time" and receiving a regular raise. None of them had more than the minimum amount of pride or loyalty toward their employer. When Caldwell was first employed, there seemed to be some hope and competition for advancement. But now she felt that only a few employees—"the ones who only worked hard when the boss was looking"—competed solely to appear that they did a good job. And, she added, since there was no real competition, the jobs became exceptionally boring.

Alice Wendell. Alice Wendell had told her supervisor that she was resigning "to seek other employment closer to home." However, her interview with Juanita Nelson seemed to suggest other motivations. Wendell stated that she had "hated" her job. Work schedules were a major reason for her dissatisfaction. The daily schedule was from 8 A.M. to 5 P.M., but during the afternoons, no scheduled break time was allowed. Further, Saturday work was required every third weekend. As far as the supervisors were concerned, they were not particularly helpful. In fact, on several occasions when Wendell had gone to her supervisor for help, she felt as if the supervisor gave her any kind of answer just "to get me off her back." Wendell thought that the departmental supervisors generally favored a few of the employees and that they were uninterested in helping the others. As a result, these "favored employees" were the ones who received the more frequent raises, even when they did not deserve them.

When asked about her impressions of the bank's overall attitude toward employees, Alice Wendell said that the employees "were nothing but numbers like in the computers." However, she inserted at this point an exception to her statement. Wendell had been told by one of her supervisors that she should contribute to an annual community charity fund. The supervisor implied that she had to give to this fund or her job might be in jeopardy. Wendell resented this type of coercion, and she said that only when the bank had something to gain was it aware of employees as individuals.

Bernice Ritchey.   Bernice Ritchey left the employment of the bank for maternity reasons. However, she, too, had some interesting comments to make in her interview. Ritchey had enjoyed her job except for the "tensions" it created and the Saturday work. Her opinion was that the supervisors were the greatest cause of discontent within the department and were responsible for most of the problems. Ritchey stated that the supervisors tended to unduly criticize employees and that they constantly made the employees feel inferior and uneasy. When asked about pay for her job, Bernice Ritchey claimed that while the bank's pay scale had risen somewhat, it was still very low and some of the new incoming employees received higher wages by comparison to the older ones. The result was that the new and inexperienced person could come in at virtually the same salary as those who had been at the bank for several years. This brought about resentment. Further, Ritchey felt that although the bank claimed that raises were based mainly on merit, an employee could do the best job possible and yet go unnoticed and not rewarded. She asserted that the bank always put itself first, and any concern for the well-being of the employees was of low priority. Since only a few of the departmental employees looked for advancement, most of them just did their routine jobs with little pride and without commitment.

Ruth Mentler.   Ruth Mentler was another case of resignation for maternity reasons. However, she, too, had not been happy with her job. She disliked the Saturday shifts, although she realized that someone had to do the work. In her opinion, the supervisors were usually too busy to take an interest in complaints or problems the employees might have. When a supervisor did offer assistance, it was always "my way or no way." Ruth Mentler thought that the supervisors had too much to do to give individual attention to employees. Most of Mentler's comments were similar to the first three interviewees' statements regarding attitudes of the employees and the bank's attitudes toward the employees. Mentler also mentioned that the situation on pay raises was common knowledge and a source of considerable discontent.

Gloria Sheetz. Glória Sheetz had resigned her position at the bank, but she actually was "forced" into this since she had knowledge of the fact that the bank planned "to let me go" due to alleged unsatisfactory attendance. Sheetz stated that she, too, disliked the long hours which often arose. Someone had to stay until the work was finished each evening, and, in many cases, this meant considerable overtime. The uncertainty of hours made the job "unbearable" to Gloria. When she tried to make suggestions that she felt might help conditions within the department, she was told by her supervisor that it was not her role to suggest changes. Sheetz said she could not remember ever hearing a supervisor compliment an employee, even when an employee was doing more than what she was told to do. It was only when someone committed an error that the employee heard from a supervisor.

Gloria Sheetz acknowledged that the bank's physical working conditions were good in general. The other employees were enjoyable to work with, but the supervisors in the department were the greatest source of employee dissatisfaction. The supervisors, she felt, were out to make themselves look good to their manager at the expense of the employees. As an example, she cited the incident concerning the "forced contributions" to the charitable fund. In Gloria's opinion, the supervisors wanted it to look as if there had been 100 percent cooperation of the employees relative to giving. Most of the time, "We were treated like dirt under the supervisors' feet," as far as Gloria was concerned. Quite frequently, supervisors had told various employees that their attitudes were "poor." She had suggested to a human resources staff person that the bank should give the supervisors training in human relations, rather than just training them to be competent on the technical aspects of the job. This suggestion was ignored.

Gloria Sheetz felt that a union was needed for this department of the bank. However, one day when she and some of her co-workers were discussing the merits of unions, a supervisor overheard the discussion. The supervisor proceeded to tell them that if management ever discovered that any of them had responded to a union's attempt to organize the bank, they would lose their jobs. Gloria also mentioned the matter of pay-raise information "leaking" throughout the department. She felt that this was another cause of resentment within the department.

Linda Ligon. Linda Ligon "resigned" for reasons similar to those of Gloria Sheetz. Ligon also disliked her job, saying that employees in the check processing department were treated as if they were located in the bank's "ghetto." She added, "It is the lowest department in the bank, and even those in other departments consider it as such."

As far as Linda was concerned, the worst problem was the supervision. She was even afraid to approach her supervisor, who never issued compliments, just complaints. Right before she left the bank, Linda was told that her attitude was bad. This only made matters worse. Linda felt that the reason her supervisor thought her attitude was bad was because she merely tried to be

EXHIBIT C–2 Interviewee Backgrounds

EMPLOYEE	AGE	RACE	MARITAL STATUS	PERIOD OF EMPLOYMENT	MONTHLY RATE OF PAY	STATED REASON FOR LEAVING BANK
Jane Caldwell	24	W	M	3 years	$1,665	RESIGNED: to stay home
Alice Wendell	20	W	M	1 year	$1,255	RESIGNED: to seek employment closer to home
Bernice Ritchey	32	B	M	1 year	$1,550	RESIGNED: pregnancy
Ruth Mentler	22	W	M	3 years	$1,470	RESIGNED: pregnancy
Gloria Sheetz	19	B	S	1 year	$1,255	RESIGNED: unsatisfactory attendance
Linda Ligon	19	W	S	2 years	$1,340	RESIGNED: unsatisfactory attendance

"honest" with the supervisors. Ligon said that she wasn't reluctant to speak her mind, and she often complained when she felt it was necessary.

WHAT SHOULD BE DONE?

After reflecting on these interviews, Juanita Nelson pondered what actions and/or recommendations she should make to higher management of Conservative State Savings Bank. She wondered if she should first interview the supervisors for their opinions, or whether this would primarily be a waste of time, with the supervisors only attempting to blame the employees for the department's shortcomings.

Travers Hospital: The Human Resources Department Secretary

BACKGROUND

Travers, Ohio, is considered primarily an agricultural community with several medium-sized manufacturing plants. The only hospital facility immediately accessible to the town's thirty thousand inhabitants was Travers Community Hospital, which had 190 beds. At the time of this case, this hospital employed approximately 530 full-time employees, a large percentage of whom were born and raised in the Travers area.

Kenneth Warner, administrator, came to Travers Hospital three years ago from a much larger hospital located in a major city in northern Ohio where he had been the administrator for about eight years. A man in his early forties, Warner felt that at a community hospital in a smaller town he would have the opportunity to manage and control the operations of the hospital more personally. Warner sought to please as many of the employees as possible, and therefore he was very sensitive to comments made by hospital employees related to the administration's style of management.

Herbert Lyon, human resources manager, was also relatively new to Travers Hospital, having arrived only a year and a half earlier from a personnel job at an industrial plant in a nearby town. Mr. Lyon made it a daily practice to walk through the hospital, once in the morning and once in the afternoon, stopping briefly to talk with various employees. Lyon believed this to be a good way of "getting a feel" for what the employees were thinking and that this would enable them to get to know him better. He came to understand very well the unusual closeness that existed among many of the hospital's employees, who were long-time residents of Travers.

Nancy Columbus was very much a part of the hospital's "family atmosphere." She had been raised on a farm just outside of Travers, and she and her husband had decided to settle in the area. Nancy came to work at the hospital some years earlier, shortly after she was married, to help her husband finance their own rodeo show that they took on weekend tours.

Nancy had received secretarial training in high school and was a proficient typist and word processor. However, Nancy's first job at the hospital was as a receptionist and switchboard operator. She was a very talkative person, and she enjoyed her work, especially because she was able to keep in touch with all the "grapevine news." After working in this position for about two years, Nancy decided to apply for one of the clerical positions in the human

---

All names are disguised.

resources department. She was very happy when she received the position because it paid more than her previous position. She was very good at her work, which consisted primarily of general clerical duties related to employee records and compensation. After two years in this job, Nancy was promoted to the position of secretary to Herbert Lyon. Nancy was thrilled with her promotion not only because of the increase in her salary but also because she was now permitted to sit in on the biweekly executive management meetings at which she took minutes for the management group, which consisted of Mr. Warner, Mr. Lyon, and six major department heads. Nancy had always wondered what these meetings were like, and now she was able to be part of them.

THE PROBLEM

Nancy Columbus's position in the human resources department enabled her to stay in close communication with many of her employee friends. Nancy was known throughout the hospital as being "softhearted" and always "sticking up for the underdog." Because of her reputation, from time to time her friends would drop by her office with their various complaints about low wages, short vacations, denied loan applications, and anything else not to their liking. Usually they would ask Nancy if there was something she could do to help them. Nancy enjoyed the fact that many of the employees came directly to her in this manner, and at times she felt very much like a "mother hen" to these people. For the most part, she would bring any employee complaints that she received to Mr. Lyon on behalf of that employee. Lyon was very patient with Nancy when she acted in this manner, but after a while he told Nancy that instead of her becoming involved in employee complaints, she should arrange an appointment for anyone who wished to discuss their concerns with him privately. Nancy decided not to follow Lyon's suggestion, for she feared that doing so would cause many of the employees to no longer confide in her. As time went on, Nancy referred only those employees who specifically asked to see Mr. Lyon, and to all others she offered her own suggestions and advice.

During this particular summer, a local union representative made contact with the hospital employees. This was a new experience for practically all the employees. News of the union's organizing activities quickly reached Mr. Warner's office, and, subsequently, reports of union contacts became a top issue discussed in the biweekly executive management meetings. The members of the administrative team were hoping the employees would not join a union, and they discussed various strategies by which they "hoped to keep the union out." Nancy Columbus became very puzzled over this attitude on the part of hospital administration. Did they not want to help the employees? The more the topic was discussed, the more Nancy came to believe that the hospital managers had no intention of helping the hospital's employees achieve some of the benefits they desired and that management would rather ignore the employees. Maybe a union was needed to force management to listen, thought Nancy. She kept her thoughts to herself, however, during the management meetings she attended.

A week of so later, as Kenneth Warner, the administrator, came to work one morning, he was greeted in the halls with repeated glares from many of the employees. When he arrived at his office, his secretary announced to him that the hospital was just filled with rumors that "management was out to get the employees who wanted a union, and that management would close the hospital if necessary to prevent the employees from unionizing." Warner became worried, and he wondered what he or any of the other members of the management group had done to create such an idea in the employees' minds. Within a few minutes, Herbert Lyon walked into Mr. Warner's office with the answer. Earlier that morning, Lyon had overheard his secretary, Nancy Columbus, discussing the union situation with a fellow employee on the telephone. Lyon said, "Many of the things Nancy was telling this woman were distorted excerpts of what we were discussing in yesterday's management meeting. I don't think she was distorting what we said on purpose. She just doesn't understand the way in which management must operate."

Lyon undertook an investigation to learn more about Nancy's possible involvement in the situation. He asked her to come into his office, where the following conversation took place.

LYON: Nancy, I'm troubled by the hostile employee attitude that I and other management people encountered in the hospital today. Can you tell me anything about it?

Nancy: Well, Mr. Lyon, they have a right to be hostile after what you, Mr. Warner, and others said about their attempts to organize a union and the requests they are making. After all, those people need some sort of protection against the outrageous and arbitrary demands made on them by some of the doctors, nurses, and supervisors around here!

Besides, their request for a 10-percent wage increase, increased medical benefits, better restrooms, laboratories, and improved pensions are only fair. Even with a 10-percent increase, they will be making only about 75 percent of what people working in the other two companies in town are making.

You and Mr. Warner said terrible things about two of the employees who are trying to organize the union. You should be ashamed of yourselves for saying what you did about the two women involved. It sounded to me yesterday as though you actually resented their taking some initiative in improving wages and working conditions around here.

LYON: Nancy, did you speak to the employees about the conversation in our management meeting?

NANCY: Well, of course, I did. After all, they are part of the hospital too.

LYON: Nancy, those meetings are confidential. You violated a very important trust we had placed in you as a management representative.

NANCY: What harm can that do? We should be open and honest with people around here. After all, this is an institution where we can help and heal people, not keep them under our thumb.

Lyon terminated the interview at that point, telling Nancy not to discuss yesterday's management meeting or any other matter concerning the union organization campaign with anyone else in the hospital. He pondered what he should do next.

The Night-Shift Group

Jean MacDuff, night nursing director of St. Amos Hospital, located in a major midwestern city, was disturbed by a memo from the administrator, Paul Seay. Reports from the controller's office indicated that linen replacement costs, particularly for bedsheets, had doubled within the past three months. A check by the day staff of the laundry room procedures and nursing floor supplies had not accounted for the continued shortages. Mr. Seay's memo concluded, "In view of rising operating costs, I suggest you institute immediate close checks on all of your personnel."

The design of the hospital included two sections with eight floors each, and one north wing consisting of three nursing units. Soiled linen was collected from two main laundry chutes in the basement of the two sections and from linen hamper trucks in the adjoining north wing. The hospital laundry operated at peak capacity for eight hours, six days per week, starting at 9 A.M. Daily supply orders were filled and checked by the laundry manager before the laundry closed at 5 P.M. At 11 P.M., the night orderlies began distribution of the loaded hampers to each of the eighteen nursing divisions and the operating room. Floor personnel stored the linen in the closets during the night as time permitted. The empty hampers were returned to the basement chutes by the orderlies before they checked out at 6:30 A.M.

The night staff was a very close-knit group, and its employment turnover was the lowest in the nursing department. Because the hospital was located in the far southwest area of the city, many of the night employees, including several of the professional nursing staff, came to work together from inner-city areas in car pools. There were many relatives and long-time employees and several second-generation nurses' aides and orderlies in the night-shift group.

The director, Ms. MacDuff, being of ample proportions, was affectionately referred to as "Miz Mac" directly and "Big Mac" indirectly. With her approval, the shift's 2:30 A.M. break had become a respected ritual; personnel birthdays, anniversaries, and pay raises were always observed with shared food and fellowship between the units. Henry Sharon, the head orderly, often added an original poem in honor of any special occasion. Of undetermined age and somewhat disabled with a lower prosthesis, Henry nevertheless was the most agile and light-hearted worker on the staff. He carried his "keys" proudly dangling from his belt, which indicated that he was in charge of laundry cart deliveries. He had been at St. Amos for more than twenty years,

---

All names and places are disguised.

and he guided new orderlies with skill and understanding of their jobs. Many student nurses learned much, too, from Henry about handling difficult patients and expirations during their early night-duty experience.

Because of the size of the hospital and her many supervisory and administrative duties, Ms. MacDuff considered the directive from Mr. Seay for an immediate check on all night personnel to be an impossibility. On rounds that evening, she simply read Mr. Seay's directive to each of the floor charge nurses and asked them to observe the handling of linen closely, to report any irregularities, and to make suggestions for changes. During the break period that same evening, MacDuff asked Henry if he had noticed any "outsiders" hanging around while the linen hampers were being moved from the laundry. Henry reminded her that there were six exits to the hospital, which fire regulations stated must be kept open at all times, and only one night watchman was on duty, and he was usually helping at the "Emergency" entrance. No suggestions or ideas were reported to Ms. MacDuff by any of the night personnel. Because there was no apparent shortage of clean linen during the 11–7 shift, nothing further was done by MacDuff and the night shift concerning the linen problem.

Two weeks later, a second memo from Mr. Seay advised that "Due to continued shortages in linen sheets, effective immediately, all linen closets on nursing units will be kept locked. Sheets will be dispensed only upon requests by the floor charge nurse, and delivery and storage of the next day's linen must be personally supervised by the charge nurse on each division."

This regulation was met with much opposition and resentment by the night staff because of the time and personnel involved in the storage procedures. Orderlies who were tied up with floor linen hamper unloading were often called off the floor, and patients' lights could not be handled as promptly. As a result of the excessive workload, the 2:30 A.M. break was frequently delayed until 3 or 4 A.M. and on some floors was omitted entirely. On two occasions, Mr. Seay was observed counting hampers and checking the basement laundry room at 6 A.M. Returned empty carts, which had never been a problem, often filled the service elevators when the day staff reported for duty. Henry Sharon explained to Jean MacDuff that his orderlies no longer had time to get the empty hampers back to the basement because the floors were too slow in unloading them. Nurses' aides reported frequent backaches from too much heavy unloading and complained that they could not guide the hampers even when they were empty and blocking the hallways.

Absenteeism, which had never been a problem on the 11–7 shift, became more frequent, and several aides asked for transfers to the day shift. One very capable aide who resigned from the hospital was questioned by Ms. MacDuff about her reason for leaving. She said, "It just ain't fun working here like it used to be. Everybody's got to be so careful and looking at each other. What do they think we would do with the sheets that are missing anyway, Miz Mac? We're all double-bed sleepers! You can ask anybody!"

The following month, St. Amos began receiving new linens with large blue-center name markings. In spite of the addition of two new guards at the employee exits and the checking of all personnel parcels, linen losses continued, although at a reduced rate.

About three weeks later, Jean MacDuff resigned as night nursing director, complaining that she simply "couldn't take all this bickering and suspicion anymore."

Six months later, the hospital administrator had not secured a qualified replacement for MacDuff. Nursing care during night hours had been reduced sharply, and many staff doctors were admitting acutely ill patients to St. Amos only if they had private-duty night nurses available to them.

CASE–5

A Denial of "Free Speech"

Jane Washington was a student at Hill City Junior College, a community college located in Hill City, Texas. She was nineteen years old and in the second semester of her freshman year. In order to support herself while attending college, Jane had accepted employment with a Gould Supermarkets store, one unit of a chain of supermarkets in Hill City.

The store in which Jane worked as a "courtesy clerk" (more commonly known as a "bagger") was located in a predominantly white community, populated primarily by blue-collar and working-class families. Jane worked approximately fifteen to twenty hours per week, during evenings and on weekends as she was available and needed. Her performance had been rated as satisfactory by her supervisors during her six months of employment.

CAMPUS UNREST

A series of events at Hill City Junior College led to a serious situation of student unrest on the campus. On one occasion, dissident minority students briefly occupied the administration building, and several protest demonstrations by several student groups culminated in a general demonstration protesting discrimination against blacks and other minorities and women in general, with specific reference to sexual harassment of women on campus and in the community. Jane Washington became interested in campus issues, and she was quite sympathetic with the student protests and political issues that had been raised. Following a student demonstration that coincided with the appearance of a major political figure on campus, she could contain herself no longer. She decided that she had to make known her feelings to everyone, including people with whom she came into contact at her job at Gould Supermarkets.

Jane reported for work on a Saturday morning at the supermarket with a black band around her left arm clearly displayed over the neat uniform that had been furnished by the store. In addition, two large buttons were attached to her uniform; one protested discrimination against minorities and women, and another was a button showing support for a major political candidate. Her supervisor, Helen Dulo, noticed these items but she said nothing to Jane because she didn't know what action would be appropriate. Dulo was a new

---

All names and places are disguised.

supervisor, having been promoted to the position of assistant manager only two months previously.

CUSTOMER PROTESTS

During the first two hours after Jane Washington had come to work, several customers whose groceries had been packed by Ms. Washington had commented on the armband and the buttons. Several went directly to the store manager, George Romero, to complain. These customers said they thought it was inappropriate for a college student to express herself politically in a store that was supposed to be neutral on political matters. Mr. Romero, after hearing the customers' complaints, agreed with them. He proceeded to tell Ms. Dulo to tell Ms. Washington to remove the buttons and the protest armband.

THE ULTIMATUM

At 11:45 A.M., Ms. Dulo asked Jane Washington to come to her office for a conference. The general nature of the conversation between Helen Dulo and Jane Washington was as follows:

DULO: We have received several complaints about your buttons and the armband. We do not care what you do or what you say off the job, but while you are at work here in our store, you must remove these and wear only the authorized uniform. All employees have been told this when they are hired by this store.

WASHINGTON: And if I choose to do otherwise? I've never seen any written store policy about this, or about our rights to express our views!

DULO: If you choose to do otherwise, we will have no recourse but to suspend or discharge you, because we need to maintain the confidence of the customers we have in this community. We will give you a little time to think about it, but before you report back to work next Monday, you'd better make up your mind. We hope you will come to work as usual without the band and buttons.

THE NEWSPAPER STORY

At 1 P.M. that afternoon, Jane Washington went to George Romero's office and told him that she was resigning her position from the supermarket. She asserted that she could not, in good conscience, work at a store where she was denied freedom of speech. After telling Mr. Romero this, she went to her home where she called a reporter at the local newspaper to relate the situation as it had occurred. She told the reporter that she had been fired because she was not permitted to exercise her individual freedom of expression while being an employee at the supermarket. The newspaper reporter contacted the supermarket manager, Mr. Romero, and asked for his version of the story. Romero replied that the company had to protect its business. He stated that no employee, while in the store, was allowed to wear unauthorized clothing or buttons that openly expressed opinions about controversial political or social issues.

The next day, the store was a front-page item in the local newspaper. On the following Monday morning, many students at Hill City Junior College were irate because of the supermarket's treatment of Jane Washington. They suggested a boycott of the Gould chain, and they organized a brief afternoon protest demonstration outside the store. Several store employees—primarily part-time students working in the supermarket—joined in the demonstration, and several employees and numerous citizens wrote letters of protest to Gould management.

Several days after the protest demonstration and the publicity in the newspaper, George Romero called a meeting of supervisors in his store as well as managers and supervisors from several other Gould Supermarkets operating in Hill City. He opened the meeting by raising several questions for consideration by the supervisors and managers:

Should we rescind our actions in the Jane Washington situation? Second, what policies do we need in order to cope with future situations of this sort? Further, should we have any different policies or rules to cover employee dress, behavior, and appearance? If so, how should these be developed, and should we put these in writing when we know that it's nearly impossible these days to get people to agree upon what is acceptable and what is not?

A Breach of Confidentiality

Unity Health Services, Incorporated, is a prepaid medical group practice located in a major metropolitan center. At the time of this case, the company employed approximately forty physicians and 160 support, administrative, supervisory, and managerial personnel; the company served a patient population of some 50,000 in five offices. Employees were eligible to receive their personal medical care on a prepaid basis at any of the company's health center locations.

Much emphasis had been placed by both management and medical staff upon the confidential nature of all medical records. The employee handbook stated that all medical information was privileged and confidential. However, an incident in which supervisors had overheard an open discussion among certain employees regarding another employee's medical condition led to an effort by the manager of the home office to tighten the practices by which employee medical information would be kept confidential. This included new rules regarding locking up employee medical records in a special cabinet, using a nonidentifiable computer code for entry of employee medical information in the databank, and special procedures whereby all labwork, claims, and hospitalization information involving employees could be handled only by supervisors. These rules and procedures were disseminated to all employees in meetings and by memo, and all employees again were told by their supervisors that confidential information was not to be discussed. A new employee handbook was distributed that included this expanded policy statement:

> *All* information gathered regarding patients is privileged and confidential material. Violation of this trust is grounds for immediate dismissal.

One of the regular procedures was that all laboratory tests and results of labwork were to be recorded by patient name and identification number in books kept in the lab. These books were readily available to nurses, physicians, and laboratory technicians so that patients could call in for results. However, under the new procedures, employee lab orders that an employee did not want recorded in the laboratory books to which others had easy access could be given directly to the laboratory supervisor. The supervisor would run the test and deliver the paperwork to the director of medical records, and it would be recorded only on the confidential medical chart.

All names and places are disguised.

Mary Alton, a medical records clerk, wished to have a personal pregnancy test run by the laboratory. Rather than follow the procedure by which she could give her specimen directly to the lab supervisor, Mary Alton asked another employee, Julie Shaak, if she could enter the lab order under Julie Shaak's name. Shaak agreed, and the lab order was entered in the laboratory book under the false name. The test came back "positive" and was recorded in the laboratory book. Several days later another employee, Coleen Luera, was asked to check a test result on another patient, which she did by referring to the laboratory book.

The next day, Julie Shaak reported to the human resources director, Emily King, that she had been approached by a fellow employee, Arthur Jacobs, who congratulated her on her pregnancy. When asked how he knew that information, Jacobs had responded, "Coleen Luera told me on the way home yesterday." When King told Shaak that this type of violation of confidentiality was considered a serious enough offense to be fired, Shaak responded, "I don't want anyone to lose their job. I just wanted you to know who always talks too much."

Subsequently, Emily King confronted Coleen Luera with the above accusation. Luera vehemently denied that she had revealed the information. She acknowledged that she did see the pregnancy result in the lab book while checking for another patient. But because she and Julie Shaak were not friendly and did not always get along well, Luera didn't really care about it or pay it particular attention. Luera also stated that she was terribly hurt by the accusation, and she believed that her long record of excellent performance evaluations should prove that she would not be involved in a situation such as this. Luera went on to state that she always minded her own business, and she did not involve herself in the "grapevine" and "gossip." In an interview with King, Art Jacobs also denied that he had approached Shaak. Instead he said that Julie Shaak had approached him with the question, "Did you hear I was pregnant?"

As Emily King pondered what—if any—action she should take, she also recognized the following additional considerations:

1. All employees involved had been with the company at least five years.
2. Julie Shaak had a reputation for being a "troublemaker" and for being difficult to get along with.
3. Art Jacobs and Coleen Luera had never had a blemish on their records, and they were employees who usually did not become involved in "gossip" and were businesslike at all times.

The IRS Investigates the Financial Consultant

THE BAD NEWS

Thad Thomas, managing partner of the Chicago office of Jordan, Anderson, and Grace Investment Services (JAG), was surprised when he picked up his phone and heard the voice of Marvin Mitner, the well-known consumer affairs reporter from *Eyewitness News*, Channel 8. As Marvin Mitner outlined the purpose of his telephone call, Thad Thomas suddenly developed a sharp pain in the pit of his stomach. It was a "worst-case scenario." According to Mitner, Steve Spencer, Thad's best friend from college and the top financial consultant for JAG, was being investigated by the Internal Revenue Service on charges of failing to file federal income tax returns. Although Steve Spencer had averaged over $700,000 in annual income in the last five years, he had not filed an income tax return during that period. Steve's penchant for fast cars, expensive jewelry, and yacht clubs had resulted in his living a life in the fast lane. His lifestyle had enabled the IRS to establish an evident paper trail of his spending and a very strong case against him. Marvin Mitner concluded his telephone call with a request for an on-the-scene interview at Jordan, Anderson, and Grace. Thad Thomas responded that he would consider this request and get back to Mitner later.

BACKGROUND

As Thad Thomas reached across his antique oak desk to hang up the telephone, he gazed out upon Lake Michigan and began to reflect on his friendship with Steve Spencer and their tenure at JAG. Thad and Steve first met when they were MBA students at Eastview University. Upon graduation from B-school, Thad was invited to join JAG, a fledgling investment firm in New York City. When Thad was asked to open a Chicago office, Thad immediately called Steve to join the firm as a financial consultant. During his employment at JAG, Steve far exceeded Thad's every expectation and had become the firm's leading financial consultant.

Jordan, Anderson, and Grace had been founded by three "refugees" from established investment houses, and the firm was considered one of Wall

This case was prepared by Professor Kristine Lanser and Professor Benjamin Weeks, both of the Graham School of Management at St. Xavier University in Chicago. All names are disguised. Used by permission.

Street's leading success stories of the 1980s. After the initial success in New York, JAG quickly expanded to Chicago, Houston, and San Francisco. Specializing in financial services to high-income clients, the firm prided itself on a personalized relationship with customers and considered trust to be one of its key assets. Although each office was managed locally, New York kept a close watch over each branch. Top management believed that a firm that sold such services should maintain an ethical climate second to none. In fact, two years ago, Thad Thomas had released another consultant for violating the firm's conflict-of-interest requirement. This dismissal occurred when the consultant recommended a stock in a company owned by his brother-in-law. The other partners suggested releasing the employee; however, they stated that Thad was the managing partner of the Chicago office and they would support his ultimate decision. All the partners of JAG believed that maintaining the integrity of the firm was essential to continuing success. At every opportunity, they emphasized the importance of a strong public image.

THE TV STORY

At 5 P.M., Thad Thomas walked over to his conference room to watch Marvin Mitner's report on the *Eyewitness News* telecast. Mitner had a reputation for dramatizing news, and this footage was no different. The camera showed a distraught Steve Spencer standing in the lobby of his "Gold Coast" condominium receiving a subpoena from a special agent of the IRS. The reporter commented that Spencer, a prominent employee of Jordan, Anderson, and Grace, would be brought up on income tax evasion charges. Mitner made comments about Spencer's reputation for tailored shirts and chauffeured limos. He even aired an interview with a staff member of the Palm Beach marina where Steve's custom-made yacht was kept. The final scene of the news report showed Marvin Mitner on the sidewalk in front of the LaSalle Street offices of Jordan, Anderson, and Grace.

During the news report, Mitner described how the IRS had uncovered and documented Steve's activities. A tax auditor of the Examination Division of the IRS had noticed that Steve Spencer had not filed a tax return for several years. The division then began to search for Spencer and was pleasantly surprised to find him working on LaSalle Street in the Chicago office of JAG. The IRS then began to establish a paper trail of Steve's spending patterns. The IRS eventually was able to document a $50,000 transaction to Goldstein's Jewelry Emporium on Chicago's "Magnificent Mile," a $3,000 monthly rental of a "Gold Coast" luxury condominium, and a monthly payment to a man in Palm Beach, Florida. When the IRS located the recipient of the checks, they found that the payments were for the purpose of maintaining Steve's yacht. The IRS established that Steve Spencer was earning approximately $700,000 per year. Given the amount of taxes due the U.S. government, the Criminal Investigation Division was eager to follow up on the criminal charges.

STEVE SPENCER'S STORY

It was a long night for Thad Thomas. The next day when he arrived at his office, a haggard-looking and exhausted Steve Spencer was waiting to see him. Steve wasted little time in trying to pour out to Thad his side of the story and how this situation had happened. According to Steve Spencer, he had had no intention of cheating the government, but he simply had become overwhelmed with work and the demands of his clients. Steve explained that he had filed for three tax extensions during his first year; but as each of the filing deadlines approached, he could not seem to find the time to attend to his own financial affairs. His clients were very demanding, and Steve felt that their needs should come first. Also, the company had regularly withheld a percentage of his pay to submit to the federal and state governments, which further justified postponing the filing. His procrastination had become easier as the situation progressed during the first year. Since there seemed to be no response or repercussions from the IRS, his failure to file was reinforced, and the issue became easier to ignore. Steve said that he continued his procrastination and thus did not file for the next four years.

Steve informed Thad that he had already contacted an attorney and that she was working to make a deal with the IRS. Steve had filed several extensions on his current income tax return. The company for each pay period had withheld Steve's taxes and submitted the amount to the federal and state governments; therefore, the attorney hoped for an easy resolution to the matter. Steve Spencer pleaded with Thad to be understanding and to grant him time to work out the problem which he assured Thad "would never happen again."

WHAT TO DO

As Thad Thomas saw the anguish in Steve Spencer's face, he thought: What should he tell Spencer about his future relationship with the firm? How should he respond to Marvin Mitner's request for an on-the-scene television interview?

CASE–8

The Smoke-Free Office Policy

It was about 10 A.M. as a taxi pulled to the curb in front of the corporate head-quarters of the Leaders International Insurance Corporation. Bridget McGovern, the corporate CEO, stepped out of the taxi, having just returned from a meeting with other executives regarding a United Way program. As she made her way toward the entrance door of the corporate building, she saw a usual group of smokers loitering near the doorway enjoying their cigarettes. But as she neared the door, she saw another group of employees chatting on a nearby bench. This drew her attention because no one in this group of employees was smoking.

"What are you folks doing here?" Ms. McGovern asked the group of nonsmokers.

"Well," replied one of the group, "our smoking colleagues have been coming out for a smoke at least hourly throughout the day, and we have been left to do the work. We figured 'what's good for the goose is good for the gander.' So we decided that whenever they take an informal smoking break, we'll join them."

McGovern was speechless. As she entered the corporate building lobby, she realized that a review of the present smoke-free office policy was in order. She remembered signing a memorandum announcing the company's smoke-free program which required all smoking breaks to be taken outside of the office building. However, she realized that what was going on was certainly an unanticipated consequence of trying to create a smoke-free environment. Bridget McGovern decided that she would immediately call Art McGinty, the company's director of human resources, to discuss a new approach.

This case was prepared by Dr. A. Ranger Curran, Professor of Management at Keene State College, Keene, NH. All names are disguised. Used by permission.

EXERCISE–1

My Best Job

Goals: (1) To enable you to become acquainted with other members of your class; (2) to help you to feel more comfortable about speaking up and participating in class activities by providing you with the emotional support of other members of your group; and (3) to learn to think about the process of employee motivation and the role of human resources management in stimulating positive employee motivation and superior work performance.

Group size: Unlimited number of triads.

Total time required: Forty-five to sixty minutes.

Physical setting: Triads should separate themselves from one another as much as possible, but they need not move to separate rooms.

Process:

1. Before class, each student should write answers to the following questions:
   a. What was the best job you ever held? (A full-time job is preferred, but a part-time job is satisfactory if you held no full-time job or if the part-time job is more relevant.) Describe each of the following:
      (1) Job title and brief description of duties and responsibilities.
      (2) Your supervisor—his or her general behavior, leadership style, and so on.
      (3) Your fellow employees—your perception of their competence, attitudes toward their work, the organization, and you.
      (4) The organization—policies, procedures, and practices. (Consider both the broader organization and the department in which you worked.)
      (5) Why was the job: excellent; very good; good; other?
      (6) What were the negative features, if any, of the job?
   b. How did this job compare with what you would have liked it to be?
2. (ten to fifteen minutes) At the start of class, form triads. The criterion for triad formation is not knowing the other members of the triad. Members of the triad should introduce themselves to each other and then, in turn, briefly describe their preferred jobs. They should allow adequate time to exchange experiences, feelings, expectations, disappointments, successes, and so on.

3. (ten to fifteen minutes) Form new triads with new people. Follow procedures outlined in step 2 above.
4. (five minutes) The instructor asks members of the class to indicate by a show of hands the number of people whose jobs fell into the following categories:
   a. Office—clerical.
   b. Sales—retail; other.
   c. Professional—engineering, law, accounting, nursing, other.
   d. Managerial, supervisory.
   e. Other:
      —Physical labor.
      —Restaurant.
      —Delivery (truck; automobile; other).
      —Health care.
      —Other.
5. (five to ten minutes) Data gathering. Instructor asks members of the class to report:
   a. Job characteristics that made their jobs good ones.
   b. How other members of their work groups felt about their jobs by age, sex, job title, and so on.
   c. Behavior of members of the group who did not like their jobs.
   d. What the organizations might have done to make the jobs better with no or very little cost.
   e. What the company might have done to change the behavior of those who did not like their jobs.
6. (ten to fifteen minutes) Class discussion concerning data gathered in step 5. The exercise might conclude with a brief discussion of the question, "What is the significance of the exercise to the human resource management function in an organization?" For example, what human resource management policies, practices, procedures, and topics are relevant to what was discussed in steps 2–5?

EXERCISE-2

Ms. Geiger: Please Respond (A)

You are Elizabeth Geiger, director of human resources for the Wiersma Corporation. The Wiersma Corporation produces and sells glass and glassware products and is located in a medium-sized city in a southern state.

You recently received several memos from individuals within the company that require your immediate attention. You are concerned about these inquiries because you believe that all of them have implications that could present problems for some of the company's human resources' and organizational policies and also have an impact upon company relationships within the community.

You have decided, therefore, to write and send memos to each of the individuals in which you will: (a) respond to their questions and (b) explain your position concerning what should and what should not be done in each situation.

The memos that you have received are as follows:

Memo Number One

To: Elizabeth Geiger, Director of Human Resources

From: Helen Hughes, Manager of Administrative Services

Subject: Christmas Party to Help Improve Morale

The secretarial pool is planning an in-house Christmas party for December 22. We would like to hold it in the company cafeteria and invite people from other departments. Frankly, with budget cuts and layoffs this past year, the internal environment has become a bit gloomy. Would the HR department help sponsor it in order to boost morale?

This exercise was developed by Professor Patrick A. Kroll of the General College of the University of Minnesota at Minneapolis. All names are disguised. Used by permission.

Memo Number Two

To: Ms. E. Geiger, Human Resources Department

From: Ellis Koloski, Manager of Engineering

Subject: Transfer of Bill Jones from the Drafting Department to my Department

I've really been impressed by the drafting work of Bill Jones in the drafting pool. Because I'm in desperate need of and have an opening for a drafting person in Engineering Support Services, I contacted Bill about transferring without talking to Bill's supervisor, Joan Dipple, who probably would oppose such a transfer.

Bill jumped at the suggestion, particularly since I hinted at the possibility of a raise in pay, too. Please take care of the necessary paperwork.

Memo Number Three

To: Liz Geiger, Director of HRM

From: George Viener, Manager of Manufacturing

Subject: Openings for Five New Assemblers

Please recruit and hire five new assemblers for the entry-grade assembly positions. You'll recall that these positions were approved by headquarters last month. You recruited for us before. Why don't you go ahead and recruit and select five for us? We've been so busy down here that we don't have time to do the interviewing. We trust your judgment.

Memo Number Four

To: Ms. Elizabeth Geiger, Human Resources Department

From: Arthur Katz, Sales Manager

Subject: Termination of Jim Lax, Salesman

I got mad at Jim Lax and told him to "hit the road." I fired him on the spot. The guy has really been getting on my nerves lately. Always seems to have a wisecrack when I'm seriously trying to explain something to him. He'll be stopping to get his last check. Don't worry about him. Guys like him we don't need around here. Incidentally, Jim is getting on in years, and he'll probably claim I discriminated against him. But he's a loser and he should have been fired years ago. I've got records to prove it.

Memo Number Five

To: Ms. Elizabeth Geiger, Director of HRM

From: Mary Hobler, Plant Security Supervisor

Subject: Demonstrators at the Gate

Twelve pickets have been demonstrating against our plant. They have even been coming on our property to protest and to confront our people. They say that our plant is polluting the atmosphere in the community, but our plant has met all emission standards that have been given to us by EPA. The pickets are demanding time to meet with top company officials and permission to speak at the annual stockholders' meeting. None of them is a stockholder.

EXERCISE–3

Frank J. Olinger, Part-Time Professor

You are Dean Herbert Hayes of the School of Continuing Education at Brookline University. You have just sat down to read your morning mail, when your eyes fall upon a letter that your administrative assistant has carefully placed at the top of the pile with a note reading, "You may want to give this your prompt attention since copies have been sent to V.P. Spangler and Dean McDonald."

Ajax, Inc.
1918 McDonald Ave.
Crestwood, Illinois

October 4, 19XX

Dean Herbert J. Hayes
School of Business
Brookline University

Dear Dean Hayes:

Last year the University very generously and kindly presented me with a certificate calling attention to the fact that I had taught fifteen years as a member of the faculty of the School of Continuing Education. Dean Georgia McDonald of that school presided at the ceremony. I sat next to Vice President Vincent Spangler at the small dinner celebrating the occasion. During the course of the evening, I asked Dr. Spangler what the University's position was on using people without doctoral degrees to teach courses in its evening classes (I have a master's degree in business administration). I asked the question because I am a member of the board of directors of a small liberal arts college. I know that prestigious universities require that virtually all members of the faculty possess doctorates. Dr. Spangler stated that experience that people like me bring to a university outweighed the lack of a doctoral degree.

I received quite a shock the other day when a student who sought to sign up for my course couldn't find it in the catalog and telephoned me

---

All names are disguised.

for help. I was very much embarrassed to find that my course had apparently been dropped from the catalog and that I undoubtedly had been dropped from the faculty. I have been quite concerned that nobody thought my position worthy of a phone call or a postcard telling me in advance of this change. It is certainly the University's business to hire the type of faculty it wants. But if this is the manner in which it conducts its business, I can understand why it has problems.

Incidentally, I have recruited and hired college students for Ajax for the past twenty years. I have repeatedly heard the criticism that college graduates tend to be steeped in theory and numbers but have no feel for the "real" world. I have also heard it said that much of this theoretical outlook stems from the fact that the full-time professors who teach them are steeped in academia and have no concept as to what goes on in business. There must be some place for the practical viewpoint in a school like Brookline.

One last thought. A teacher always likes to hear that his students have made use of what he has taught. I frequently meet former students who say, "What you taught me about human resource management is one of the most practical things that I learned at the university." The word has apparently gotten around that mine was an interesting and useful course. In fact, I had earlier telephoned Dean McDonald requesting that registration be limited to thirty-five. Last year I had forty-eight students.

In summary, I am not trying to tell Brookline how it should conduct its affairs. I guess that I am more than a little upset at the way the University treats people.

Best wishes for success at whatever is going on.

Very truly yours,
Frank J. Olinger
Vice-President—Human Resources

cc: Vice President V. O. Spangler
Dean Georgia McDonald

When you finish reading the letter, you recall that you met Frank Olinger last year at a dinner honoring long-service adjunct faculty. You can recall no other contacts with Olinger, however. When your administrative assistant, Millie Rap, enters your office, you say: "The part-time faculty is so large, and we never hear from them unless there is a problem. Please call this Frank Olinger and set up a luncheon appointment for me with him at the earliest date possible."

EXERCISE–4

The Reluctant Researcher

You are Robert White, manager of the Madison, Wisconsin, plant of the Biotechnics Corporation. You are waiting for one of your plant research staff members, Dr. Ronald Smith, to come to your office. As you wait, you review the chain of events that occurred prior to this meeting.

ORGANIZATIONAL BACKGROUND

Biotechnics, Inc., is a leading biotechnology company that utilizes recombinant DNA and monoclonal antibody technology. Its major products under development include cancer therapeutics, cholesterol-lowering agents, antihypertension drugs, and congestive heart failure drugs. The company is in the forefront of research and has several name-brand drugs on the market that have been well received by both physicians and the public.

Because of its high emphasis on research, its plants tend to be small, averaging about ninety persons, almost one-third of whom are engaged in research. The ten plants are all located in cities with important research-oriented universities and teaching hospitals. The principal office is located in the city of New York, and the total number of employees in the organization is approximately one thousand persons. While the principal source of revenue to the company is from the sale of drugs, about 15 percent of revenue is derived from research grants from the federal government and private foundations. The industry has been growing rapidly, and competition for highly competent research personnel has been keen at all levels.

Biotechnics, Inc., is quite decentralized (see Exhibit E–4). Both plant managers and the research groups have wide latitude in the decision-making process. Production planning and coordination are managed through quarterly meetings with Isaac Waldron, vice-president of production, and research is managed in the same way. Plant managers do not exercise direct line authority over the research staffs at their respective plants. However, because of the great distance from the New York office and the need for production and research to cooperate on mutual problems on a continuing basis, the two groups like and respect each other, especially at the Madison facility. The president of the company believes that this high degree of freedom contributes greatly to the company's success in all functional areas of the organization.

All names are disguised.

THE NEED FOR A NEW RESEARCH DIRECTOR

The current administrative director of research located in New York recently resigned to accept a lucrative position as vice president for research with another company. Competition in the industry plus rapid developments in research make it essential that the vacancy be filled promptly with a very competent person knowledgeable in genetic research and having good managerial potential. The company has decided to search first within the organization for such a person. A memorandum was sent by the vice president of research, Dr. John Appleby, to all plant managers and research personnel who might possess the necessary qualifications, or who might be in a position to recommend a qualified candidate.

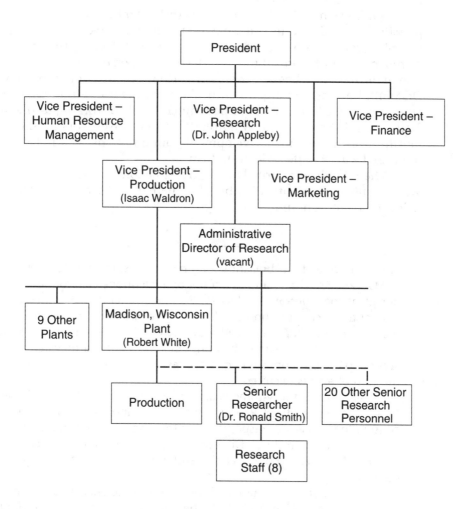

EXHIBIT 4   Partial Organization Chart of Biotechnics, Inc.

THE CANDIDATE

When you, Robert White, manager of the Madison plant facility, received the memorandum, you immediately thought of one of your outstanding researchers, Dr. Ronald Smith. Smith seemed to possess the ideal qualifications. You immediately telephoned Isaac Waldron, vice president of production in New York, telling him about Dr. Smith, and you followed up this telephone message to Waldron with letters to Dr. Appleby and several other executives in the company who knew of Dr. Smith's accomplishments.

After Dr. Appleby conferred with Waldron and several other senior executives, it was agreed that Waldron, who was planning to visit the Madison facility the following week, would meet with Dr. Smith to learn more about his qualifications and interests.

Waldron's meeting in Madison with Dr. Smith was cut short by other pressing demands on his time; however, Waldron took an immediate liking to Smith. You drove Waldron back to the airport. During this trip, Waldron commented that he hoped that Smith could be persuaded to accept the position in the New York headquarters office. However, Waldron also told you that Dr. Smith had shown no great enthusiasm for the position in New York, and Smith had talked mostly about how much he liked working at the Madison facility. Smith also had told Waldron that while in New York for the quarterly meetings of the research development committee, he was not particularly impressed with the life style in that city.

When Waldron returned to New York, he told Dr. Appleby and the president about Dr. Smith and distributed to them and other senior executives the following memorandum:

I met with one of our brilliant young researchers, Dr. Ronald Smith, while in Madison a few days ago as a result of a telephone call from Bob White, our plant manager at that facility. Bob recommended that we consider him for the vacant position of administrative director of research. It would mean, of course, that he would move here. While he did not seem overly enthusiastic about leaving Madison, I believe that his ambivalence about accepting the position was largely the result of the suddenness with which this turn of events occurred.

Dr. Smith is thirty-three years old; a graduate of Harvard University (B.A.), the University of Pennsylvania (M.A.), and the University of Wisconsin (Ph.D.). He was responsible for the discovery and development of one of our major products, Dimezerin, which has been widely accepted as an agent for lowering blood cholesterol. He has several other projects under way.

I believe that he could lead these projects to successful completion while working in New York, but I believe that his greatest contribution

---

would be made in inspiring and leading our other researchers in the company to move in the most productive research directions. Bob White speaks of him as an "idea man." My very brief conversation with him leads me to agree with Bob.

Based on Isaac Waldron's strong recommendation, the urgency of finding a new person to fill the vacancy, and the support of Dr. Appleby who knew Dr. Smith quite well, the executive committee agreed to offer the position of administrative director of research to Dr. Smith. Dr. Appleby telephoned you about the committee's decision and asked you to inform Dr. Smith about it as a preliminary step.

You, of course, are enthusiastic about the decision. You like Ron Smith and are pleased to be able to provide him with this opportunity to make his creative talents available to the entire organization. You also realize that it could aid your own career opportunities by having an important ally at the New York office. However, you are worried that if Smith should decline to accept the position, this could be an unfavorable incident in your record as plant manager and for your future career.

You telephoned Dr. Smith's office and asked his assistant to have Smith come to your office at 2 P.M. While waiting for Smith to arrive, you consider how to "break the good news" to Smith.

People at Work

CASES

EXPERIENTIAL EXERCISES

The behavior of people at work is frequently difficult to understand or assess. Certainly, much of the behavior that is observable is *goal-directed*—that is, employees are seeking to satisfy wants and needs important to them. But it is often hard to discern the causes of specific behaviors, to see the connection between the behavior and the goal sought or the need being manifested, or even, on occasion, to perceive the behavior as being functional at all. Sometimes, in frustration, or because of a lack of knowledge, managers may reach for simplistic explanations based on classifications or stereotypes. Such attempts at labeling or stereotyping individuals usually serves neither the manager nor the employee, since the manager fails to see the differences in individuals and likely diagnoses behavior human resource problems erroneously. Managers need to remind themselves constantly that human behavior is caused and that individual people are different. If we recognize the differences in people and are cognizant of the strengths and weaknesses in each individual, we have a much-improved prospect of successfully addressing and solving work-related problems.

The workplace is a source of confusing challenges. Managers are faced with pressures for output and standards of performance, but they also should recognize their responsibility to attempt to provide their people with satisfying work opportunities. Yet, for example, employees may feel keenly the need for improved job security and health benefits at the same time that the organization is seeking to cut employment costs in the face of domestic and global competition. Communications can be misinterpreted and misunderstood. Formal and informal organizations may not be evolving toward consistent purposes. Behavior of both employees and managers may give rise to ethical questions—questions of what is right or just. Sometimes people at work are burdened with personal problems—difficulties that not only affect their work but affect their lives and their relationships with family, friends, and co-workers as well. Managers may then be called upon to play a counseling role, at least until appropriate professional services may be engaged. These types of always-interesting, always-perplexing panoramas of people at work are the subjects of the cases and exercises in Part Two.

Hammond General Hospital: The New Contract Food Service

Hammond General Hospital was a 334-bed general hospital located in a small southwest town of approximately 45,000 people; it served a county-wide population of approximately 140,000. The area was heavily dependent on manufacturing and supported several industries. At the time of this case, there was considerable unemployment and good jobs were not readily available.

The hospital was one of the largest employers in the city. The administrative team was fairly young and aggressive, but administration also felt a genuine obligation to provide a safe, pleasant, and positive work environment for hospital employees.

THE CONTRACT FOOD SERVICE DEPARTMENT

Dave Smith came to Hammond General Hospital in October to become director of food service. Smith was employed by Universal Hosts Company, a large, national food service corporation that had just been awarded the management contract for the department. The previous director of food service had been employed by the hospital in the same capacity for the last twenty-eight years and had been a registered dietitian (R.D.). Prior to this, the hospital had always operated its own food service.

At this time, approximately 15 percent of all hospital food service departments in the country were contracted. Universal Hosts Company had approximately 50 such contracts, making it about fourth in size in this industry. The general procedure was for the contractor (Universal Hosts) to supply a director and an assistant director, as well as to provide support systems such as recipes, production systems, and accounting procedures. The company charged the hospital for the salaries and benefits for the management team and the negotiated fee for all other services. The director would report to the hospital's administrator as well as to the company's district manager.

When Universal Hosts Company assumed management responsibility for Hammond's food service department, the department had fifty-eight full-time equivalents (FTEs). This consisted of forty full-time employees and twenty-five part-time employees (see Exhibit C–9A for an organization chart

---

All names and places are disguised.

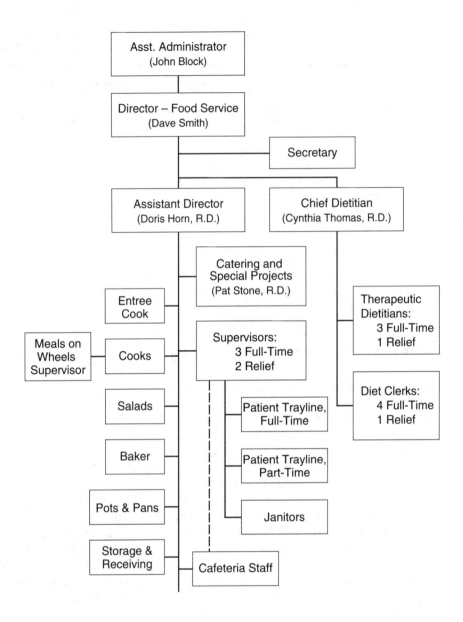

EXHIBIT C–9A   Hammond General Hospital: Food Service Department

and Exhibit C–9B for selected managerial profiles). Dave Smith and Doris Horn were the two managers employed by Universal Hosts. All others were hospital employees.

The clinical staff was headed by Chief Dietitian Cynthia Thomas, R.D. It consisted of three clinical dietitians and four diet clerks.

EXHIBIT C–9B   Managerial Profiles

Dave Smith: thirty-two years old. Held a bachelor's degree in business administration (BSBA) from an eastern state university; had been with Universal Hosts Company for almost seven years, five as an assistant director of food service at two other hospitals.

Doris Horn, R.D.: twenty-five years old. Held a bachelor's degree in nutrition from a state university in Illinois; had been with the Universal Hosts Company for only one month but had been an administrative dietitian in another hospital for two years.

Cynthia Thomas, R.D.: twenty-six years old. Held a Bachelor's degree from a state university in Michigan; had been a clinical dietitian at Hammond for three years before becoming chief dietitian.

Pat Stone, R.D.: fifty years old. Held a Bachelor's degree from a private institution in the East; had been assistant director of food service at Hammond General for ten years; prior to that, had been an administrative dietitian in the military service.

Operations were to be headed by Universal Hosts' new assistant director, Doris Horn, R.D. Her responsibilities included food production, sanitation, patient traylines, and the employee cafeteria. Three supervisors reported to her, one each for mornings and afternoons and one as a relief supervisor.

Pat Stone, R.D., was placed in charge of all catering events and was made responsible for coordinating new projects and changes that would come with the change in management.

RESISTANCE TO THE NEW DEPARTMENT MANAGEMENT

Dave Smith described his reception at Hammond General Hospital[1] as follows:

Prior to assuming official control of the department, I spent a week there just getting to know the people and learning the current system. I immediately met resistance from the acting director, Pat Stone. Stone felt she should have been promoted and that an outside food service was not needed. She had been acting director for six months and prior to that had been the assistant director for ten years. Further resistance was quickly made obvious by the entire dietitian staff, who all felt that the

---

[1]Comments from other supervisory and employee interviews are included in the following section.

director should be a registered dietitian (R.D.). There was also concern among the nursing staff at the hospital that a man had taken a position that traditionally had been held by a woman.

After encountering nothing but resistance wherever I went, I made an appointment to see the assistant administrator to whom I reported at the hospital. His name is John Block, and he had been at Hammond General for only one month himself. In fact, his first assignment was to hire an outside contract company and then approve me as the director.

Upon hearing my problems, John smiled and said, "That's nothing, I understand the entire city is upset that a big company has taken over the food service department. The hospital's board of directors is having second thoughts, and the president of the hospital, Dan Schultz, is not comfortable with my selection of you as director."

But John Block then explained to me the reasons for contracting with Universal Hosts to run the department were:

The department was considered to be overstaffed by ten FTEs;

The food and supply costs were excessive in comparison with industry standards;

Department morale was at an all-time low; the department had supported a recent unsuccessful attempt by the Teamsters to unionize all hourly employees in the hospital;

The medical staff was unhappy with the quality of the cafeteria food;

Overtime pay in the department was the highest in the entire hospital;

Performance evaluations had not been taken seriously for several years;

Ordering of food lacked systematic procedures and was not well related to dietary planning or cost estimates.

Block summed it all by saying that the department was run last year the same way it was twenty-eight years ago. There have been no new systems, improvements, or changes in management philosophy for more than a quarter of a century.

A few days after this interview, John Block was admitted to Hammond as a patient for emergency surgery, and he would be out for two months. "I am now virtually alone to succeed or fail," said Dave Smith.

INTERVIEWS WITH SUPERVISORS AND EMPLOYEES

Following his talk with Block, Dave Smith conducted a series of interviews with selected supervisors and employees. The following comments were made in these interviews.

Sally Manley, A.M. supervisor: We are supervisors in name only. We make no decisions, take no disciplinary actions, are not involved in performance appraisals, and are not involved in interviewing new hires. If we do discipline someone, it is usually overturned.

Jane Harper, P.M. supervisor: The morning shift does everything wrong. There is no procedure that we do the same as them. People that cross shifts don't know what to do. When we ask management for a decision as to what to do, they say "do whatever will work for you." Also, we have no authority to discipline, so no one pays any attention to us.

Sheila Rafferty, relief supervisor: This place is a zoo. No one knows what in the hell they're supposed to do. There is no direction and no management whatsoever. The employees do what they damn well please, and nobody does anything about it.

Millie Park, head cook: I have been here for twenty years, and this place gets worse each year. No one in there [the office] ever comes out here. I'll bet they don't even know what's on the menu today. They order food and don't even take inventory; they do it sitting on their butts. I'll bet there is $30,000 in outdated food in the basement. Also, no one else can cook. They pay dishwashers as much as cooks, so we have two cooks who can't even read a recipe—if we had recipes, which we don't.

Pat Baker, cook: We never have enough food to cook what is on the menu. We are always running out and we get blamed. We can't cook what we don't have. Also, everyone else in the other departments thinks everyone in the kitchen is a stupid jerk, when they are the only stupid ones [management].

Lora Lee Butram, cafeteria cashier: We run out of food halfway through lunch. No one in the kitchen knows what is going on. Everyone in the hospital thinks everyone in this department is an idiot.

James Wilson, janitor: They want us to clean the kitchen. I don't even have a good broom or a mop. Half of the time, I don't even have soap to use on the floor. How the hell can I clean the kitchen?

Jean Allen, diet clerk: They want us to have a high school diploma plus a year of additional schooling. Yet, we don't make any more money even though we do as much as dietitians.

Ed Norton, maintenance foreman: They should close food service and have McDonald's deliver. No one in that whole department can do anything right.

Allie Crow, head nurse: The patients don't get what they ordered. The trays are late and incomplete, and the food is cold. If a patient has a problem, we can't get a dietitian to come visit them.

Noreen Watson, housekeeping supervisor: We are supposed to clean the cafeteria at night. Food service is supposed to clean it during the day. They don't. It is a mess, and no one can do anything about it.

Delphine Mason, director of human resources: I think there are a lot of good people in food service. I think they care, but they need help and a lot of it.

THE MANAGERS MEET

Several days after assuming responsibility for the food service department, Dave Smith met with his assistant director, Doris Horn. Her comments were:

Let's bomb this place and go home. It's hopeless! Look what we face:

No one wants us here.

Our budget is unrealistic; it's based on having people that can, at least, walk and chew gum at the same time.

Pat Stone, the previous assistant director, thinks she should be the director, and she hates you for taking her job.

The chief dietitian is 100 pounds overweight (great example, eh), and she is afraid of her "old school" dietitians who don't want to leave their desks.

There are no systems of any kind.

The place is filthy.

The whole hospital hates the department.

The supervisors can't manage people and don't.

Administration thinks we will have the best food service department in one year because our salesman said we would.

Why did I take this stupid job?

Dave Smith replied. "We will fix this department the same way you would eat an elephant, one bite at a time. Let's get'em all, managers, dietitians, and supervisors, in here and start right now."

Filmore Electric Company (A): The Machine Shop

THE ACCIDENT

George Whitmore, an experienced machinist for the Filmore Electric Company, had worked in the machine shop many years without an accident. About 9:30 one Monday morning, he appeared at the door of the combination shop office and supply room with an injury. His hand was wrapped in a dirty handkerchief and was bleeding badly. "Say, Bill, where's that first-aid kit? I nicked my finger a while ago—need some stuff to wrap it up in," he said to the foreman, Bill Webster.

"Well, I never thought it could happen to you, George. Let me see it! Oh, never mind—go up to the medical office—Beth Jones can fix you up. I haven't sent her any business yet this morning," replied Bill.

"Takes too long up there. Just give me that first-aid box. I'll wrap it up and go back to work."

"Okay, but let me take a look. Sometimes those cuts are worse than you think," and Bill stepped toward a cabinet to get the first-aid kit.

George began to unwrap the handkerchief but was still trying to keep it partially covered and stop the bleeding by holding the base of the injured finger. Bill stepped back from the cabinet and was preparing to use the gauze when he stopped suddenly, saying, "Hell's fire, George, that finger's really bleeding. Keep hold of it and go on up to medical."

"Naw, I don't want to do that, Bill. Dab it with that red stuff and tie it up for me," he said.

"No, George, you know the rules—anything worse than a scratch has to be reported and treated upstairs. Besides, that finger's almost cut to the bone."

"But Bill, I don't want to go up there," objected George.

"You've got to, George—it's an order. Get up there before you bleed to death. Go on, maybe I'm saving your life or something," he said laughingly.

"Well, if you insist, I will—but I don't want to. Now don't do anything about the work at my machine. I'll be right back and take care of it," and somewhat grudgingly George strode off to the stairway still clutching his hand.

All names are disguised.

A PUZZLING REPORT

The incident was almost forgotten by Bill until Beth Jones, the nurse, called about 10:15 A.M. She reported that she had done the best she could for George's finger, but she was insisting that he wait and see the doctor. A stitch or two might be taken in the wound. The doctor was due in the office any minute, but sometimes it was 10:30 or 11:00 A.M. before he arrived. George didn't want to wait but had been persuaded to do so. He had asked her to tell Bill not to bother the work at his machine, as he would take care of it as soon as he got back.

Bill thought it was a little strange that George, who had never seemed to complain about any rules or regulations, was reluctant to visit the medical department. It was odd too that he seemed worried about the work at his machine. But the nurse had indicated that he was not hurt too badly so it would work out all right.

A short while later Bill was walking down the aisle and passed the cylindrical grinding department. He noticed George's machine standing idle. Another grinder, Sid Stone, saw Bill and asked, "How's George, Bill? He sure got a nasty cut!"

"He's all right, Sid, but the Doc may take a couple of stitches in his finger. If he's not back before long, I'd like to get Mike over here on this machine. Mike's crying his eyes out to get on a grinder since he spelled you guys during vacations." And with this remark Bill looked around the department. He spotted a tote pan under the bench beside George's machine. He gave it a kick with his foot—said "ouch" and then pulled it out into the aisle. "What's this doing under here, Sid? These shafts have a Saturday schedule for grinding. Must be four dozen here."

"I don't know, Bill. George put them there, I think," replied Sid.

Walking away from the grinding department, Bill thought it was unusual for George to be as much as an hour's work behind schedule. All the operators in cylindrical grinding were on piece rate—they all made good bonus earnings, especially George, and the dispatcher would seldom permit a Saturday schedule on a batch of work carried over to Monday. These considerations left his mind as he thought of dependable George. He could always count on George. Everything would be taken care of unless he was sent home by the doctor. He would check on that after lunch.

THE TRUTH COMES OUT

Other matters absorbed his attention during the remainder of the morning, and Bill did not plan on checking with George until lunchtime. On returning to his desk from the cafeteria, he found this note written hurriedly in pencil:

Bill—Sid tells me you found that tote pan under my grinder. You probably found out I counted that on last week's production. I'm sorry because I haven't done it very often. This finger throbs like blazes, and I don't feel good. I'm going home and I'll talk to you later.

George

Bill began to realize that George had cheated on the previous week's bonus earnings. He was sitting and thinking about it, trying to analyze the situation, when Sid Stone appeared at his door. "I've been watching for you, Bill. George came back a while before lunch. I told him you'd been around and found those Saturday shafts. He was really pretty sick and went on home. I hopped on those shafts and finished them up. They're back on schedule."

"That's good, Sid. But won't you be behind today?"

"No, I'd like to talk to you, Bill. Those lousy rates are getting us all down. The whole damned time-study department has studied our jobs—and it seems to get worse every time they come around. You've got George hooked—and I want you to know that once in a while we all do what he did. We try to keep our bonus about the same each week, but you can go to town with rotors and you get behind on shafts. George got stuck Saturday, and last week's report shows he finished 'em Saturday. He would have cleaned 'em up this morning if he hadn't cut his finger. I was on rotors, and I had half a pan done Saturday that I didn't report. We keep our sheet about even. I guess we're all wrong, and maybe it's good you found out. Why don't you give us all a dime raise and throw out this damn piece-rate system? Think of the fancy engineers' salaries the company would save. I don't see how you can do anything about George when we all do it."

"OK, Sid, I'll have to think this thing over. Are you speaking for all the grinders or just for yourself?"

"Well, at lunch the boys told me to tell you. Everyone was there except the newer men. We decided that you couldn't do much about George if you knew we were all doing it," and with that Sid walked away.

"Say, Sid," called Bill, bringing him back, "send Tom Horton over to see me."

"Oh, no, Bill, don't tell that guy about this! He still wants to be our boss—and we can't stand him. If he plays the big shot around us much more, we'll run him clear out of grinders," complained Sid.

"All right, he's not your boss, but maybe I need a foreman over there. You and George both turned the job down, and Tom has gotten to be a pretty good set-up man. He's willing to set up and break in new men. I'm not making Tom an assistant foreman yet, but maybe I've got to do something," explained Bill.

"We get along pretty good, Bill. We like you for a boss. Unless George wants the job, I don't think we need anyone. Let Tom have the set-ups and training, but for God's sake don't make me take orders from him. Do you really want to see him?" asked Sid.

"Yes, I do. Send him over," said Bill.

A short while later Tom Horton, a skilled mechanic, came to Bill's office. Tom was younger and had several years' less service with the company than George or Sid. "You want to see me, Bill?" he asked.

"Yea, Tom—what do you know about George's injury this morning and the work on his machine?"

"I know the whole story, Bill, and I'm sorry George cut his finger. But it's about time you found something like that pan of shafts. I guess you knew about the boys adjusting their weekly reports on Saturdays, didn't you?" asked Tom.

"No, I didn't know about it, Tom. Why didn't you tell me?" queried Bill.

"Why didn't I tell you? How do you get that way—I'm not supposed to report everything that goes on around here, and besides, I thought you probably knew. Anyway, I'm not an assistant foreman so I don't have any say over those guys."

"No, you're not an assistant but you are the set-up man for everyone but the old-timers—and you break in new people on grinders and engine lathes," said Bill.

"Yea, I'm just a set-up man, but I haven't any real say. If I were assistant foreman, like Pete on the punch presses, a lot of things would be different," complained Tom.

"We went all through that last year, Tom, and we set up four assistant foremen—punch presses, drill presses, lathes, and screw machines—but we decided that everybody else would report directly to me," stated Bill.

"Oh, yea, and you yourself counted fifty-six men that you boss. You said it was too many … and I've been studying up on that. I know it's too many … fellows in the front office told me so."

"Well, Tom, I just can't go through that again now. You know that Sid and George and the other boys don't want you as a boss now. Maybe later it'll be different. But I want to get this bonus business settled," said Bill. "Sid says the standards are no good. Rates on shafts are too tight and rotors are too loose. What do you think?"

"Well, I really think Sid is just an old fox. The rates are probably too loose on both shafts and rotors. He sits there all day, taking it easy, making a big bonus. And, he turns in a bonus report that fills his pocket. When the time-study man comes around to change the rate, he slows down to where you'd think he was dead. There's nothing I can do about it—they even get the new men acting that way. They all do it, and poor old George gets caught and a sore finger to boot. Hell, I don't want to be the boss of a crazy gang like that!" and with that outburst Tom stomped out of the office.

WHAT TO DO?

Bill continued to sit at his desk and consider the problems in the grinding department. He wondered if he had been right in talking to Tom Horton. The shop really did need better supervision. Maybe Tom could supervise the benchwork—eighteen or twenty of those fellows on broaching, filing, and hand jobs and half of them "horsing around" all the time. But putting Tom over there would take him off of machines. Tom was a good set-up man. Suddenly Bill stood up and left the office, saying to himself, "I'm going to talk to Anderson about these problems. He's superintendent around here—let him worry some for me. I've got four assistant foremen, but forty or fifty guys yell at me all the time. I need two or three more supervisors just for insulation. Wonder what the supe will say about George and those rates on the grinding machine? And, who—if anybody—should get disciplined for all of the cheating that's been going on? Will I get blamed for it, too!?"

CASE–11

The MBO Game with One Player

Gerald Richards was director of the research section of a large state government department responsible for disbursing funds for programs related to medical assistance, mental health, drug and alcohol abuse, and welfare assistance. The primary function of Richards's section was to provide periodic statistical reports pertaining to past and projected expenditures for these programs. In addition to these routine reports, the section often responded to departmental requests for special research projects such as cost-benefit studies of specific programs. Richards constantly tried to find additional ways in which his section could provide better informational support to those responsible for decision making in the various program areas.

There were seventeen employees in the section:

Three unit supervisors, each responsible for information regarding one of the following program areas:

1. Medical services.
2. Mental health and retardation.
3. Drug and alcohol abuse.

Three research analysts in each of the three units.

One clerical supervisor with authority over three clerks.

One administrative assistant (secretary), who reported to Richards.

This case was prepared by Professor Charles W. Boyd of the Department of Management of Southwest Missouri State University in Springfield as a basis for class discussion rather than to illustrate either effective or ineffective handling of an administrative situation. All names are disguised. Used by permission.

Two of the research analysts were men. All the other employees were women.

Gerald Richards had formerly worked in the research bureau of a large university. He was well advanced toward a Ph.D. degree when he accepted his present position about a year ago. Since becoming a section director, he spent a good deal of his spare time reading management literature. He became very interested in the possibilities of applying *Management by Objectives (MBO)* to his section.[1] This approach appeared to suit his style of leadership, which was characterized by a desire to develop his subordinates' full potential through careful delegation of authority and responsibility. In addition to the expected benefits to his employees, he believed that MBO, integrated with good planning, would improve the section's performance.

With these goals in mind, Richards began the task of educating his employees concerning the concept of MBO during special training sessions. He also devoted part of the weekly staff meeting to MBO training. A consultant was employed to instruct in the initial training sessions, and a few articles by well-known writers on the topic were circulated among the employees. The four clerical personnel were asked to attend the initial session so they would be aware of the nature of the new program. Attendance at future sessions was made optional for them, and all four chose not to attend.

Richards felt that his unit supervisors and research analysts had a sound basic understanding of the MBO process after the training sessions and their independent study of the subject. For the next phase of training, he asked them to practice writing some tentative objectives for the next year. He first provided them with his own set of goals for the section. Each unit supervisor reviewed the objectives written by her research analysts.

Richards in turn reviewed the objectives written by the three supervisors. The purposes of the review sessions were to ensure that the goals were stated in measurable terms and that they could be accomplished within six months to one year. Richards wanted his personnel to go through this practice experience with as little pressure as possible. He felt that spending this extra time would result in a better set of initial objectives and a higher goal accomplishment rate. He was sure the process would go faster during the next cycle of objective setting.

The research section was the only part of this state department that was actively involved in an MBO program. Other section directors typically developed their objectives with little or no input of subordinates. Throughout the department, there were few directed discussions between superiors and subordinates concerning the establishment of objectives. The approach being taken by Richards and his employees was unique for the department.

While some of his personnel still lacked confidence in their ability to write good objectives, Richards felt they were learning and that they were reasonably enthusiastic about the MBO program. However, before they began writing and finalizing a set of operating objectives, Richards and all of the

---

[1]See Appendix to this case for a brief introduction to MBO.

other section directors received an unexpected memorandum from his boss, the manager of the state government department. The memorandum asked that all section directors submit within one week a set of objectives for the next five years relating to their top five or six goals. A sample set of objectives from one of the department's sections was attached to the memo.

Upon receipt of this request, Gerald Richards called a meeting with his unit supervisors. The group decided that the supervisors would work with their research analysts and attempt within the next three days to write their unit objectives based on Richards's section goals. The supervisors would then have one-to-one discussions with Richards in order to finalize the objectives. He would then add his personal objectives and write the required response to the department manager.

As he wrote the responding memorandum, Richards was concerned about the effect of his subordinates being suddenly forced to change their planning horizon from one year to five years. He realized that there had been very little time for them to make the mental adjustment of thinking that far into the future and developing solid, measurable objectives. As a result, he did not feel confident about the set of objectives being presented to his boss as he would like to have felt. He also became aware that the successful accomplishment of some of his section's objectives was contingent on certain events transpiring in other sections of the department, most notably in data processing. The following comment in his memo reflected this concern:

> In the case of the research section, its planning is highly interdependent with that of the data processing section. Some of our objectives reflect this interdependence.

Objectives were submitted from each section, and none of the section directors received any feedback about them. Although his response had apparently been acceptable, or at least not unsatisfactory, Gerald Richards wondered how he should proceed with his section's MBO program from this point.

APPENDIX

Management by Objectives (MBO) is a system of management in which managers at all levels of an organization jointly identify common goals, determine each manager's major areas of responsibility in terms of specific results to be expected, and use these objectives as the primary guides for managing each organizational unit and evaluating the performance of each manager.

MBO-type approaches are often called by other designations, such as *managing for results*, and *results-oriented management*. Such approaches may be an integral part of organizational efforts that utilize *total quality manage-*

ment (TQM), employee empowerment, and other participative management approaches.

A firm's approach to MBO will reflect the preferences and circumstances of the organization. Usually, however, an MBO system involves the mutual setting of target objectives between a manager and his or her subordinate supervisors prior to a budget year. Objectives must be written in terms that are measurable (quantifiable) or verifiable. These objectives may be adjusted during the year if necessary to reflect changing conditions. At the end of the year, the manager and subordinate mutually compare the objectives that were agreed upon with the performance results achieved. This appraisal of performance results is the major basis for determination of salary adjustments, bonuses, and other rewards.

CASE-12

An Alcohol/Drug Problem within a Drug Company

Siegman Pharmaceutical Company manufactured and marketed a line of non prescription and prescription pharmaceuticals as well as bulk chemicals. Company headquarters were on the East Coast of the United States, and six sales regions were carved out of geographical areas of the United States. The company was competitive worldwide; at the time of this case, the company employed some 26,000 people in operations in some 115 countries.

Founded in the early 1900s, the company's steady growth had resulted in ample profits and continued market dominance in several key medical applications, such as antihypertension pharmaceuticals and lipid (cholesterol) regulating agents, along with an over-the-counter line of cold remedies. Net sales in the last year had been approximately $3 billion, and net income after operating costs was about $305 million, up 12 percent from the prior year.

Within the eight-state Midwest sales region, sales of both prescription and non prescription pharmaceuticals were up 18 percent from the previous year. The regional sales manager, Julie Jaworski, was especially encouraged by this trend; she felt that her sales force was one of the best throughout the entire company. Miles Blain, the district manager of one of her sales districts centered in Terre Haute, Indiana, had left her a message to call him as soon as possible to discuss one of his pharmaceutical sales representatives.

THE FIRST CONVERSATION

Julie Jaworski returned the call to Miles Blain on a Monday morning after returning from a trip to corporate headquarters the previous week.

JAWORSKI: Hello Miles, I got your message. You have a problem with one of your reps?

BLAIN: Julie, I received a call on Saturday from a sales representative's wife. She said her husband had checked into a program for drug and alcohol abuse over the weekend.

JAWORSKI: Who was it? Did you know he was having this sort of problem?

The names of the company and its locations and the names of all individuals are disguised.

BLAIN: Julie, it was Sheldon Briggs, a young guy we recruited from a prestigious Ivy League university two years ago. He had been one of the top producers in my district since joining us, and this really came as a shock to me. In fact, I had met with him only three weeks ago and reviewed his performance. We went over the objectives we had agreed upon, and he had met or exceeded all of them. He didn't seem to be having any trouble that I could see, and I asked him for his inputs on any problems he had.

JAWORSKI: Well I had better call corporate headquarters and alert them to the situation. I'm sure Carl Tufts, our HR head, will throw a fit over this. You know what he thinks about drug rehab programs and people with drug or alcohol problems. He will probably want to know why we didn't spot this problem before it came to this. I'll get back to you after I talk with him.

BLAIN: Okay. I hope we can get an answer soon. This whole situation really caught me out of the blue. Again, Julie, tell Tufts that Sheldon Briggs's performance has consistently been above his objectives, and I have not received any complaints or information that he was not handling his accounts in a professional manner.

THE CORPORATE HR CONVERSATION

Julie Jaworski called corporate headquarters to talk with Carl Tufts, human resources director for all sales and marketing personnel.

TUFTS: Hello, Julie, it was nice to see you when you visited last week. What can I do for you?

JAWORSKI: Well, Carl, I wish I were calling on a positive note. I just talked with one of my district managers, Miles Blain, in Terre Haute. He informed me that one of his pharmaceutical sales representatives named Sheldon Briggs had checked in to a drug and alcohol treatment center over the weekend.

TUFTS: Julie, was the guy performing his duties while all this was going on? Why didn't anyone notice this? Surely his performance must have suffered. We have to make sure we abide by all Food and Drug Administration (FDA) regulations that pertain to selling prescription and non prescription pharmaceuticals. This type of incident doesn't help our situation. It's even worse that he was driving a company car during all of this. What if he had killed someone while under the influence of whatever he was doing? We would be liable.

JAWORSKI: Well, Carl, Miles Blain said that Briggs was one of his top sales reps, and his past performance verifies this. Evidently Briggs had continued to service his accounts without any incidents. What is the policy towards this situation? This is the first such case in my region since I moved into my current position.

TUFTS: It depends on the person and the circumstances involved. For some of our personnel, we have covered the costs involved in a treatment program, but we've found that these programs usually don't work and are a waste of a lot of money. They can cost between $10,000 to $15,000 for the usual stay. Personally, I'd advocate immediate termination of this individual, because sooner or later down the road he's likely to return to doing drugs or drinking. This places us in a terrible position with our customers and the government. All I can tell you is that you and Blain have a decision to make regarding this guy. I need to be appraised quickly of whatever you decide to do. I've seen more of this in the last two years than in the previous twenty years I've been with this corporation. Maybe we need to do a better job of picking people.

THE THIRD CONVERSATION

With this in mind, Julie Jaworski called Miles Blain to tell him of her discussion with Carl Tufts.

JAWORSKI: Hello, Miles. I just talked with Carl Tufts at corporate headquarters, and he was not very pleased with what I had to tell him. He recommended that we immediately terminate Briggs, but he said we would have to make the final decision ourselves on what to do.

BLAIN: Julie, I think we need to consider the circumstances as well as Briggs's past performance before we make a hasty decision. In my opinion, Sheldon Briggs could be salvaged if we support him through this and show some confidence in him. After all, he did admit himself for treatment on his own, so maybe he really is serious about getting help. Besides, didn't Carl Tufts recently tell us that it was important to attract and retain bright and promising people? Briggs is very bright, and our own records indicate that we invest about $28,000 of training costs in each of our sales reps.

JAWORSKI: That's true, Miles, and, yes, Briggs is bright and was a top performer. But the FDA regulations associated with our business, as you know, are very stringent. And, think of the consequences that could result if we allow him back and he goes back to his old mode of behavior or worse. Miles, we need to set up a meeting and decide on our course of action. Carl Tufts wants us to keep him updated on what we are doing. Can you come to the regional office on Thursday of this week? We can talk then.

DECISION TIME

On Thursday morning, Miles Blain drove to the regional sales office in Chicago to meet with Julie Jaworski to discuss what should be the final decision regarding the future of Sheldon Briggs.

CASE–13

Stan Ballard, CPA, and the Upset Client

Stan Ballard was an honor graduate from a state university in Virginia, where he had maintained a 4.0 average and majored in accounting. Many of his faculty felt he was the best overall student to attend the business school. His score on the CPA exam ranked him among the top five in the nation. He was a member of two national honor societies and two local ones, and he was the pianist for the university concert orchestra. Besides playing the piano, his chief avocation was reading.

Ballard was sought by the major CPA firms and accepted a position with one of the largest accounting firms in its Atlanta office. He didn't start work until September because he spent the summer in Europe. He was initially assigned to an audit team. On his first day with the audit team in the field, his supervisor, Dan Thomas, was informed by Terry Davis, manager of accounting of the Allen Paper Company, which they were auditing, that Stan Ballard had a strong tendency to annoy the employees by talking down to them. Dan asked Terry specifically what he meant. Terry replied, "His tone of voice and choice of words in asking questions comes across like he is talking to a simpleton. It is like I am asking a simple person a simple question which hopefully he will answer. Three of the women he worked with today complained of his attitude. I am telling you so you can square him away." The next day, Dan met with Stan and at the end of the day said, "Stan, try to remember at all times we are paid to ask questions, and the people we deal with can make the job easy or difficult for us."

THE CLIENT'S COMPLAINT

The next day, all things appeared to be normal. Dan Thomas was scheduled to be in his office on Thursday and Friday because of previous commitments. At 3:00 P.M. on Friday, he received a call to come to the office of Peter Zacker, partner in charge of the Atlanta office.

Zacker said to Thomas, "I just received a call from Sam Allen, president of Allen Paper Company, telling me to remove Ballard from our audit team at his firm or we will not have his firm as a client. In fact, he has given me

This case was prepared by Professor Thomas L. Wheelen of the University of South Florida at Tampa, and by Kathyrn E. Wheelen, Research Assistant at the University of Tampa. All names are disguised. Used by permission.

until Tuesday to get Ballard to apologize to a Ms. Brown that he insulted. He is adamant about this apology. Sam and I are good friends, but I am not sure I can calm him down without the apology.

Dan Thomas asked, "Pete, what transpired to cause this mess?"

Zacker replied, "It seems Ballard was dealing with a Myra Brown, who has been responsible for accounts payable for the past twenty-two years. He asked her several questions and it seems she didn't answer the questions to his liking. He said, "How can anyone do such a menial job so long and not know it." She got up and went straight to Terry Davis's office and reported the incident. She was so upset, she cried. Terry knew you were at our office, so he went out and found Ballard still at Ms. Brown's desk. He told Ballard to apologize to Brown. Ballard asked, "For what reason should I apologize? I haven't done anything wrong. What am I accused of; at least let me know that." At this point, Davis blew his lid and told Ballard "Get the hell out of this office and don't ever come back. You are an arrogant snob." Ballard packed his attache case and left the office. Davis had then proceeded to call Zacker and relay the whole story to him. Zacker concurred on Davis's handling of the incident. It seems Ms. Brown had just been honored at a party for thirty-five years of outstanding service to the company; in fact, Terry Davis made the presentation. He said, "Myra Brown is one of our most loyal and most faithful employees and no young college genius is going to insult her. He will apologize and then never enter our offices again, or I will get a new accounting firm to handle our business."

Zacker pointed out to Dan Thomas, "This is one of our largest clients and we have had the account for fifteen years, so I don't want to lose it. Also, Sam is a very close personal friend. I told him that I'd look immediately into the matter and get back to him on Monday. I have scheduled a meeting to see him at 11:00 on Monday. I think we have all the facts, but check them with Ballard. I hope he has enough sense to come straight back to the office. I don't want to lose this client since I am the one who brought this account to our office."

STAN BALLARD'S SIDE OF THE INCIDENT

Dan Thomas returned to his office; Stan Ballard was waiting for him. Thomas said, "Stan, what did you do? All hell has broken loose around here. I thought we had agreed on how to handle the client's employees." Stan answered, "Wait a minute, Dan, I didn't do anything wrong. I simply asked her four simple questions in a row that she said she would have to look up. So, all I said was, "Forget it, we can do it later; let's do the simple things first, then you can look up the answers to these questions. At that point, she got up and walked away. I thought she was going to look up data, so I ignored it. Next thing I knew I was being chewed out by Mr. Davis and being told to apologize to Myra Brown. He never said for what. So, I couldn't see why I had to apologize since I didn't know what I was accused of. When he said to leave, I figured it was best for me to get back here and see you. Honestly, that is all that happened." Dan said, "It was smart not to say much. I will call Terry and try to see him before he leaves the office or at his home tomorrow. If you think of anything, please let me know since Mr. Zacker is meeting with Mr. Allen at 11:00 Monday over the incident. It seems if you don't apologize to Ms. Brown, we will lose the Allen account. So, is there anything else I should know?" Stan replied, "Well, Myra Brown is very touchy about being asked many questions. She told me she didn't know how I could ask her questions with my experience and age." Dan Thomas responded, "Stan, I have to give a recommendation to Mr. Zacker on Monday morning. You might have to apologize just to save the account for the firm. See you on Monday." Stan replied, "I won't apologize since I didn't do anything wrong. I'll see you Monday."

Dan Thomas called Terry Davis. "Terry, can we meet today about the Ballard problem?" Terry replied, "No, I am going out of town for the weekend with my family. I am adamant that Ballard apologize to Ms. Brown. He is arrogant, and must take his medicine. He really upset her. She is a very mild person and never had problems like this before, so it has to be Ballard."

THE ULTIMATUM

On Monday, Stan Ballard met with Dan Thomas and Peter Zacker in Thomas's office. The following conversation took place.

ZACKER: "Stan, my boy, both Mr. Thomas and myself feel the best way to resolve the problem is for you to apologize to Ms. Brown. I recognize you may not be completely at fault, but it would simplify the whole matter. The firm and I would truly appreciate your assistance in this sticky matter. The incident will not be held against you. It can be chalked up to a learning experience. I must go but I will be in contact with Mr. Thomas."

BALLARD: "Mr. Zacker, I would like to discuss the entire situation with you since your solution is wholly unacceptable to me."

ZACKER: "You and Mr. Thomas can discuss the alternatives, but I feel this solution is the only acceptable one to our client. I will see Mr. Allen at 11:00 and see if we can reach another solution. I must go."

With that, Peter Zacker got up and closed the door as he exited from Dan Thomas's office.

CASE-14

Too Many Bosses

In February, the major jig and fixtures department of a large manufacturing company had opened a group of jigs to production. Some of these tools had been built by outside contractors and shipped in, presumably ready for use in building parts, although this was only the ideal. In practice, many "bugs" had to be ironed out, and in some instances it was even discovered that subcontracted tools had been built to obsolete tool design. This meant that major reworking would be required—occasionally even rebuilding the tool involved.

Where this was necessary, production was delayed until the tools could be ready to build the production assemblies that were needed to turn out parts in quantity. This might require as little as three days or as long as four weeks, depending upon the amount of rework required. It is no wonder that this condition generated a great deal of pressure on the tooling organization from some of the upper echelons of management (See Exhibit C–14.)

During the peak of this confusion, Fred Larson, a supervisor, found his operation to be one of the hottest spots. Jess Bradley, his division superintendent, inaugurated the practice of walking through the shop a couple of times a day to see how things were moving along. At first, he always came with Phil Hawthorne, Fred's foreman, and discussed the job chiefly with the supervisor in charge. Pretty soon, however, he was coming by himself, and if the supervisor wasn't around he might talk at length with a lead person or even one or two of the workers. Then as time went on, he went a step beyond talking and asking questions, requesting job builders to tear down a set-up in order to incorporate some of his ideas.

Fred's was not the only work station in the tooling organization to receive this treatment. All of the operations reporting to Phil were also on Jess's itinerary, as were several of those for which other foremen were responsible, and Phil and his foreman colleagues well knew what was going on. The straw that broke the camel's back, so to speak, was an incident that occurred in Fred's area about ten days after all of this started. Already the morale of the workers was at a low ebb, since they did not know any more whether to go ahead with a planned set-up or wait for Jess Bradley to tell them how to proceed. Then one day Fred returned to his station after a brief absence to

---

This case was prepared by Professor Howard R. Smith of the College of Business Administration of the University of Georgia at Athens. All names are disguised. Used by permission.

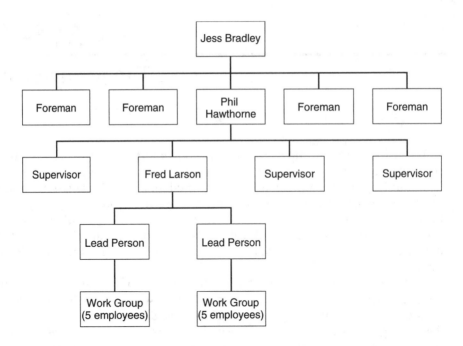

EXHIBIT C–14 Jig and Fixtures Department Organization Chart

learn that scheduled operations on a large job had just been changed, and that two days' set-up time for seven men had thereby gone down the drain.

Profoundly disturbed and thoroughly angry, Fred decided that things could no longer go on this way.

Friction on the MIS Project

James Albertson headed one section of a department of state government staffed by twenty-one employees. Sixteen of these personnel worked in four small units, each having a different set of responsibilities. Four of the other personnel were secretaries or administrative assistants, each assigned to one of the four units. The remaining member of the section was Marion Jackson, Mr. Albertson's personal secretary.

Albertson was experiencing some pressure to provide his section's input to a new management information system (MIS) that the department was developing. This involved specification of the records, files, and data elements necessary to automate a large portion of the department's data. The task had taken approximately ten hours of Albertson's time during each of the past two weeks. His superior expected him to finalize his input to the new MIS in three more months. Meeting this deadline would continue to take a large amount of his time.

Marion Jackson had been assisting Albertson with the MIS project, but he had not been very pleased with the progress that had been made so far. He found that he had to provide her with rather explicit and detailed instructions; as was true of her regular secretarial work, she did not exercise much personal initiative. On the other hand, he was pleased that Marion, a fifty-year-old married woman, was extremely loyal to him and that her word processing and other work were of above-average quality. Nevertheless, he felt that the nature of the MIS project with its rather short deadline required that he have administrative assistance from a person willing and able to exercise more initiative and thus requiring less personal guidance from him. He believed that this would also provide more time for him to manage the day-to-day operations of his section.

James Albertson thought that Linda Williams, a secretary for one of the four units in the section, could provide him with the type of administrative assistance he was looking for. Linda was a young, personable, single woman with excellent skills who had demonstrated initiative and a desire for more responsibility. She kept the personnel in her unit informed concerning the due dates for reports they were required to write. She was an extremely fast and

---

This case was prepared by Professor Charles W. Boyd of the Department of Management of Southwest Missouri State University in Springfield as a basis for class discussion rather than to illustrate either effective or ineffective handling of an administrative situation. All names are disguised. Used by permission.

accurate word processor and a good editor as well. Personnel in her unit often delegated to her the task of writing routine memos and correspondence, which she always handled in a capable manner.

As a result of her speed and efficiency, Linda often had periods of two or more hours at a time when she had no pending workload. She frequently complained about this to the personnel in her unit and to Mr. Albertson. This was another factor that led Albertson to feel that he could utilize Linda as a part-time administrative assistant on the MIS project without seriously affecting her work output for the unit to which she was regularly assigned.

Basing his decision on the above-mentioned factors, James Albertson decided to discuss with Linda the possibility, of utilizing her on the MIS project. She expressed great interest in serving in this capacity because she felt it would occupy her time more fully and be more challenging than the comparatively routine work she did for her unit. She assured Mr. Albertson that the efficiency of her performance would not suffer as a result of the increased responsibility. Linda's supervisor agreed that she should be able to discharge the unit's work even with the sacrifice of time that the MIS assignment would require.

Albertson's next step was to meet with Linda and Marion in order to clarify the roles of the two women. He explained to Marion that Linda would be assuming the responsibilities of the MIS project, and that Marion would continue to function primarily as his secretary. Marion appeared disturbed by this decision and asked if there had been some problem with the way in which she had handled the MIS assignment. Knowing that Marion had a strong sense of loyalty to him and was always concerned that her work pleased him, Albertson responded by indicating that the main issue was time; Linda had more time to devote to the MIS project than Marion did. As the discussion concluded, Marion told Linda, "Be sure to share your work with me when things pile up. I believe you are taking on more than you are going to be able to handle."

Two weeks later, James Albertson was not sure that he had made the right decision. Linda had made significant progress with the MIS work while requiring minimal direction from him. At the same time, the quality of work she did for her unit had been maintained. Despite this, Linda did not seem happy on the job. She conversed less with the other employees and with him, going about her work in an almost mechanical fashion. Marion had initiated two conversations with Albertson in the office during this period. On these occasions, she questioned him further concerning his satisfaction with her work, and asked him if there were any ways in which he felt she could improve her performance. He tried to assure her that he was not unhappy with her work, but that he did hope that she would be able to handle more of the smaller details of the job without specific direction.

Linda burst into Mr. Albertson's office one afternoon during the third week following her assignment to the MIS project. Through tears she said, "I must talk with you!" Albertson took her to a nearly, deserted coffee shop on the lower floor of their office building. Beginning to cry again, Linda told him,

"I just can't stand it! Marion never speaks to me anymore. Sometimes I see her whispering to one of the other women, and then they look at me. I'm sure they're talking about me. I know that Marion can't stand me, but I don't know why. I'm just trying to do my job!" Albertson tried to comfort Linda by telling her that if Marion really did have ill feelings toward her, time was often the best healer of such emotions. After he had talked with her for about thirty minutes, she regained her composure. He told her to take the remainder of the afternoon off and get some rest.

When he returned to his office, James Albertson spent some time reflecting on this problem and trying to decide what action he should take, if any. He also wondered about the rumor he had heard from Linda's unit that she was looking for another job.

CASE–16

Frazer's Department Store: A Communications Challenge

Ann Fiske, executive vice president of Frazer's Department Store, returned from a conference held by a national retailers' association, where she had been impressed by a talk on the subject of communications. Soon after her return to the store, she discussed the conference with Sterling Stone, the human resources manager, and gave him the notes she had made. Stone agreed that relationships among members of the organization might be improved if more attention were given to management-employee communications. (A management organization chart, Exhibit C–16, is presented at the end of the case.)

A young woman, Gloria Prentiss, had recently joined the human resources department and was being trained for the position of employment supervisor. She was a graduate of a state university and had worked in a chain discount department store while in college and for two years thereafter. She came to Frazer's directly from that position. It occurred to Stone that it would be good training and experience for his new assistant if she made a thorough survey of the methods of communication used by the store personnel.

Gloria Prentiss discussed this assignment with both Mr. Stone and Ms. Fiske. Gloria was given the notes that Ms. Fiske had prepared at the conference, and she was told that she could interview any executive in the store. She was given permission to dictate her report for Mr. Stone's secretary to word process. Gloria was asked to complete the survey within a week.

Five days later, Gloria Prentiss presented the following report to Mr. Stone and asked permission to discuss it with him after he had read it.

All names are disguised. The store was located in a small midwestern city.

Store Communications—Report
by Gloria Prentiss

Like many other department stores, Frazer's has established various channels for two-way communications between management and employees. There is a need for making these means of communication more effective. This report suggests that improvements in store communications might result in greater employee understanding of store problems and could increase productivity, lower operating costs, and result in greater store profits.

Means of Communication

Various types of communication are currently used at Frazer's. They include the following:

A. *Written communications.* Several media make up this part of the formal system used by management to supply employees with information.

   1. *House organ. Frazer's Family* is a monthly publication largely written by store employees. It is edited, printed, and distributed by the employee services department. It's a very attractive magazine featuring many employee pictures and brief copy. It concentrates on the "human element" and attempts to build group solidarity among store personnel. The store management makes little or no attempt to use this medium to tell employees of its philosophy or its problems.
   2. *Door handouts.* The employees receive these bulletins when they sign in for work at the beginning of the day. The handouts announce special events such as an evening softball game, or they emphasize important sales promotions, Christmas sales, and other events. The handout bulletins are issued once or twice a week and primarily serve as reminders of store events. They frequently give employees information or instruction from management.
   3. *Paycheck inserts.* Another reminder that emphasizes important promotions, charity solicitations, or policies is a brief message placed in each employee's paycheck envelope. This method is particularly effective when the store is in the process of a charity drive. In general, the messages in pay envelopes are carefully written and do not offend the reader when he or she is being asked for a contribution. Several supervisors feel that these inserts are less effective when used each week.

4. *Bulletin boards.* Eleven bulletin boards, placed in strategic locations throughout the store, contain important and current information. Some workers pay very little attention to these postings. Perhaps the material could be presented in a more interesting and readable form. Some employees complain that items on the bulletin board are seldom changed and that current notices are carelessly posted.

5. *Intrastore messages and correspondence.* Probably the most widely used channels of communication consist of intracompany messages, correspondence, and reports. Written matter, electronic mail, facsimile messages, and the like permeate throughout the store. The majority of messages usually concern operating problems and policies, but they frequently clear up misunderstandings and solve problems that are part of the human-relations aspects of communications. Unfortunately, many individuals in the store do not write letters, memos, and instructions as well as they should. Further, many employees complain about "information overload"; that is, they feel that too many messages are trivial and a waste of their time.

B. *Meetings.* Department and store meetings constitute another segment of Frazer's formal communication system.

1. *Departmental meetings.* In departmental meetings, employees receive merchandise information and hear about changes in operating procedures. New selling techniques are presented. The primary motive is to stress store operations, policies, procedures, and merchandise.

2. *Store meetings.* Occasionally, a meeting is held on the main floor for all dayshift personnel of Frazer's. Everyone is expected to come to work ten minutes early on the days of these meetings, but half or more of the store personnel either miss the meetings or come in late. New policies or special promotions are briefly discussed. Detailed explanations are given at the department level. The purpose of the mass meeting is to develop a feeling of group solidarity and to give employees the opportunity to hear a message from "top management." Supposedly, the employees will think that they are in "one big happy family," and thereby accept the submitted information more readily. These meetings are not as successful as the speakers think they are. Many employees complain about the early starting time. Employees who work other shifts and part-time employees complain that they miss out on these meetings and get the information "secondhand" from dayshift supervisors.

C. *Counseling.* In connection with employee attitudes and performance, there are two types of counseling: a six-month interview and the attitude survey. The objective of both methods is to determine and improve employee job satisfaction and job performance.

   1. *Six-month interviews.* Every six months, each employee is rated by his or her supervisor and then is interviewed by the supervisor and next by a staff person from the HR department. An attempt is made to see if an adjustment between job and employee is needed. Compensation problems, promotions, benefits, and transfers are the main topics considered. It is the responsibility of the HR department to cooperate with an employee's supervisor if any action is needed after the interviews. The interviews have more form than substance. In many cases, the employee and the supervisor or HR counselor differ in their opinions as to needed adjustments. The interviews seem to be guided too much by what management feels is important. These impressions have been obtained from conversations with several employees.
   2. *Attitude survey.* Occasionally, management attempts to determine general employee attitudes toward store policies and operations. A questionnaire has been developed that is used as a guide by a member of the HR department to conduct a question-and-answer interview with each employee in those departments in which morale or productivity seems to be low. Some employees think the attitude surveys are a waste of time. Some of the younger sales clerks take the interviews as a "joke," and the information is probably very unreliable.

D. *Informal communications.* Some supervisors and departmental heads at Frazer's seem to be unaware of the fact that good management-employee relations depend on continuous satisfactory relationships. These managers are frequently skilled technicians in merchandising or sales, but they fail to realize that the cooperation and good will of their employees and associates are necessary to have an effective department. Lower levels of management in the store do not appear to be convinced of this.

   1. *Manager-employee relationship.* A wide variance of supervisory effectiveness is seen from department to department. In a few departments, the employees seem to be reasonably content and productive. Their managers treat them as individuals and are willing to listen to their problems and questions. Too many Frazer supervisors do not know how to develop this open atmo-

sphere. Their employees seem to be afraid and seldom care to speak with their bosses. Some even refused to talk frankly with the author of this report.

2. *Grapevine.* Frazer's grapevine is, perhaps, the quickest means of communication in the store. It travels up and down the management-employee ladder at a rapid rate. Many instances occur in which the grapevine has information long before the supervisors find out what is going to happen in their departments. Unfortunately, the grapevine also has been known to spread rumors and gossip, which have been embarrassing to certain individuals involved.

Conclusions

Some potential channels of communication in the store have not been included in this study. One of the most significant of these are relationships between the training division's personnel and between departmental supervisors and employees. The activities of the store's training division could be a more effective channel for management communications. In training new employees and in training regular employees for transfer, the training supervisor and the departmental supervisors could pass along more information regarding management policies and practices. In addition, the training supervisors could collect ideas, suggestions, and other information from employees that would be helpful to management. The meetings organized by the training supervisor for department managers and supervisors could be more effective. Apparently, higher-level executives have seldom participated in these meetings. One supervisor stated that he was sorry that his boss couldn't hear what was said at the last supervisory conference.

At this time, two suggestions might be appropriate as part of this report. First, it is recommended that the suggestion system, which was discontinued several months ago, be reconsidered. With careful study and reorganization, it might be operated successfully to the store's advantage. Second, this report could be carefully reviewed in management and supervisory meetings. Improvements in communications in the store can be made if the key people in the organization give their attention to the challenge.

Respectfully submitted,
Gloria Prentiss

Within an hour after the report on communications was submitted to Sterling Stone, he called Gloria Prentiss to his office.

STONE: It's a good report, Gloria. You've covered a lot of ground. Don't you think you've been a little too critical in some spots? You've been pretty tough with our counseling program.

PRENTISS: Well, I hope not, Mr. Stone. I just didn't know how to write the report. I couldn't sleep night before last, worrying about it. I could have made it sound better, but I decided to call a spade a spade and tell you just exactly how I felt.

STONE: Oh, it's not so bad—but, take something like the early morning meetings. A few employees gripe about the ten minutes' early start, but do our better people mind? Don't the meetings do more good than harm? We pay them for it if they attend.

PRENTISS: Possibly so, Mr. Stone, but I just feel that there have been too many lately. Mr. Bauer had two last week.

STONE: Well, Art Bauer is superintendent over the whole store, but he probably does call too many meetings. Did you talk to him about the survey? How did he like it?

PRENTISS: I think he was too busy to really understand what I was doing. I had a hard time seeing him, and when I did have a chance to get into his office, I waited behind a line of three other people. I don't think he liked the survey.

STONE: But what did he say about communications in his department?

PRENTISS: He said they were good; he thinks there is no problem. He says that when he wants to communicate, he just goes out and talks to whomever he wants to communicate with. Of course, I couldn't ask him many questions.

STONE: I know what you mean, Gloria. I need to reach him this morning. I've called three times, and I can't get him on the phone.

PRENTISS: Well, I want you to know, Mr. Stone, that I appreciated the opportunity to make this survey. If I seem critical, it's just because I want to be of help. I don't expect any place to be perfect. I like Frazer's, and I think I have a good job here.

STONE: I'm glad you feel that way. We want you to get into these store problems. I'd better mark this report "Confidential"—and we'll see what Ann Fiske says about it. She started all this, anyway. Is there anything else you have to say about it?

PRENTISS: Yes, there is, Mr. Stone. As long as I'm sticking my neck out, I might as well go all the way. I met an old schoolmate of mine working on the first floor in men's clothing. He's only been there two months, but he's not sure who his boss is. He says that he takes orders from two buyers and also from his department supervisor and the first-floor manager. Much of the time, he just does what he thinks is right. It seems that both the buyers and the operating managers think they supervise the salespeople. He told me that he'd been in the department about a week when a new woman came to him about 12:30 one day and asked him if it was all right for her to go to lunch. He looked around and saw the floor was clear, so he said, "Yes, I guess it's all right." She went to lunch, and for several days after that she thought that he was the boss. It may not be a problem of communications, so I didn't see how I could put it in the report. But I did want to tell you about it.

STONE: That's a good story, Gloria, and I'm glad to hear it. We really depend on our buyers' expertise, but some of the operating managers still don't like it. But then maybe the supervision of salespeople is weak when merchandisers have a lot of authority and influence. If that's a communication problem, it's a tough one. Let me give this report to Ms. Fiske, and I'll see you later.

PRENTISS: Thanks, Mr. Stone.

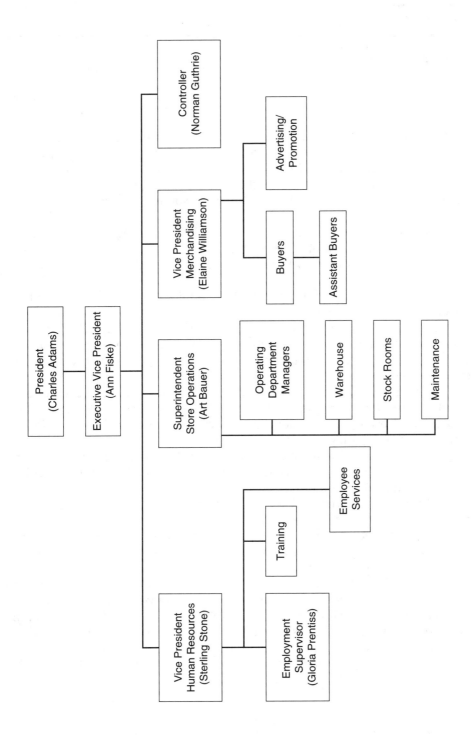

EXHIBIT C–16 Frazer's Department Store Management Organization

CASE–17

See, We Were Right!

Joe Grant said, "Bull, I think we could make a few minor adjustments to this die and turn out the part for the new model."

"Joe, if we can, it'll be the first time. But it's worth looking into. After all, a new die costs in the neighborhood of $14,000. With the way the brass has been crying the blues over our costs lately, it would be a real plus if we can pull it off."

Joe Grant, supervisor of the production line at the Able Manufacturing Company, and his foreman, Bull Jones, spent the next few hours examining the specs for the new part and evaluating the possibilities of the adjustments on the die.

Finally, Bull spoke triumphantly, "We can do it, Joe. It'll work. I'll tell the boss in the morning."

The Able Company supplied parts for a major automobile company. When new models came out each year, new tools were usually required because of changes in the parts; but this year's new part was very similar to that supplied last year.

Bull Jones wrote out his suggestion and took it to his department head, Chad Hodges, director of manufacturing. Hodges thanked Bull and promised to see that the engineering department was informed of the idea. Hodges forwarded the suggestion as he had promised.

Two weeks went by and nothing was heard from the engineering department regarding the proposal. Hodges, after questioning by Bull Jones, called the chief engineer, Karl Milentz.

"Are we clear to readjust the old die to make the new part when we get ready to run that order?" queried Hodges.

"No," replied Milentz. "My people say that it is impossible to do it correctly with the present die. We've ordered the new one, and it will be here in time for running the order."

Both Bull Jones and Joe Grant were very unhappy over the turn of events. They felt that higher management was completely ignoring a suggestion that would save a large amount of money. Further, they felt that the engineering department had questioned their knowledge of their job.

When the new die arrived, the production department did not install it. Instead, Bull Jones and Joe Grant adjusted the old tooling and turned the

---

This case was prepared by Dr. A. Ranger Curran, Professor of Management at Keene State College, Keene, NH. All names are disguised. Used by permission.

parts out on it. The parts met all specs, and the engineering department was not aware of the change.

About a week after the order was completed and shipped out, Chad Hodges' telephone rang. He answered only to hear the irate voice of the plant manager, Willis Whitney.

"Hodges, what in hell is going on? The tool crib just called to ask what should be done about disposing of the new die for our auto parts order. They say it's still in the crate!"

CASE–18

Too Many Personal Calls

THE ORGANIZATION

John Dixon, vice president of operations for Consolidated Stores, Inc., was responsible for the Springdale region. Forty-four retail apparel stores and outlets in four midwestern states were in the region, which was divided into three districts. Each district was supervised by a district manager and an assistant district manager. Managerial, accounting, merchandising, and advertising activities serving the stores were carried on in the Springdale regional office. An administrative services group in the Springdale office served all managers and supervisors and was located on the second and fourth floors of the company building. A spacious, well-appointed lounge, used by office personnel, was located on the third floor along with the cafeteria and restrooms.

At the time of this case, John Dixon had more than thirty-five years of service with the company. During his five years as regional manager in Springdale, he had been very successful in meeting the problems created by shortages of facilities and by an increase of nearly 40 percent in store sales. Service and operating results for the region were above average for several years, and the current year had shown improvement over the corresponding months of the previous year.

In addition to the district managers and their assistants, several other managers and supervisors maintained offices in the Springdale building. A controller, a merchandise manager, and an advertising director each had private office space. Although many employees worked directly for the various managers and supervisors at Springdale, other employees reported directly to several office supervisors who, in turn, reported to the office manager, Harriet Black.

Because most managers and supervisors traveled frequently to the stores, all clerical services employees were responsible to Ms. Black for office procedures, practices, and discipline. Harriet Black was an experienced manager who had been in the Springdale office for more than fifteen years. She generally was recognized as being exceptionally capable, and other supervisors and managers often consulted with her for help on problems. All other

---

All names and places are disguised.

office supervisors were formerly employees who had been promoted and trained during the previous five years.

THE PERSONAL CALLS PROBLEM

John Dixon devoted some time each week to operating and personnel problems within the Springdale office. Sometimes he observed various office activities jointly with one or more of the managers and supervisors, but he also made it a frequent practice to observe certain operations by himself.

Over a period of weeks, Dixon became increasingly aware that many personal telephone calls were being made by the office supervisors and certain employees from their desks. He noticed that this was not peculiar to any one unit but seemed to be a general practice. On several occasions when he was in the various offices, he had to wait for supervisors to finish their personal calls before he could discuss business matters with them. One morning, as he was observing activities alone, he noted that a supervisor's telephone was tied up for almost an hour with two successive calls that Dixon believed to be personal in nature. He was not always sure that he was able to distinguish a personal from a business call, but it was obvious that company telephones were often used for other than business communications.

Company policy was not to prohibit personal calls, but such calls were to be strictly limited so that the telephone lines would be available for calls from stores, suppliers, customers, and other business people needing to communicate with the regional office. Several complaints from store managers had been received by Dixon to the effect that it was difficult "to get through" to the regional office by telephone. Consequently, on two different occasions earlier in the year, Dixon had discussed the policy on personal calls in regular meetings with his management personnel, and he believed the policy was generally understood. Further, Dixon felt that the office supervisors and managers through their own observations should have been aware of the excessive number of personal calls currently being made by their people.

THE NEW POLICY

It seemed apparent to Dixon that the corrective action—if any—taken by the managers and office supervisors had not been effective. He decided that prompt personal action on his part was needed.

To dispose quickly of the problem, as was his usual practice, Dixon issued the following memo, a copy of which was distributed to every person in the Springdale office: "To keep our telephone lines available for business calls, all personal calls by supervisors and employees should be made from the telephones that have been placed in the lounge." Dixon then arranged for four additional telephones to be connected in the lounge the same afternoon.

PROBLEMS WITH THE POLICY

During his observations the following week, Dixon did not discern any personal calls. However, early one morning about two weeks after he had issued his directive, Dixon received a call from Janet Smythe, one of the most reliable word processors in the office services pool. He invited her to come right up to his office. Ms. Smythe had been a "Class 1" word processor for three years; she was frequently called on for special assignments because she was popular and well liked by everyone. As she walked into his office, Dixon noted that she seemed to be quite upset.

Ms. Smythe, in her usual low voice, commenced by saying, "I would like to question the fairness of your ruling on personal telephone calls." She went on to cite her own experience on the day before. She had been informed of an overtime assignment by Harriet Black, late in the afternoon. Feeling obligated to let her family know that she would be late, she started for the lounge to call home, when Ms. Black questioned her as to why she would be leaving her desk since she had already taken her afternoon rest period break. After explaining her reason for leaving, she was told by Black that the only time personal calls were allowed was during a normal rest period.

Dixon promptly told Janet Smythe that the directive had been issued for the purpose of stopping excessive calling from the supervisors' and employees' desks, and he had not intended it to be interpreted as it had been in her case. He told her that he would like to investigate this incident and that he would get in touch with her later.

Several days later Dixon discussed the situation at a regular meeting of his managers and supervisors. He found that the supervisors and managers were unanimous in disagreeing with his directive. They pointed out that the instructions permitted no flexibility and were too severe. Dixon apologized to the group for not discussing the problem with them prior to issuing the directive, and he asked for their suggestions.

A supervisor in accounting was emphatic and insisted that the directive should be rescinded in its entirety. She said, "Really, Mr. Dixon, if you expect an order like that to be enforced by us, you should have let us give the instructions to the people ourselves!" The advertising department director commented, "This whole matter is ridiculous; it's a waste of time! Why not let employees make personal calls? To stop excessive calls would cost more than they are worth!" One of the assistant managers suggested that the employees should be allowed to make personal calls only with the approval of their supervisors. Several members of the group immediately disagreed with this suggestion, stating that the responsibility for policing personal telephone calls should not be placed on supervisors who are trying to motivate their people positively.

After a prolonged discussion of the telephone-call problem and other matters, Dixon adjourned the meeting, stating that they would hear from him or the district managers at a later date about the problem of personal calls.

As he returned to his office, Dixon wondered what alternative procedures could be used to reduce the time wasted and the expense of excessive personal telephone calls. In addition, he began to speculate on what methods of communications or supervisory practices could be used to help him obtain better reception of management policies and decisions.

CASE-19

Theft in the Office

Veronica Richards, manager of a local office of a major insurance company, had just composed a memorandum to her boss, Leslie Greenberg, who was a divisional manager in the company. In her letter, Richards outlined a series of events that had recently occurred in her office. In relevant parts, the letter included the following:

Memorandum

RE: Dorothy Friday

On October 16, employee Mary Olson reported $15 missing from her purse; she was quite sure the money was stolen during her morning break. Olson, like most of our clerical employees, had left her purse in her desk drawer because we do not have any lockers in which employees can put their purses or other valuables.

On October 30, there was a second occurrence of theft; $15 was stolen from another employee's purse.

On November 6, I had a meeting with all of my office employees. During the meeting, I warned them to try to keep their money on their person. I indicated that if we did find out who was stealing the money, this person would be subject to immediate termination. I also asked for any information that might be helpful in determining who was taking the money.

On November 8, we had a third theft; this time $12 from still another employee's purse.

On November 15, a wallet was stolen; the employee reported it missing immediately after the theft. I began a search of the office for this missing wallet—while most of the employees were at lunch. Eventually, I found it in the desk of Dorothy Friday. The wallet was well concealed in the bottom drawer of Dorothy's desk. My search had begun while

---

All names are disguised.

Dorothy was gone on her noon lunch break. Dorothy Friday is one of our word processors, and she has been employed by us for only about six months.

I interrupted Dorothy's lunch break to interview her in my office regarding the missing wallet found in her desk. She denied taking the wallet, and she indicated that she had not been in the area where the theft occurred. Dorothy was very calm and poised during the interview, and she did not seem as concerned as one would have thought for the type of discussion we were having.

After Dorothy had left my office, I considered the matter further. About an hour later, I called Dorothy Friday in my office again, and I asked her for her resignation at that time. Although I never directly accused her of theft, I told her that with the current situation it would be better for her, since her credibility was in doubt with me and her fellow workers. For the morale of our office, she should end our employee-employer relationship.

At that point, Dorothy Friday became very angry and upset. She said that she would not resign because she was innocent; that someone else must have planted the wallet in her desk; that I had no real proof concerning who took the wallet; that she should be given a polygraph test to prove her innocence; and that if I terminated her, she would get a lawyer to sue me and the company for falsely accusing her. She then left my office and returned to work.

Leslie, what do you recommend that I do next?

Veronica Richards placed her letter to Leslie Greenberg in the mail to be sent by special delivery.

CASE–20

Tom Mendola

Tom Mendola was employed in the machine shop of the Thornton Manufacturing Company when he was seventeen years old. His parents had asked him to leave high school in his third year to go to work and help support the family.

Tom's first job was miscellaneous assembly, filing, and benchwork in the shop. After a few months, he was placed in a job where he could learn to operate a drill press. At first, Tom was very enthusiastic, and he seemed to learn the work very quickly. Soon after the first month, however, he began to tire of the monotony of the machine, and he spent a great deal of time going to the tool crib, to the washroom, and looking for excuses to be away from his machine.

When his foreman noticed the drop in Tom's learning speed, he reprimanded Tom and told him to pay better attention to his work. During the next month, second and third reprimands were necessary, but Tom still did not seem to take an average interest in his work. Tom was also tardy and absent from the job several days during this period.

In talking to Tom again, the foreman found out that Tom's wages were badly needed at home because his family was in very poor circumstances. Tom said that he was the oldest child in a family of ten children and that his father had been in poor health and unable to work regularly for the past year. Tom also said that he did not believe that he could get interested in the drill-press job, and he would like to have a transfer to the assembly department. He said he was very interested in one job—spraying parts in the assembly department. He said he was sure that this was the kind of work he would like.

The machine shop foreman discussed Tom's case with the assembly department supervisor, and they agreed to give Tom a transfer to the spraying unit of the assembly department.

When Tom first started his new job, he showed considerable interest and enthusiasm for the work. But once more this interest lasted for only about a month. Part of Tom's work in the spraying job was to deliver parts to the different departments in the factory. Tom soon acquired the habit of visiting and loafing in other departments, which also kept other employees from their work. Tom was again reprimanded, and the assembly department supervisor made it plain that she would not tolerate such actions. It was later necessary for these reprimands to be repeated because Tom did not improve in his work.

All names are disguised.

Tom was finally told that he would have to be released. Tom made a plea that it was necessary for his family's sake that he hold his job. He said that he now wished that he had kept his job in the machine shop because that would offer him the opportunity to become a machinist. He appealed to the supervisors of the shop and assembly departments and also to the human resources manager for another chance on the drill-press job.

EXERCISE–5

Jasper Water Company

You are Ronald Pierce, a superintendent in the operating division of the Jasper Water Company, a municipally owned company serving an eastern city of 275,000. The city has grown steadily in recent years, and the company is consequently pressed to increase capacity and to lay new water lines as subdivisions are developed. Because parts of the city are old, a large number of the existing lines either need replacement because of deterioration or should be enlarged. You are in charge of the section responsible for the water lines in the outlying subdivisions of the city. You have approximately sixty management and other personnel in your section. (See Exhibit E–5).

You have been ill and at home for the past three days. This is Saturday, July 15, and you have just arrived at your office. The time is 8:30 A.M.; you must leave in 30 minutes to catch a plane for Chicago at 9:35 A.M. A special industry conference committee meeting, of which you are the chairperson, is scheduled there for 4:00 P.M., necessitating your early departure. You will be out of your office until 8 A.M. next Friday, July 21.

Your secretary, Ann Jordan, placed a folder of materials on your desk before she left town yesterday afternoon. She indicated in the folder that she felt you should review the materials before leaving.

The following materials were left for you by your secretary. You should go through them and indicate in writing whatever action you think is appropriate. You can write your responses on the correspondence if you wish. Indicate how each communication is to be conveyed as you assume the role of Ronald Pierce.

Mr. Pierce:

Do you want me to reserve your return flight from Chicago on the 5:15 or the 5:30 P.M. plane?

Ann

All names are disguised.

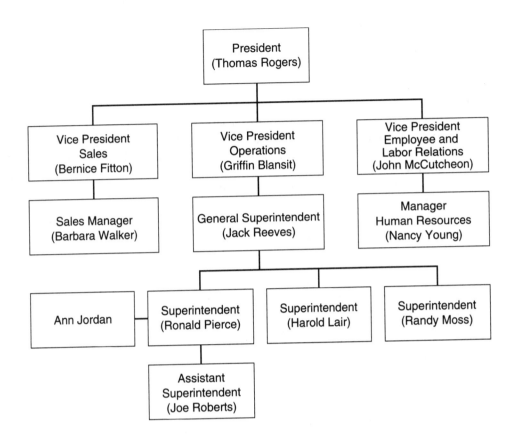

EXHIBIT E–5 Jasper Water Company—Partial Organization Chart

From the desk of: Griffin Blansit

Ron:

Please attend an emergency meeting in my office at 8:00 A.M. Monday.

G. B.

July 14

Mr. Pierce:

After inspecting the building this morning, the city fire marshal reported that you are violating a fire ordinance by keeping an accumulation of oily rags in your stationery storeroom. I told Joe Roberts about this twice in the last month.

When are you going to do something about it?

Fred Forester
Building Supt.

From the desk of: Griffin Blansit

July 13

Ron:

Please give me a report on Friday morning, July 21, on how many employees have been absent this month.

G. B.

From the desk of: John McCutcheon

Ron:

Please make your recommendations for the proposals we should make to the union in contract negotiations that start August 7.

J. M.

R. P.

Here is the letter you asked me to write, for your signature.

Ann, July 14

July 14

Dear Mr. Jones:

Replying to your complaint of May 16, in which you said that water pressure in your house in Fox Hunt Subdivision is too low, I want you to know that I cannot understand your problem. I personally checked the water pressure at our main at that point and it measures 60 psi, which is much higher than the 50 psi we set as a minimum. So far as we are concerned, we have met all requirements. Your plumbing contractor must have made a mistake somewhere. Why don't you contact him?

We have done our part in providing you with a satisfactory water supply. It's now up to you to find the cause of your low water pressure and to correct it.

Sincerely,

July 12

Ron:

You will recall that during last summer we had considerable difficulty with the lawn watering system at the house of Mr. John Miller. Miller is next-door neighbor to Tom Rogers, our CEO.

I understand the Millers are out of town now but are returning Friday. Will you please go out Monday with a serviceman and see if we can't get that thing working right before they return. (G. B. called me about this after he got a call from Rogers.)

Jack Reeves

July 14

Mr. Pierce:

I have handled all the correspondence I could and left you only the letter I didn't know what to do with. All of your other appointments have been postponed until Tuesday, July 25, or Wednesday, July 26.

Since you will be out of town next week, I would like to take the last three and one-half days off. If this is OK, I'll work all day Monday and Tuesday morning.

I know you won't mind. You have always been so fair.

Have a nice trip.

Ann

July 14

Ron:

One of your presupervisory trainees—Jim Reilly—was involved in another argument on the job this morning. This is the second time in the past two months. I have felt for some time that Jim was not cut out for this training but have been willing to go along, on your high recommendation of him.

We are meeting at 11:00 A.M. on Monday (the 17th) to take some kind of disciplinary action. Would you like to sit in on the meeting? (You're the one guy who seems to be able to get through to him.)

Jack Reeves

July 14

Mr. Ronald Pierce:

Because of a sudden switch in schedule, I am now free to attend that Illinois University program the week of the 17th after all. Nancy Young in human resources told me you would be the one to check to see if they can still take me. If so, please make the necessary registration, room reservations, etc.

The program is *Safety and the Supervisor* (in the Conference Center on the campus, July 17–21).

Barb Walker

July 12

Ron:

I've been trying to get the feel of this job of being a new foreman, but I'm not quite clear on where my authority begins and ends. We've run into a few situations where some kind of written detailed statements of our responsibilities would have been useful.

The job descriptions in the manual are so vague that I don't get much practical help from them.

I would appreciate something more definite about what you expect from me on this job. Incidentally, do I report directly to you, or do I also report to Joe Roberts?

Alan Berndt
Foreman

EXERCISE–6

Who Reports to Whom?

The Oscar Metz Tool Company is a closely held manufacturer of bottling and canning equipment located in a large southern city. The company was founded in the early 1920s and in recent years has experienced considerable growth. The company hopes to double sales in the next ten years. At present, Metz employs approximately three hundred persons. It manufactures bottling and canning equipment to order. The entire management group takes great pride in the quality of their products and in the company in general.

You are a management consultant who was contacted and hired by the executive vice president to investigate the organizational structure of the manufacturing division of the company. Your initial investigation revealed the following problems: (1) tendency on the part of lower echelon managers to try to shift decisions up to higher management; (2) confusion on the part of most front-line supervisors regarding the functions and authority of the management levels above them; and (3) a tendency to bypass intermediate levels and to take problems and complaints to the vice president of manufacturing and even to the president.

Permission was then granted to you to make a more complete study of the situation. Your investigation, which required numerous interviews, resulted in the discovery of the following organizational problems.

THE ORGANIZATIONAL PROBLEM IN THE SHOP

The management group in manufacturing consisted of a vice president of manufacturing, a shop superintendent, a night general supervisor, nine day supervisors, and four night supervisors. Although the manufacturing functions of the various supervisors are clearly defined and do not appear to offer a major problem, there are few clear-cut lines of authority. The shop superintendent believes that he reports to the president, but the vice president of manufacturing believes that the shop superintendent reports to him. The shop superintendent believes that the nine day departmental supervisors report to him, but his opinion is not shared by many of the supervisors. They made the following comments:

This exercise was prepared by Professor James C. Hodgetts of the Fogelman College of Business and Economics of the University of Memphis. All names are disguised. Used by permission.

1. The supervisor of the miscellaneous machining department says that he reports to the vice president of manufacturing.
2. The supervisor of the lathe department also says that he reports to the vice president of manufacturing.
3. The supervisor of the grinding department says she reports to the vice president of manufacturing and to the miscellaneous machining supervisor.
4. The supervisor of the milling machine department says he reports to the production control manager and to the vice president of manufacturing.
5. The supervisor of maintenance says that he reports to the shop superintendent and to the vice president of manufacturing.
6. The supervisor of the drilling department says she reports to the shop superintendent and to the vice president of manufacturing.
7. The supervisor of the tool and die room says he reports to the vice president of manufacturing and, to a minor degree, to the chief engineer.
8. The supervisor of assembly says he reports to the president, to the vice president of manufacturing, and to the shop superintendent.

In summary, it appears that only one of the nine day supervisors reports entirely to the shop superintendent. Only three acknowledged a partial responsibility to him, and five did not even mention his name when asked to cite their immediate boss. About the only undisputed authority the shop superintendent appears to have is in connection with the heat treat department, but he believes that he is in charge of the entire shop.

THE ORGANIZATIONAL PROBLEM IN PRODUCTION CONTROL

The production control manager says that she supervises the work of the shipping supervisor, the final inspection supervisor, and six clerks. Both the final inspection supervisor and the shipping supervisor say they report to both the production control manager and the vice president of manufacturing. The milling machine department supervisor says that he reports to the production control manager as well as to the vice president of manufacturing. Other comments from the various production supervisors also indicate that the production control manager has some authority over them. The production control manager reports to the vice president of manufacturing.

THE ORGANIZATION PROBLEM ON THE NIGHT SHIFT

Discussions with the four night supervisors, the night general supervisor, the vice president of manufacturing, and the shop superintendent indicate differences of opinion relative to lines of authority on the night shift. The vice president of manufacturing believes that the night general supervisor reports to him. So does the shop superintendent. The shop superintendent believes that the night general supervisor also reports to the president, but the night general supervisor says this is definitely not correct and that he reports to the vice president of manufacturing. The vice president of manufacturing believes that the night lathe supervisor reports to the day lathe supervisor. The night general supervisor does not believe a night lathe supervisor has been appointed but believes this should happen and that he should report to him. The person who believes that he is the night lathe supervisor says he reports to the night general supervisor. The vice president of manufacturing believes the night supervisor of assembly reports to the day supervisors of both assembly and milling. However, the night supervisor of assembly says that he reports both to the day supervisor of assembly and to the night general supervisor. The night general supervisor says he reports to him. Both the night shipping supervisor and the night milling machine supervisor say they report to the vice president of manufacturing, but the night general supervisor says that he is their immediate supervisor.

YOUR ASSIGNMENT

The executive vice president has requested that you develop an organizational chart for the Oscar Metz Tool Company in order, to improve the organizational structure and working relationships among managers and supervisors in the manufacturing division. You also are to make whatever recommendations you feel are appropriate as a result of your investigation and analysis.

EXERCISE–7
The Designer's Dilemma

You are Joan Thomas, age twenty-eight, and you are in charge of a design section at Timely Togs, a manufacturer of women's sportswear. You are already established in the industry as one of the most talented new designers of women's casual wear, and you find the work both stimulating and challenging. You recently told one of your colleagues, "There is always the excitement associated with being just one step ahead of the market, as well as the apprehension that I may be 'so far out' that the public will not accept my work." You do not find the technical part of the job nearly so difficult as the human part, however. In fact, George Randall, president of the company, is one of your principal problems. You are sitting in your office pondering how this came about and what you should do next. You are trying to picture a conversation that may take place between you and Randall.

BACKGROUND

George Randall had hired Joan Thomas away from a competitor two years ago after discovering that it would cost him about 30 percent more to hire a man of comparable experience and talent. All his previous head designers had been men. Randall liked Joan's work; in fact, partly as a result of her designs, the past year was the best in the company's history. In spite of her success, Randall still did not quite believe that Joan Thomas could be "that good." Randall did like her creativity, and he respected her sound judgment. But the combination was something he hadn't expected or previously confronted in a woman who he had supervised or with whom he had worked closely.

The garment industry is highly competitive and has even been called "cutthroat." For example, stealing designs from competitors is commonplace in the industry.

Although Thomas was friendly and easy to work with, she succeeded at an early age not only because she was talented but also because she could be tough with those who tried to stand in her way. She was always careful to treat Randall with respect, but she also did not hesitate to stick to her guns when she felt that she was right.

Joan Thomas had always found it difficult to communicate with Randall about design and production matters. She felt that he was distant and aloof with her at the office, and that he did not take her comments seriously.

All names are disguised.

On the other hand, she had found him friendly and easy to talk to at off-the-job social functions. For example, she found Randall cordial and friendly when she and her boyfriend, who was also a successful designer, met Randall and his wife at a benefit at the local art institute a few months earlier.

Thomas had noted that Randall tended to exclude her from important business meetings involving top managers of the company, most of whom were men. This created problems because these managers discussed many matters that required coordination with her department. For example, last week they discussed the possibility of using a new fabric in the fall line of women's blouses. Such a decision could not be made without her participation, because the fabric was an important design ingredient.

Thomas wished to attend the spring women's ready-to-wear market exhibit in New York the following week. Designers need to attend this function because it provides them with an opportunity to meet other designers and to compare one another's work. And, on this occasion, manufacturers display their new lines and take orders from retailers for subsequent delivery. She spoke with Randall about going to New York, but he was reluctant to permit her to attend. He told her that three other company representatives would already be there and that she was needed to assist in the start-up of production on a new line of slacks—(high-speed production techniques frequently require slight last-minute design changes). After much persuasion, he finally acquiesced to her request to go New York.

JOAN THOMAS'S PROBLEM

You (Joan Thomas) recognize that your relationship with George Randall is interfering with the optimal use of your talents by the company. You are becoming increasingly concerned about your ability to develop professionally under present circumstances. You know that you should discuss your concerns openly with Randall, but you are not sure about when and how to proceed. You also believe that George Randall senses that something is amiss between the two of you and that sooner or later you will both have to talk about your work relationship at Timely Togs.

EXERCISE–8

The New Sales Clerk

Shortly after graduating from high school, Mary Roberts went to work in the receiving department of Robinson's Department Store as a marking clerk. Her job consisted mainly of checking price labels against computerized data and, after receiving necessary instructions from her supervisor, attaching them to merchandise before it was moved to the selling floor. She liked her associates in the department and enjoyed the casual and informal manner in which everyone dressed. However, the work was quite routine and Mary soon felt that it lacked challenge. Besides, she always associated retail stores with selling and meeting people. She learned through a friend in the store of an opening for a sales clerk in women's sportswear. Mary Roberts applied for the job and after a short interview was offered the position. She received a brief orientation to the job that included instructions on how to make a sale and various policies relating to absence, sick leave, and employee discounts on purchases in the store. She was also given a copy of the employee handbook, which stated, "You are expected to be neatly groomed and to dress in a manner appropriate to the department in which you work and/or the type of work to which you will be assigned. Your supervisor will provide you with more specific instructions."

Robinson's considered itself to be the "quality" store in town. It was somewhat conservative, although it also was a style leader in the area. Mary was very excited about her new job and devoted much time to selecting the outfit she would wear that first day.

YOUR PROBLEM

You are the manager of the women's sportswear department. It is 10:15 A.M. You have entered the department to pick up some fabric samples to show at an important meeting of merchandising officers and department heads called by the president, George Robinson, for 11 A.M.

As you make a quick observation of selling activity in your department, you spot your new employee, Mary Roberts, waiting on one of the store's best clients. To your dismay, Mary is not only busily chewing gum, but she is also dressed in a very loud and "tacky" looking blouse and skirt. Worse still, it even appears to you that she may not be wearing a bra. You are distressed by this, and you ponder what you should do.

The names of the company and the individuals have been disguised.

PART THREE

Managing Employment and Performance

CASES

EXPERIENTIAL EXERCISES

The selection, training, appraisal, and development of people are not separate organizational activities but parts of a continuous process of managing employment and performance. The process begins with the identification of the types of skills, knowledge, and capabilities needed in the organization and a time schedule for their acquisition. Next, a comprehensive assessment of available sources of the needed talents must be made and followed by effective communication efforts to attract applicants from these sources. This recruitment stage leads to a process of selection from among those applying to determine the persons best suited to meet current and future human resource needs. All of these subprocesses are carried on in a fairly continuous or, at least, systematic and logical way.

Training and development could be said to start when a job applicant first has contact with the potential employer. In these first contacts, through advertising and initial visits to the employment office, an organization is communicating something about its views, values, and philosophies concerning people. In a formal sense, however, training begins in the orientation stage and continues through introduction to the job, on-the-job training, skill-enhancement training, preparation for promotion, and special developmental opportunities for selected purposes. The focus of training and development is to provide the organization with the talents it needs and to give individuals the opportunity to maximize their accomplishments and satisfactions.

In order to ensure a proper match of skill and knowledge to job performance requirements, continuous assessment of employee performance is needed. This process is generally called performance appraisal, and it usually consists of both written and verbal analysis of job performance. For some managers, performance appraisal is looked upon as a "necessary evil" to be dealt with quickly in order to make compensation or other decisions. This is unfortunate, because performance appraisal is one of the strongest developmental opportunities any manager and organization can utilize in an effort to improve performance. Of course, the discussion of performance should be a regular, almost daily activity, seen by organizational members as a natural, useful, nonthreatening process. Performance appraisal contributes to many additional organizational decision processes, such as promotions, transfers, reassignment, coaching and counseling, and compensation. And, the performance-appraisal process contributes to continuing decisions about training and development. It provides important data that can lead to internal and external training and development programs, including training and development programs for supervisors and managers.

The cases and exercises of Part Three primarily focus attention on these and such related areas as recruitment policies, selection procedures, applicant credentials, marginal-performance problems, and issues of promotion and development.

CASE–21

Paragon Pulp and Paper Company, Ltd.

Paragon Pulp and Paper Company's office manager, Bill Gilroy, doubled as employment manager and carried out the actual interviewing and evaluation of job applicants. John Humphrey was manager of the newest of the Paragon Pulp and Paper Company's two Vancouver plants. The plant, which he had designed and which he now supervised, had been completed several years ago to produce a heavy-duty kraft stock for use in making boxes and containers. About three-fourths of its average plant workforce of 275 employees were male.

Paragon Pulp and Paper maintained a standard personnel selection program at each of its plants. This method has been worked out by a management consulting firm, together with the company's industrial relations vice president, a former Austrian who held degrees in psychology and law. Company management attributed a considerable portion of the company's low turnover rate—among the lowest in the industry—to its personnel selection method. Both John Humphrey and Bill Gilroy felt that their success in attaining an efficient level of production six months ahead of schedule was, in large part, as a result of their use of this method.

The formal paperwork required in Paragon's selection of plant personnel consisted of three main parts: an application form, a test of reasoning ability, and a patterned interview form. Evaluations resulting from these three sources and from face-to-face contact were recorded on a summary form. Bill Gilroy, office manager, had spent three days at a course given by the management consulting firm to instruct potential users of the selection methods.

The functions of the overall system, in Bill Gilroy's opinion, were to determine, insofar as possible, an applicant's reasoning power, personal compatibility, and stability, and, on the basis of the final summary, to permit selection of the proper persons for jobs in the plant. Each step in the process served as a screening that started when an applicant obtained an application form from the office receptionist and continued until an employee had successfully completed the required one-month probationary period in the plant. This latter final screening was spelled out in the company's union agreement.

This case was prepared by Professor William A. Preshing of the University of Alberta in Edmonton, Canada. It is based on a case originally prepared by W. S. Carrick, formerly of the University of Alberta. All names, dates, and locations in this case are disguised. Used by permission.

"You'd be surprised," said Bill Gilroy in describing the first screening, "but we've had people come in for a job who are obviously drunk. We don't waste much time in dealing with them. Similarly, we'll get applicants who might be what I call miscast—their social tendencies might be bad. This is the type that says in a loud voice to our receptionist, 'Get me the big boss—I don't want to speak to the office manager.' Finally, there are the one-armed, the cripples, the paraplegics, and so on. The physical requirements of the jobs we have to offer are beyond the abilities of this disabled group. In most cases I go out and tell them that at present there are no openings, but to leave their name—'we'll call you, you needn't call us'—you know the routine."

The next step in the process required the filling out of the standard application form. Bill said, "We're looking for several things here, some general and some specific. As an example of the former, take the way a man fills out the form. You can tell if a man's careless and sloppy, or if he's ambitious enough to take a little care when he fills in the form. Basically, the application form gives me a brief look at the man before the interview. Take his date of birth—this gives me an idea of what job he can hold. What about his residence? If it's a fashionable address, what's he doing here? How long has he lived in the same place? This gives you an idea as to a man's stability. Of course, if he has been working in the construction field, I expect him to have moved around a lot. What kind of earnings does a he expect? If he wants $12.50 an hour, why? I'm going to offer $7.00.

"Another thing I check for in the application form is the number of children a man has. If he's got too many, he's out. You can't support six or seven kids in Vancouver on monthly wages of $1,300, but a man's not going to make any more than that when he starts with us. So he just couldn't do it without some other income; unrest and trouble would eventually result. I also find out in the interview what type of car a man has, because where we are, just outside the city, you really need a car. Of course, a man doesn't have to have a car, but it helps. To get back to the application form, I want to know how much education a man has had. We're not looking for men with university degrees, either. I've found that if a man with a degree applies for a job in our plant, getting that degree was probably the last constructive thing he did in his life. But if a man has been to trade school, or a business school, that's okay.

"Then I take a look at a man's extracurricular activities, if any, and especially at any offices he might have held. This gives you an idea of a man's initiative, and willingness, and desire to lead. Similarly, as far as a man's military service goes, I look for a man who was promoted—indicating some ambition. I begin to wonder about the man who went in and came out a private—professional privates', they call them.

"Finally, I look at a man's record of employment, on the back of the application form, especially the last five years. There are eight spaces, and if a man says that's not enough for five years (unless he's been in construction work) we don't want him. We seldom bother to check a man's references if it involves anything more than a phone call."

The next step in the selection procedure is the use of the test of reasoning ability. This test, on which there was no time limit, had five sections of twelve problems each. "We don't want the erratic type," Bill Gilroy commented, "and people can be erratic whether they're brilliant or not. Almost every time I've hired somebody whose test result on two individual sections or more was off by more than two from the norm, thereby indicating he was erratic, there's been trouble. One example is a man whose test results showed him to be erratic; I hired him, and found out later he was an alcoholic, a highly excitable type. Another man, who was a fork truck driver in the plant, all of a sudden blew up at the plant superintendent one day, and we had to let him go. The funny thing is, though, he'd formed a social club among some of the fellows in the plant, and it collapsed when he left.

"Basically, with this test we're looking for employees who can reason. Anyone below a test score of Grade III is automatically out—with rare exceptions—and we fell flat on our face in every one of them. One good example involved a young woman who came to Vancouver from Edmonton with her six-month-old child. She told me she'd left her husband, who was twenty or twenty-five years older than she and who wasn't taking good care of her. She really needed a job. Even though she was Grade IV on the matrices test, I gave her a job plus an advance in wages. She told me she felt she hadn't done her best on the test, so a couple of weeks later I let her take it again, and she barely made Grade III. Then she started being absent for sickness—either she was sick or the child was sick. Well, we reserve the right to let a person go if her absentee rate indicates that the work is adversely affecting her health, so I called her in and pointed that out to her. She was okay for two or three weeks, but then it was the same old story, so the plant supervisors were forced to release her.

"I've found that people who score Grade III on the test are the workers, while people with Grade II have the top jobs. Some of the applicants in Grade III appear stupid in the interview as a defense mechanism, but I've found this type often makes a good routine worker. Of course, you can't equate reasoning power alone with ambition and the desire to take responsibility.

"We will take people with a score of Grade I, subject to their having the right background. They're too mentally active for the type of job we have here—they tend to ask questions that aren't necessary to get the job done. We have a woman in that category. Similarly, because of our seniority clause, we're cutting down on the number of Grade II's we take. We can, if the highest seniority employee is not qualified to take the responsibility, jump him or her. We haven't had much trouble with this situation, however, because usually an unqualified, although senior, employee will refuse the promotion."

The next step in the screening process for a job application involved the patterned interview conducted by Bill Gilroy. The interview ordinarily took twenty to thirty minutes, unless, as Bill said, "the applicant is frightened, reticent, or opposed." Before the actual interview starts, each person is assured that they do not have to answer any questions they do not want to. Bill said, however, that anyone who did not want to answer all the questions directly would be subject to indirect questioning to determine the necessary information.

"In the interview," Bill said, "I look for quite a few things, as you can see from the form. The main thing the questions bring out is their stability, and as far as personal compatibility goes, I get a good idea of that by the way they come across in the interview. Then, of course, there's the thirty-day probationary period on the job. I'm always thinking of the summary sheet as I go along.

"They have to prove themselves in the interview. For example, if a man is obviously trying to gain sympathy from me, say by telling me about his aches and pains, I usually don't want him. This type of thing will carry over to the job. One question I think is pretty important is, 'When did you have your last drink?' Typically a man will hesitate a moment, and then remember the beer he had a few nights ago, and then he might mention the drink he had at his birthday party, or something like that. But when they say, 'I had my last drink at two o'clock on such and such day and year,' watch out! This type, ninety-nine out of one hundred times, is, or was, a confirmed alcoholic. Anyone that can tell you to the minute the last time he or she had a drink is the worst risk from the alcoholic point of view.

"I deliberately hired two alcoholics not long ago. When they're sober, they'll work twice as hard as anyone around them—to punish themselves. You can't put them on the line, because when they're out there will be a hole. Maintenance, stores, and so on, are okay for this type. One of the two I hired had been a major league pitcher, and had owned his own furniture manufacturing outfit. I thought he'd be able to transfer his knowledge, but he couldn't do it; the job was too broad for him.

"Another thing I definitely look for is the type who is accident-prone. That's the only way I can think of saying it, but I don't like the expression. I check on health, car accidents, and the last accident on their former jobs. Of course, somebody with too many accidents tries to hide it, but it usually comes out.

"I also look for a smooth domestic life. It's almost a prerequisite. I like to see a good healthy home life, too. For one thing, with poor health in the family, they usually need extra money. As far as our plant goes, we have voluntary medical service insurance with the cost carried by the workers, but no hospitalization insurance. The city of Vancouver has a plan that helps out there.

"We have some fringe benefits, but don't forget this plant is still growing, and right now we can't afford to commit ourselves to these expenditures. Take our wage spread—from a base rate of $7.00 up to $13.65. The $7.00 might be a little low, but we deliberately tried to start low in anticipation of union demands.

"Notice the questions about an applicant's financial situation. Here I'm looking for those in the middle. You'd be surprised how many people come in here and tell me about the farm their father left them, from which they're earning $20,000 per year. It's not hard to predict that these people aren't going to be the steadiest workers in the world. They just aren't hungry. On the other hand, we can't take people who are too hungry, with many mouths to feed, as I mentioned before.

"Single women on their own are especially bad. It's typical of them to say, in answer to my question as to how much they need to live a week, 'Oh, I can live on $250 a week.' Then when I ask them about the payments on the coat they're wearing, and their car, rent, and so on, they'll say, 'Oh, gosh, I guess I can't live on $250.' Eventually, they realize it will be tough for them to get by on the wages that we pay."

The final step in the selection process required Bill Gilroy to fill out the Selection and Evaluation Summary Form. Bill completed this form from information and opinions he obtained from the application form, the test, and the patterned interview. Applicants were rated "outstanding," "good," "marginal," or "poor" in comparison with employees actually working in the plant, and not against any outside standard. Bill explained that the ideal applicant would have a series of checkmarks distributed among the first three categories—"outstanding" to "marginal."

"We don't want them with too many 'poor' checks," Bill said, "but neither do we want them who are the opposite—too outstanding. It just would not work out.

"I first used this method," Bill said, "a couple of years ago when we were just starting up. Another fellow from the company was helping me then. Then last year, when we added a second shift, the other fellow and I had to hire another sixty workers, and we had over three hundred applicants. Ordinarily, though, I'd say we reject about 65 percent of the people who apply for jobs. Right now we're back to one shift, so we've got a backlog of employees with experience on our seniority list who aren't working right now. During the last six months we've only accepted a few applicants each month.

"Even though on two occasions we needed a lot of workers in a relatively short time, I can think of only one instance in which we hired someone who didn't pass through the selection procedure, and that was due to coincidence. A foreman called me up and said he needed help on the line right away, and at the same time, a fellow was outside just starting to fill out his application form. He was out in the plant before the ink was dry.

"There are some people in the plant now that I wouldn't hire today. They're chiefly the ones in the forty-five to sixty age bracket. They're able to reason, but they are not as alert physically as they should be. Older workers sometimes lack a certain something that is necessary on production jobs requiring continual judgment and endurance.

"What we try to do, if possible, is to give these types 'prestige' jobs, though we have only a few. One example is our first-aid man. Although he's in a low-paying job, he gets a bonus—$.40 per hour—for his first-aid job. He's between the devil and the deep blue sea, which is where we want him. You see, we have a spread between rates, and if this man were promoted up one notch, he realizes he'd probably lose the $.40 bonus—in other words, he'd be out $.24. So he's happy right where he is.

"Sometimes you have people who hunger for authority. We occasionally put an individual on the safety committee to satisfy this hunger. The union's the same way—they provide positions that have the prestige and authority.

"The important thing is to keep the plant operating efficiently," Bill concluded, "and if it is not operating, all this red tape and all our records are meaningless. We are attempting to keep it going as efficiently as possible. The plant is the be-all and end-all."

Ajax Electronics Company: The Projective Tests

Art Johnson was hired as human resources manager of the communication services division of Ajax Electronics Company. This was a new division to be established in Salt Lake City, Utah, and would require the hiring of several hundred engineers, technicians, and assemblers over the next eighteen months.

The new top management of this division, transferred from the headquarters in Chicago, was very concerned that careful selection procedures be used in the appointment of managers and supervisors. They were aware that Art Johnson was trained, qualified, and licensed as a psychologist, and they urged him to use his professional knowledge and techniques to improve the selection of several dozen supervisors and managers needed for this new division.

At this time, there were numerous consultants operating throughout the country who were assisting in the selection of managers and executives. Many consultants advocated using a variety of psychological tests to assist them in evaluating supervisory and managerial candidates sent to them by various clients. Included among these tests were the two most widely known projective tests—the Rorschach Ink Blot Test and the Thematic Apperception Test.[1] Art Johnson, however, refused to administer these tests to applicants on ethical and legal grounds, to the considerable disappointment and irritation of his superiors. Chicago headquarters human resources staff had been using psychological consultants for several years to assist them in managerial selection, and the corporate HR staff felt that results of projective tests provided valuable information on personality factors crucial to managerial success.

When the headquarters HR staff heard of Johnson's refusal through the general manager of the new division, they recommended to the general manager that one of the local psychological services consulting firms, which they had used, be called in. This particular consulting firm had a small office in Salt Lake City staffed by a psychologist who was qualified to administer these projective and other tests.

Art Johnson protested the use of this firm on the grounds that various aspects of candidates' personalities would be revealed by the tests, yet no steps or effort were planned to explain the findings to the candidates. He argued

---

This case was prepared by Professor James A. Lee of the College of Business Administration of Ohio University at Athens. All names are disguised. Used by permission.

[1]See Appendix.

that since some of these results might reveal serious personality problems or neuroses, the communication of findings to candidates could be extremely disturbing or require far more counseling time than the company was willing to provide. Johnson was also concerned about possible legal complications that could come from improper use of test information obtained from minority and female candidates.

The company decided to proceed with the engagement of the consulting firm anyway, and Art Johnson was trying to decide whether to acquiesce or jeopardize his job by pursuing his objections further.

APPENDIX

Professor Dale S. Beach has discussed projective personality tests as follows:

> A projective personality test is one in which the subject is asked to project his own interpretation into certain standard stimulus situations. The meaning he attaches to the stimulus depends upon personal values, motives, and personality. Theoretically the number of responses that various people can give to a single stimulus is infinite. Two well-known projective tests are the Rorschach and the Thematic Apperception Test.
>
> The Rorschach test, developed in 1921 by Hermann Rorschach, consists of ten cards, each containing a different inkblot. These inkblots are of various colors. The person is asked to explain what he sees in each blot. The explanations provide clues to personality. A full evaluation can be made only when the analyst knows about the subject's family background, education, past experiences, and has evaluations obtained from others who know the individual.
>
> The Thematic Apperception Test, developed in 1938, consists of a series of twenty pictures, there being a different set for men and women. The person tested must interpret each picture by telling a story about it in terms of what that person believes is happening and what will be the outcome.
>
> All projective tests must be administered individually. Interpretation of the results is a job only for a qualified clinical psychologist or a psychiatrist. The interpretation is highly subjective and unstandardized. In a sense it is impressionistic. Quantitative scores are not developed.[2]

---

[2]Dale S. Beach, *Personnel: The Management of People at Work*, 5th ed. (New York: Macmillan, 1985), pp. 162–163.

Simmons Specialty Stores: Selecting an Auditor

Harry Jamison, employment manager of the Simmons Specialty Stores national chain, returned to his office from a luncheon engagement with two assistant controllers at which several important matters had been discussed. Among them was the company's expansion program, which included the establishment and acquisition of new stores throughout the southwestern part of the country. These changes, plus the normal amount of turnover, had greatly increased the need for additions to the company's accounting and internal auditing staffs.

Several of the traveling auditors had been promoted to more responsible positions, some were made regional controllers, and others were brought into the Chicago office as department heads. Two experienced auditors had retired during the past year, and four had left the company to take positions with other companies. As a result of these changes and the difficulties in hiring replacements, eight requisitions for either experienced accountants or auditors were in the employment office. It was desirable but not necessary that the auditors be certified public accountants.

The assistant controllers were convinced that ten years of accounting or auditing experience were necessary for an individual to qualify as a retail chain store auditor. Harry Jamison believed that it might be possible to employ college graduates with specialized training in accounting, place them on a planned job-rotation program, and develop them into auditors in five or six years. Simmons's policy, however, was to hire only experienced personnel, so Mr. Jamison usually sought auditors through newspaper advertisements and private employment agencies.

The pressing problem of the moment was to fill the immediate vacancies with qualified people. In recent years, Jamison had experienced extreme difficulty in hiring new auditors. Part of the problem was that the starting salary paid to a new auditor was somewhat lower than the prevailing rate in the Chicago area. Jamison believed, however, that most of the problem lay in the nature of the job itself. Simmons's auditors were required to travel extensively and to be away from their homes for long periods of time, sometimes several months. Even though the company paid most of the travel expenses so that they could come home on weekends, numerous qualified accountants with family responsibilities objected to the potential long absences from home and often turned down positions at Simmons because of this problem.

All names are disguised.

Several auditors had resigned in the past specifically because they disliked being away from their homes on extended assignments.

Harry reached into his pocket and pulled out a newspaper clipping that the chief controller, Al Griffin, had given to him. It was a section from the want ads and was heavily marked with pencil. It read:

Wanted

Position in accounting or auditing work by well-qualified man with twenty-five years of financial experience with two corporations and one bank. Long service in responsible positions marred by one human error, an embezzlement. Interested in discussing employment with corporation executive needing the services of good accountant, controller, or auditor. Single. Will travel. Box M-103.

The penciled notation indicated that Al Griffin was willing to talk to this man. However, Harry knew that Griffin was aware of the company's unwritten policy against hiring people with prison records. In addition, this applicant was probably in his late forties or early fifties, and the company seldom hired auditors over forty-five years of age if younger applicants were available.

Just then the telephone rang. It was Al Griffin.

"Harry," said Griffin, "how about my requisitions for accountants and auditors? Look, boy, this thing is getting serious. We need people and fast."

Jamison answered, "Griff, I've been saying for years that we need to establish some type of policies or training program in regards to where, when and how we're going to get and keep qualified auditors. It's going to be a tough proposition to find eight experienced auditors right away."

"Maybe so," replied Al Griffin, "but the problem is that we need auditors today. I say, let's get whatever people we can get today and worry about the policies some other day when we can afford to think about them. Do you think we should talk to the guy in the want ad who has the prison record?"

False Credentials

Case Characters

Jenny Young: Manager of Accounting Department, Willows Discount Stores

Amanda Nerl: Staff Accountant

Jack Wiley: Staff Accountant

Holly Lee: Director of Human Resources

Jenny Young, had served for about five years as manager of the corporate accounting department for Willows Discount Stores, a chain operation involving dozens of outlets in several midwestern states.

Amanda Nerl and Jack Wiley were staff accountants who worked for Young. Both were hired at about the same time two years ago. The job specification for their positions included requirements for a college degree, personal computer skills, and, preferably, some accounting work experience. Compensation for this position was competitive and reflected these requirements. The employment applications of both employees clearly indicated that they claimed they possessed all of these requirements. Amanda Nerl and Jack Wiley also had signed waivers allowing the company to verify all information provided on their application forms. However, this was not done when they were hired.

It had been about two years since they were hired. Jenny Young felt that during that time Amanda Nerl's performance had been stellar. Nerl frequently performed above and beyond the call of duty. For example, Amanda recently suggested a software change that would save the company $25,000 per year. By contrast, in Jenny Young's opinion, Jack Wiley's performance had been average, at best.

Recently, Jack Wiley reported to Jenny Young that he had learned that Amanda Nerl had falsified her employment application form by stating that she had a college degree. Young talked with Amanda Nerl, and Amanda admitted that she did not have a degree at the time of her employment. However, Amanda indicated that she had been attending night school and she would graduate with a B.S.B.A. degree in approximately three months.

In a subsequent meeting that included Jenny Young, Holly Lee (director of HR), and Jack Wiley, Wiley expressed his anger and frustration about this

---

All names are disguised.

situation. He claimed that Young had shown favoritism in job assignments and compensation to Amanda because she was a woman. He was very angry and demanded that Amanda Nerl be terminated immediately. Wiley emphasized that the company's employment application form which he and Amanda had signed included a specific statement that if any information was false or a major misrepresentation, this would be grounds for later discharge.

After this meeting, Holly Lee told Young that the HR department would support her in whatever decision she reached regarding this matter.

Dr. Allen's Request for Promotion

As he looked out his window, the president of Argay Co. thought, "What should I do?" Dr. Albert B. James had assumed his responsibilities as president of the company less than a year ago. He had already successfully negotiated labor agreements with several of the unions in his company, but two more had to be negotiated within the next twelve months. One of the unions with a contract expiring soon represented Dr. Allen, the employee in question.

Dr. Ivan R. Allen had joined the chemical research division of Argay Co. four years ago as an assistant research chemist. Before that, Dr. Allen had spent three years at the University of Illinois earning a Ph.D. in chemistry. Before doing his doctoral work, Dr. Allen had received a B.Sc. as well as an M.Sc. in chemistry and had been a very successful salesman for a major chemical company. He had left his career in chemical sales after nine years because his goal of working in the sales training area had not been achieved. His manager had intended to place Ivan in the next sales training slot that opened up (a lateral move), but Ivan left the company to pursue his doctoral studies before an opening was available.

Since joining the chemical research division of Argay, Dr. Allen had greatly impressed his associates as well as his managers. He was responsible for research in the synthetic fibers department, and the manager of his department, Dr. Gwen G. Brandt, remarked in her annual evaluation that Dr. Allen was the best at his job that she had ever seen. As a researcher, Dr. Allen was also expected to present papers at chemical research conferences and publish papers. He had only performed at an acceptable level in the presentation and publishing aspect of his job.

The synthetic fibers department was unionized, as were the other research departments. Although he was not required to be so, Dr. Allen was a member of the union, but had not been very active. The union and top management had agreed to a general—although not "iron-clad" policy—that promotion from assistant to associate research chemist normally took place in five years. If a research chemist was doing a good job, promotion was almost automatic after five years. Dr. Allen had requested that he be promoted one year early. If granted, the promotion would result in Dr. Allen receiving a salary increase of about 10 percent. This would be in addition to an annual

This case was prepared by Professor Irvin A. Zaenglein of the Cisler School of Business of Northern Michigan University at Marquette. All names are disguised. Used by permission.

raise of approximately 6 percent. Dr. Allen earned $59,000 last year. His earnings while in sales had been higher, but Dr. Allen appeared to love research.

The promotion request had received a positive endorsement from Dr. Allen's Departmental Review Committee. The committee comprised three research chemists from the synthetic fibers division. Likewise, Dr. Allen's request had received very strong support from his department head as well as from the manager of the chemical research division of Argay. A committee composed of one researcher from each of the three departments within the chemical research division had also given their blessing to the promotion request.

The promotion had to clear three additional hurdles before becoming effective. The research review committee, which had one researcher from each of the nine research divisions, had to approve the request, as did the president, Dr. James. The final step was the vote of the board of directors. The board usually endorsed the promotion recommendations of the management team.

The hang-up came from the research review committee. That body had voted against Dr. Allen's request for promotion and had so informed him. Dr. Allen appealed the decision to the president. The president could overrule the vote of the research review committee, but this was an unusual situation. Ordinarily, potential conflict arose when the research review committee—the researchers on this committee were all union members—wanted a union member to receive a promotion or wage increase and a department head, division manager, or the president did not feel that the promotion or wage increase was justified.

Dr. James had met Dr. Allen several times, but did not really know him. Dr. Allen had developed several products that had received praise from Argay's customers. Dr. Allen felt that his nine years in sales made him better able to understand the customer's needs, compared to most of his research colleagues. In fact, it was his sales experience on which he had based his request for promotion at the end of his fourth year at Argay.

The president wanted to promote people who genuinely deserved it, but there was the consideration of the research review committee. If Dr. James overruled the committee's recommendation, he was obligated to explain his reasons. Then too, there were the upcoming negotiations with the researchers' union. Most people agreed that if Dr. Allen did not receive the promotion this year, he would surely receive it next year.

Rambusch Company: An Executive Choice

BACKGROUND

Louis Dashman had been working at the Rambusch Company for eight weeks, having accepted the position of operations manager. At this time, Dashman was thirty-two years old. He had finished his B.B.A. from Churchill Business School and his M.B.A. from a major state university B-school. Among his prior work experience was a stint at Stenson-Forsgren, an R&D company, where he gained extensive experience in computer design and construction. He came to Rambusch because of the potential career and financial opportunities it offered him. Dashman's long-run goal was to become a top corporate executive.

The Rambusch Company, Inc., manufactured a wide range of products associated with the computer world. The firm started some twenty-five years ago at a time of intense growth of the computer and computer-components industry. A major breakthrough came for Rambusch when it gained a contract with Zerom, one of the largest computer design and manufacturing firms in the world. Recently, the firm had been expanding, and its latest step had been into the office equipment field (or "office of the future," as *Business Week* labeled it). A major current contract had been with the Department of the Navy for specialized office equipment, and designing and producing entire office systems, and for including copiers, word processors, data storage, and the like. The Navy contract was negotiated after two years of experimenting, testing, and bidding. At present, the contract was on a nine-month trial basis. If accepted beyond this trial period, it could mean major business revenues for Rambusch for at least four years running.

Rambusch products were designed and manufactured in western Massachusetts. There were two plants in Turners Falls, one in Sunderland, and a fourth in Greenfield. The central office was in Deerfield, which was centrally located between the four manufacturing units. This also allowed the Turners Falls plants some badly needed expansion space made possible by the evacuation of the executive offices.

This case was prepared by Professor Martin R. Moser of the College of Management of the University of Massachusetts at Lowell. All names and certain data are disguised. Used by permission.

THE CONTROVERSIAL VICE PRESIDENT

Gilbert Winston was the vice president of the Rambusch Company. Winston was forty-four years old, twice divorced, and currently single. He was a dapper, well-dressed, and very flamboyant man. He had an M.B.A. degree from the University of Massachusetts, and his work was very efficient. He began at Rambusch at the lowest management level, and worked his way up through the ranks. Some said his pull in certain places finally helped Rambusch get the Navy contract, but nobody knew for sure.

Earl Anderson had been the operations manager before Dashman. During his job interview, Winston said to Dashman, "You will probably hear rumors about how Earl left Rambusch because of a personality clash between him and me. Earl left because Dillman Corp. offered him almost twice the salary he was getting here, and also for some personal reasons that I am not at liberty to discuss with you. A lot of people around here don't like me. It has nothing to do with the quality of my work or the way I treat my subordinates. It's a matter of my style. It seems to offend people that I am not exactly as they think I should be. They are all curious about my personal life and what I do in my spare time. But as far as I am concerned, that's nobody's business except my own. I want to be square with you and also give you my perspective about what it would be like to work here. People will want a lot of information about me from you because you will be working for me. They will not be satisfied with purely work-related information. This can be a hard situation to deal with, because unless you give them what they want, they isolate you. But on the other hand, there is great opportunity here at Rambusch. Our contract with the Navy is just the beginning. I am quite sure that we will get the four-year contract. Let's just say my intuition is very good. And there are a lot more potential contracts on the horizon. Rambusch will be growing larger and probably within the next few years. But that's between me and you, and if anyone asks me how I know, I'll say I never said a thing!"

Winston was correct about the employees at Rambusch not liking him. During Dashman's first few weeks on the job, more people spoke to him about Winston than about work. Jack Kozenski was a line manager who reported directly to Dashman. Kozenski was a Polish immigrant and nearing retirement. He was a very intense, withdrawn, and austere person, prone to occasional outbursts of temper. He wore thick, steel-rimmed glasses that made Dashman feel as if Kozenski was looking straight through him. Self-made and self-educated, Kozenski began with Rambusch as a maintenance man. He was married and had seven children. One day during a conversation with Dashman, Kozenski said, "I have a cousin like Winston. We never understood him. He never married, but became a successful lawyer. Always dressed sharp. When he was a young boy he never played with the other boys. He read and played his piano. But he is smart, a good lawyer, and he makes a lot of money."

Pauline Johnston was one of five supervisors on Kozenski's line. She was twenty-nine years old, originally from New Orleans, and was the first black female supervisor at Rambusch. She had been with the company for six years, did very high-quality work, and was well liked throughout the organization. Pauline was currently going to night school to complete a college degree. Dashman was at the Sunderland plant when Johnston said to him, "I want to give you some advice. Play your cards close to your vest. People around here let their imagination get the best of them. That was the reason Earl Anderson left. He thought that everyone was talking about him because he worked so closely with Winston. Truth is, he was right. What people should be doing is judging people by the work they do, not by the color of their skin or what they do in their own time. But people talk, and they imagine. I just wanted to let you know what you are in for."

DASHMAN'S PROGRESS

When the employees talked about Winston, Louis Dashman tried not to listen. Dashman made a "contract with himself" that he was at Rambusch to work hard and that he wouldn't get involved in petty office politics. Besides, in the eight weeks he had been working at the company, Winston had been extremely helpful in phasing him into the work process. Winston had been open and straightforward with him, and Dashman felt, at least so far, he was an excellent person to work for.

Dashman's first priority was to establish himself at Rambusch. He liked western Massachusetts and would be happy to settle there. His fiancée, Anne Weston, also liked the area. She would be finished with her doctoral studies in two years and there were many schools in the area at which she could teach. Anne wanted to be out of the city. She was born in Boston and had been in New York for the past seven years. They both wanted to restore an old New England farmhouse. The opportunity to work at Rambusch fit into Dashman's plans, and if Winston's comments about the future at the company were true, he felt he might have found the almost perfect opportunity.

Since the work that Rambusch was doing for the Navy was so specialized, there was a need for a lot of personal contact. Winston made frequent trips to Washington, D.C., to discuss engineering and design issues. He usually made these trips alone, but in July he asked Dashman to accompany him. "I want to let you know that I am aware of the excellent work you have been doing in your six months with the company. I think that it is important that you get more involved with my contacts in D.C. and also get some experience in playing the government contracts game. The future of Rambusch is in these government contracts. I've been working on my sources in D.C. for over ten years and it's starting to pay off. We are at the stage where it's becoming too much for me to handle alone, and I would like to get you involved. We will go down to Washington next Monday and return on Thursday. Get things in order so that you can get away for a few days."

Dashman was fascinated by the way Winston worked in Washington. Winston seemed to know everybody at the Department of the Navy, and at a meeting with a vice admiral, it was confirmed that the four-year contract had been awarded to Rambusch. Both men returned to Massachusetts in very good spirits.

In September, Winston and Dashman made another trip to Washington to meet with officials from the Department of Defense. The Defense Department representatives were interested in getting a bid from Rambusch on a contract for advanced office systems. The dollar value of the contract was twice as large as the Navy contract. The meeting with the Defense Department officials was very informative, and Rambusch, under the guidance of Winston, submitted a proposal in October. In the following January, a five-year pact, worth approximately $3.8 million per year, was awarded to the Rambusch Company by the Department of Defense.

THE CONVERSATION AND OFFER

Winston and Dashman celebrated their success by going to lunch at Judy's, the most expensive restaurant in western Massachusetts. "I've also been informed by the chairman of the board of Rambusch that I am going to be promoted," said Winston. "President Jameson is going to retire in March, and the board unanimously voted for me to be his successor. I've also got approval to hire an assistant to help me work on obtaining and managing the government contracts for the company. I would like to promote you to that position. You will also be involved in shaping the expansion plans of the company, as well as in recruiting and hiring new people."

Dashman was delighted. "I'm overwhelmed. I don't know what to say. It's an incredible opportunity for me."

"There are some other things that you need to know before you decide whether or not you will take the promotion," said Winston. "I've been waiting for this opportunity for some time now. I've made a very important decision that has to do with my personal life. It might affect you if you decide to accept the promotion, or even if you decide to stay at Rambusch. I'm telling you this now because I like and respect you and I want you to be informed. I am a member of a gay political action group. The members of this group are all professional people, men and women who are respected community members. They include lawyers, business people, doctors, a political leader, a judge, and so on. We have decided to hold a news conference and to declare our alternative sex preference openly. The group has been waiting for my promotion, which I had anticipated. We're not sure how this will affect our professional lives, but we all believe the time has come for us to stop hiding and to acknowledge who we are openly. This is an important step for all of us. I told Earl Anderson about this decision, and that is one of the reasons he went to Dillman. I'm telling you now because I want to give you some time to think it over. We will hold our news conference in March after I have signed my new contract as president of Rambusch. As you know, the business is very secure for the next five years. You have the opportunity to gain invaluable experience in this new position as well as to profit financially. The news conference might attract a lot of attention. To my knowledge, this is the first time an organized effort like this has ever been done. It might also blow over without any real hullabaloo. In any case I'd like to know what your decision is in one week."

LOOKING FOR DECISION ADVICE

Louis Dashman decided to seek the advice of a former professor about his available courses of action: "I have to be pleased at the career opportunities open to me in the new job and the obvious growth potential of the company. Yet, I wonder if the military people will be as persuaded by Winston once he announces his status. They seem to have a decided distaste for people like him and may quietly cut him off after he comes out in the open. Should I try to persuade Winston to forget this group of people he is associated with, or at least not come out in the open as he plans to do? On the other hand, maybe if he is going to blow himself out of the water with this scheme of his, I should stick around. If he fails, I will be ready to move up and take over in a strong managerial position. I have already established myself favorably with the Navy and the Defense people, and if I assure them that I am straight and not one of Winston's group, will they hang onto the contracts and renew them on my ability rather than Winston's? I also have some concern about my reputation inside the company. Perhaps I should quietly talk to the important people inside the firm and let them know that I am not affiliated with Winston in any personal way and that my contacts are purely professional. But, they may not believe me. I may even be worrying too much about the effect of this thing; it may all go away without creating more than a temporary sensation, and I will have worried for nothing. I understand that gay rights is on the rise and there are many states and cities in which gay rights laws are in effect, and a federal bill has been discussed. However, I have to remember that we aren't located in a big city like San Francisco or New York and that western Massachusetts is quite provincial. What do you think would be the best course for me?"

The professor, a gray-haired gentleman, tamped the tobacco in his pipe. "As I understand it, you are wondering whether you should accept the promotion."

CASE–27

A Conflict With Official Duties

Gary Davis was the human resources manager for Merchants and Farmers Bancshares, a large bank and financial services holding company with offices throughout several southeastern states. As part of his compliance duties, he was responsible for overseeing the firm's "standards of conduct" policies and procedures. These were written in a booklet that provided detailed guidelines for employees on different topics including press relations, employee borrowing, acceptance of gifts from customers and vendors, and part-time employment. The section on part-time employment read as follows:

> Employees of Merchants and Farmers Bancshares are expected to devote full business time for which they are employed to the effective accomplishment of the duties to which they are assigned. They shall not accept part-time employment that could conflict with official duties or impair their ability to perform their jobs in a totally impartial manner.

When hired, each new employee received a copy of the firm's current policies and procedures manual entitled *Standards of Conduct*. All employees would be sent memos that described any changes and additions whenever new policies or procedures were to be implemented. Annually, each employee had to complete statements certifying that they were in compliance with all of the firm's employment polices. When completed, these statements were reviewed by each branch office manager and then sent to Gary Davis for his review and filing in each employee's personnel file. Davis's recent review of these statements on January 30 had yielded no conflicts with employee activities and company policies.

On February 14, Gary Davis received a phone call from Barbara Chester, a branch manager in Barrell City, one of the holding company's many small-city branch offices. Ms. Chester told Gary that she had discovered that one of her loan officers, Frank O'Neil, had been "moonlighting" as a life insurance agent for another firm. Some of the products O'Neil was selling directly competed against the credit life products sold by Merchants and Farmers Bancshares to its own customers to cover loan balances in case of death. Barbara Chester had found this out when a customer inquired as to why the policies sold by Merchants and Farmers Bancshares didn't have as attractive premiums as those O'Neil was selling on behalf of another firm. Chester also relat-

---

All names are disguised.

ed to Davis that Frank O'Neil's work had been "substandard" and that at his last six-month performance review, she had placed O'Neil "on probation." Chester told Davis that O'Neil was fifty-two years old and that he had been an employee for over twenty years. O'Neil had been transferred to Barrell City and had reported to Chester for a little over one year.

Chester wanted to know if Davis felt O'Neil had violated company policy and, if so, if it was grounds for dismissal. Chester said that she never had experienced a problem like this before, and she didn't know how to handle the matter. Further, she was concerned about O'Neil's age and length of service with the firm, since she had heard that another employee who recently had been dismissed had sued the company on grounds of age discrimination.

CASE–28

The Controversial Sales Representative

Lawrence Scott joined the field staff of Stuyvesant Drug Products Company as a "detail person" (also known as a medical sales representative) early in 1991. He was a college graduate, having majored in physical education; although extremely interested in sports and athletics, he did not pursue a teaching career as he had originally planned.

Scott was first interviewed by Edward Graham, central division manager. At the time, Scott was working as a salesman for a business education publishing house. As a result of his credentials and his performance during the interview, Scott impressed Graham as an aggressive, hardworking book sales representative who appeared eager to gain prestige and higher earnings by entering the pharmaceutical industry. Graham decided to consider Scott for the Louisville territory and immediately instituted a personnel check through the Personal Credit Investigating Company. Character references and former employers spoke well of Scott and reported nothing unfavorable. However, Personal Credit reported that Scott had been employed by the post office in his home town, Freeport, following his graduation from high school 1981. (His application for employment stated that he graduated from high school in 1982 and made no mention of his employment by the Freeport post office.) The report stated that during February 1982, a quantity of mail was found on

This case is based on a case originally developed by the late Professor Emeritus Charles L. Lapp of the John M. Olin School of Business of Washington University at St. Louis; the case has been subsequently revised. All names, dates, and locations are disguised. Used by prior permission.

a creek bank near Freeport that had never been delivered even though it had passed through the Freeport post office. Upon investigation, a postal inspector discovered that Scott had disposed of two bags of mail by throwing them into the creek. Scott claimed that he had a date that night and had thrown the mail away to avoid being late. Scott was discharged by the post office for this offense, but no charges were pressed by the authorities.

In spite of this report, Graham decided to employ Scott and arranged to train him in the technical aspects of the job and familiarize him with reporting systems and other paperwork necessary to carry out his functions as a medical sales representative.

Scott's territorial performance apparently pleased Graham. About a year after joining the company, Graham wrote Scott:

March 21, 1992

I should like to commend you on your splendid performance during the last half of 1991. You finished this half with 104.7 percent attainment of quota. What is even more impressive, Larry, you attained 106.8 percent of your quota in old products. Very nice work. I know you will do everything possible to retain or better this position next year. Best of luck to you.

Edward Graham

During the ensuing months, Graham was heard by other representatives to remark about Scott's outstanding performance. Scott received salary increases in July of 1991, January of 1992, and again in July of 1992. Although this was considered unusual and was not in accordance with company policy, Graham insisted, and the exceptions to policy were made.

Scott seldom corresponded with the home office except for routine matters. The only knowledge the home office had of his performance was obtained through copies of memoranda from Graham to Scott.

By the end of 1992, Stuyvesant Drug Company had grown rapidly and had expanded its field staff considerably since the early part of the year. As a result, several new sales divisions were to be created. Scott received word from the home office in December that effective January, 1, 1993, he would be responsible to Douglas Rathbone, the newly appointed Cincinnati district manager. Rathbone was highly regarded by the home office and was considered to be very capable by Harry Lane, his regional sales manager.

Soon after his appointment to division manager, Rathbone went to Louisville to work with Scott and to get acquainted with him. Because he was eager to get acquainted with all the representatives in his district as soon as possible, Rathbone spent only two days during this field visit with Scott. Following this trip, Rathbone reported to Lane:

February 17, 1993
To: Harry Lane
From: Douglas Rathbone
Subject: Field Visit with Lawrence Scott

Detailing—Not too strong here. Tries to cover too much in the allotted time. Didn't have calling cards with him.

Accounts—Very good support and cooperation with direct retailers and wholesalers. They all like him. He should know the names of more of the personnel in the stores.

Comments—Makes an excellent appearance—neat. Well groomed. Has good general knowledge of his territory. He appears conscientious and a willing worker. *Ambitious.*

Doug Rathbone

About two months later, Rathbone again worked with Scott and reported:

April 23, 1993
To: Harry Lane
From: Douglas Rathbone
Subject: Field Visit with Lawrence Scott

Detailing—Weak. His detailing lacks enthusiasm, and his delivery needs more modulation and variety. A dull and uninspiring detail.

Accounts—Has good wholesaler support. Could stand improvement with some of the retailers.

Comments—On the favorable side, the man has a nice appearance and is well groomed. He is also sales-minded.

On the negative side is his manner of expressing himself in the physician's office. Definitely a candidate for a Dale Carnegie course or Toastmasters. He was so advised.

His organization is just fair. His car and detail bag were poorly organized. We repacked his detail bag and I advised him to organize his car better. The man has the basic qualifications but needs development to become a first-rate detail person.

Doug Rathbone

During a telephone conversation a week or two later, Rathbone expressed to Lane his disappointment in Scott's performance. At that time, Rathbone was busy training the district personnel in sales. However, he intended to devote extra time in Louisville just as soon as he completed training new sales representatives and a group of medical students he had employed for the summer.

On June 4, Lane received an announcement from Scott that his wife had delivered a baby girl, Louise, on May 29.

Rathbone had been traveling extensively during the month of May and by early June was in the midst of training summer students. On Wednesday, June 6, he was in Centerville, a town located on Swan River, about three hundred miles from Louisville. Centerville was known to be a resort town offering various types of amusements and sporting facilities. Although he was training two students, Rathbone called Paula Norris, a local company representative, to accompany him on an afternoon appointment he had with the manager of a local wholesale drug firm. As Rathbone and Norris were driving toward the outskirts of town at about 4 P.M., Rathbone thought he saw Scott on a miniature golf course with an unidentified young woman. Scott appeared to be attired in bathing trunks and an open shirt. As the two passed the golf course, Rathbone asked Norris to drive around the block. Upon returning to the scene, both Norris and Rathbone were certain that it was Scott who was playing golf. They did not stop, but continued on their way to the wholesaler.

As Rathbone drove home to Cincinnati that evening, his thoughts concentrated on the Lawrence Scott situation.

CASE–29

Alexander Memorial Hospital: The Termination of Susan North

Alexander Memorial Hospital was a major medical center located in a midwestern city. At the time of this case, it employed approximately nine hundred people. The hospital had expanded over the years and added to its building a number of times.

The comptroller's department of the hospital was managed by the comptroller of the hospital, Richard Kuntz. (See Exhibit C–29). Rita Burrows was the director of accounting services and reported directly to Richard Kuntz. Two of the accountants in the department, Susan North and David Sheldon, shared space in a small office. North was in charge of accounting for hospital investments and also maintained files for the hospital's malpractice liability fund. She reported directly to Burrows, although Kuntz also assigned some work to her. North's job entailed reconciling various asset accounts, including cash and investment accounts, and preparing standard journal entries. Sheldon, a CPA, had joined the department only six months ago. He reported directly to the assistant director of accounting services, Debbie Marx. Sheldon supervised two clerical positions and was primarily responsible for the general ledger and fixed assets.

SUSAN NORTH: PROBLEM ACCOUNTANT

Susan North had been with the hospital for about two and one-half years. She had been hired by Ralph Hughes, who was the comptroller at that time. North had a Bachelor's degree from a small liberal arts college, where she had majored in accounting. North had worked for one year at a major CPA firm before coming to work at Alexander Memorial. The CPA firm had contacted Hughes to inquire about placing North in a position at the hospital because she was going to be terminated because of "problems with the technical aspects of her work." Hughes was contacted because he had worked for this CPA firm in the past. Susan North was a sociable and well-liked person who came from a very prominent family in the community. Susan's father was president of a local company that used the services of this CPA firm, so the CPA firm was interested in helping her to find employment.

Rita Burrows, who at that time was an assistant director, was responsible for training Susan North for the position of investment accountant. However,

---

The names of the hospital and of all individuals are disguised.

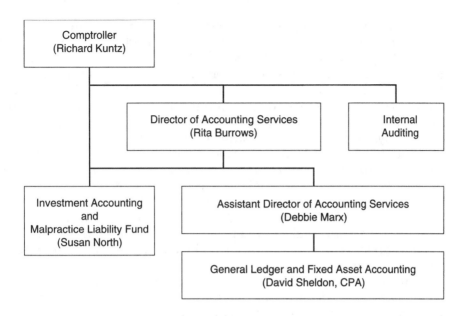

EXHIBIT C–29 Organization Chart of Comptroller's Department (after Organizational Changes and at the Time of the Case)

Susan North was assigned to report directly to the comptroller, Mr. Hughes in an administrative assistant capacity. Rita Burrows felt that Susan North did not have a good understanding of what she was doing in her training period. After approximately six months had elapsed, Rita believed that Susan had been given sufficient time to learn the job. Burrows also believed that Ralph Hughes should have been more involved in supervising Susan North, since North reported to him for other duties.

Susan North's six-month probationary review in Februrary was "favorable." Ralph Hughes did note on the evaluation form that she needed to learn more about the hospital and the work in the department, but he stated that she was "making adequate progress" and she eventually would be "an excellent employee."

In May, because of lack of office space, Susan North was asked to give up her private office to provide an office for a new internal auditor position. North was distressed about losing her own office, and she complained to Ralph Hughes that this was an indication that she was "going to be terminated." Hughes assured her that the move did not have anything to do with her job performance and that she did not have to be concerned about being terminated.

During these months, however, Ralph Hughes had noticed that Susan was spending considerable time on the telephone. She was also away from her desk for periods of time and took extended lunches. Rita Burrows and the accountant in charge of processing journal entries had reported to Hughes a number of errors that Susan North had made. North was confusing debits with credits, and she did not always check her work. At times, her entries were in error, or there were transposition errors in account numbers. Once when Ralph Hughes talked to Susan North about some of these problems, Susan North became very upset and cried. Several clerical employees started joking among themselves about Susan's "easy tears."

In July, Hughes started a program of cross-training and development for all accountants. Susan North was assigned responsibility for reconciling cash accounts, clearing accounts, and prepaid accounts. These accounts were assigned to North because Hughes believed they were straightforward and required only a basic knowledge of accounting.

At the year's end, Ralph Hughes reviewed the accountants' work papers; he found that North had not made sufficient journal entries to correct her accounts and several entries that she had made were incorrect. Several bank accounts assigned to North had not been reconciled. Hughes did some of the work himself to get the accounts up-to-date for the year-end audit. Subsequently, he discussed with Susan North the problems he had found with her work and explained how the work should be done.

In January of the next year, Ralph Hughes gave Susan North her first overall annual performance review. Before completing the evaluation form, he discussed North's situation with Rita Burrows. Burrows was aware that North still did not have a good understanding of what she was doing. Burrows had reviewed the journal entries, and she discovered that North sometimes tried to cover up her mistakes. Burrows had tried to work with North to help her improve her work, but North seemed to resent Burrows offering to help her. Burrows encouraged Hughes to "be firm with Susan" and make certain that she was aware of the seriousness of the problems so that she would be motivated to seek help and improve her work. Therefore, Ralph Hughes stressed the problems that Susan North was having with her work during the performance-evaluation interview. He noted that she was taking too many extended lunches and was away from her desk too often. He also mentioned that she should try to seek the assistance of other people in the department and improve her working relationship with Rita Burrows and the other accountants. Nevertheless, his overall evaluation of Susan North as stated on the evaluation form was that she was an "average" employee who had "high potential for considerable improvement."

ORGANIZATIONAL CHANGES, BUT NO CHANGE IN SUSAN

In July, Rita Burrows was promoted to director of accounting services. Susan North was told that she now was to report directly to Burrows. At the same time, Richard Kuntz replaced Ralph Hughes as comptroller. (Hughes had left the hospital to direct an accounting division in a large corporation.)

Burrows met with North to determine the status of her work and to encourage her to seek assistance and improve her working relationships. North expressed a desire to have her job upgraded because she was near the top of her salary range. Burrows explained that the job could not be upgraded because it had not changed substantially since it was first established and evaluated. She encouraged North to expand her knowledge of accounting by taking some review courses or by reviewing some of her school texts and by taking on new assignments. Burrows assured North that if she expanded her responsibilities and became more knowledgeable of other areas in the department, she would be considered for an upgrade. However, Burrows also told North that she would not be considered for an upgrade or promotion until she showed improvement in her work and took on more responsibilities.

Susan North expressed her dissatisfaction because her position was not going to be upgraded. During the ensuing months, Rita Burrows could see no improvement in North's work or in her attitude toward Burrows. North did not ask for additional work assignments, and she spent considerable time either on the telephone or talking to clerks in the office. Although Burrows was concerned about North's performance, Burrows didn't say anything to North about it because she wanted to avoid any further confrontation or acrimony with North.

In November, Rita Burrows asked Susan North about the status of her work papers and accounts; North responded that they were up-to-date and accurate. Susan North said that she was working "on something" for Mr. Kuntz at the moment, and she would get her papers together as soon as she finished his work assignment. Rita Burrows talked to Richard Kuntz about the situation, because Kuntz had assigned work to North without Burrows knowing about it. Kuntz denied that he was giving Susan North much work, and he stated that at times he had to "hound Susan" to complete the few assignments that he had given her. When Rita Burrows asked for Kuntz's opinion about Susan North's competence, he said that she was an average employee who participated in too much office gossip. But Kuntz also said that he thought North was a "sweet person" and that he liked her "preppy look." He stated that he thought there should be enough work available in the department that North was capable of doing, and that with "a little closer supervision," he believed "everything would work out."

Rita Burrows became even more concerned about the status of North's work when the hospital received a notice from one of the banks that one of the hospital's accounts was overdrawn. Rita Burrows reviewed the bank reconciliation forms. Susan North brought her work papers to Burrows, and then North admitted that she didn't know how to reconcile the account and that it was a "real mess." Rita Burrows told North that she would try to bring the reconciliation up-to-date; she also asked to see all of North's accounts so that they could be reviewed before the year-end closing.

It again was January, and it was now Rita Burrows's responsibility to prepare the annual performance evaluation of Susan North. On the performance-evaluation form, various problems in North's work were cited, including her reluctance to seek help from her supervisor or the other accountants in the department. Burrows gave North an overall evaluation of "below average" as compared to other personnel in the department. When Burrows met with North to discuss this evaluation, Susan said that it was "totally unfair" because it didn't have "anything good in it." North felt that the evaluation should have included something about "all of the work" that she was doing for the comptroller. North then asked Burrows if this evaluation would result in her being terminated. Burrows told her that she wanted North to be aware of the seriousness of the problem, and that if there was no improvement in her work, this might lead to North being terminated. However, Burrows said that if North would work more closely with her, improve her work, and take on additional responsibilities, then North wouldn't have to worry about being terminated.

Susan North was given a copy of the evaluation, but she was not required to sign it. No record was made of the conversation between North and Burrows other than a date on the form. A copy of the evaluation form was sent to Richard Kuntz for his information.

A "TIME LOG" LEADS TO A TERMINATION DECISION

In March, Rita Burrows met with Debbie Marx and David Sheldon to discuss the status of several projects and the reassignment of duties among some of the department positions. During the meeting, David Sheldon voiced concern over what he believed was a problem of morale with some of the personnel in the department. There had been several major changes over a relatively short period of time, and he said that some of the employees had "problems adjusting." In particular, Sheldon stated that he heard quite a few negative comments about the "situation" in the office, which he assumed Burrows and Marx knew about. He stated to Rita Burrows, "There is something I think you should know, if you don't already, and it's that Susan North is keeping a log on your time in and out of the office. She was showing it to me, and she wanted to know my opinion about whether I believed that you were really on hospital business when you weren't in the department. I told her that where I worked before, my boss was gone a lot of the time in meetings and just because I didn't know where he was, I didn't have any reason to believe that he was not on company business. I don't want to cause any trouble for anyone, but I thought you ought to know this."

Both Rita Burrows and Debbie Marx were amazed to learn that Susan North was keeping a time log on her boss. Burrows commented, "I've been with the hospital for five years, and I've always worked a great deal of overtime. Who does that gal think she is?"

After learning about the time log that Susan North was keeping on her, Rita Burrows decided that things had gone too far and that Susan North should be terminated. Since her evaluation several months ago, Susan North had apparently spent more time on her work, but she continued to make errors and she was still spending time gossiping with clerical employees. Also, North hadn't shown any interest in taking on additional work or responsibility.

Rita Burrows contacted Richard Kuntz and told him about the time log. Richard Kuntz was enraged. Then he revealed to Rita that an anonymous caller had telephoned the president of the hospital several weeks prior to this and had told the president that Rita Burrows was frequently absent from her work and that Richard Kuntz was "trying to cover up for her absences." Kuntz said he felt sure that Susan North had something to do with this call, and he agreed that North "had to go."

That same day, Rita Burrows and Richard Kuntz contacted the director of human resources, Ellen James, and discussed the situation with James. James told them that she was aware of the existence of the time log, because Susan North had shown it to her several weeks before. However, James said that she believed that North was within her rights to keep such a log and that it should not be used as the sole grounds for termination. They discussed alternatives to a termination, but Rita Burrows stated that she thought any action less than a termination would not be acceptable. Kuntz inquired about the possibility of letting North resign, but Ellen James stated that the hospital had adopted a policy that no one would be offered the choice of "termination or resignation" unless the employee was given the option of staying if they did not choose to resign. James stressed the point that if Susan North filed a grievance, Burrows would have to be prepared to justify her decision to terminate Susan North to the hospital grievance committee.[1] Rita Burrows stated that she felt confident that she could get support for her decision. Thereupon, Ellen James agreed to the termination, and it was decided that Susan North would be terminated that afternoon.

Rita Burrows met with Susan North to inform her that she was being terminated and to give North a letter stating that she was being terminated because of "problems with her work and her lack of satisfactory improvement." North became angry, and she accused Burrows of not giving her enough time to improve and of not helping her. Burrows then questioned North about the time log she had been keeping and which North had shown to other hospital personnel. North said, "I've got a right to do that. You can't fire me for keeping records on you that are accurate!" Burrows then said, "And I guess you don't know anything about a telephone call to the president of the hospital?" North responded, "I don't know what you're talking about," and she proceeded to leave Rita's office. As a parting comment, North said, "You'll hear from my lawyer about this!"

---

[1]The hospital had an internal grievance procedure by which employees could protest management decisions. The procedure provided for several steps, with the final step being a hearing before a committee of employees and supervisors, which made a final determination.

A THREAT OF LITIGATION

Several days later, Rita Burrows was summoned to Ellen James's office. As HR director, James had received a letter from Olivia Harris, a local attorney, in which Harris indicated she was representing Susan North in regard to her termination by the hospital. In Harris's letter, she stated that she was prepared to file an unjust (unlawful) discharge lawsuit against the hospital. Harris requested a meeting with hospital management within the next ten days. When Ellen James met to discuss this letter with Rita Burrows, James said, "Rita, we've got a real problem on our hands. Can we justify what we've done, or should we back off and settle this in some way as fast as we can? And, what if North goes to the media about this? How would we explain our position, especially with her family connections?"

The Problem Employee
in a Governmental Agency

THE AGENCY SITUATION

The "Governmental Sixty Public Employment Department" (G6PD) was orig-inally established by the state of Minnesota to help secure employment for out-of-work people who were over sixty years of age. The office where this case occurred was located in a small city that was in the ore mining area of Minnesota. It was logical to have this G6PD office expand its scope of opera-tions to help thousands of unemployed miners when the iron ore industry began to slide.

The overall mission of the G6PD was to help workers of all ages find employment. Unfortunately, at the time of this case, most of the jobs that the agency seemed to be able to assist workers in finding were low-paying in nature. The low wages were difficult to accept for many unemployed miners who previously had been making excellent incomes. Although most of the unemployed miners had completed high school, they usually had no specific skills that were readily transferable to other careers.

Randy Russell was the manager of the local office of the G6PD, and he was well aware that his marketing representatives (or "reps") faced a difficult job in getting people placed in jobs. His reps were actually a sales force that represented an unusual product—people. The job of the rep was to match the skills of the unemployed with the needs of specific jobs and then to convince the employers to "buy the product"—that is, to hire the worker. The job was made a little easier by the fact that part of the worker's wage would be paid by the state during a training period in the new job.

Randy Russell had been a marketing rep for several years before being promoted to the position of managing the office of people who had been his co-workers. Russell had a good working knowledge of the job of a marketing representative. He really wished that Madelyn James had a better under-standing of what she should be doing as a marketing rep.

This case was prepared by Professor Irvin A. Zaenglein of the Cisler School of Business of Northern Michigan University at Marquette. All names are disguised. Used by permission.

THE PROBLEM EMPLOYEE

Madelyn James had moved to the area some years ago when her husband moved his office there. Her husband, a local doctor, was loved and respected by the community. In fact, when Dr. Archie James purchased a new automobile a few weeks ago, Madelyn had remarked that it was absurd for the doctor to buy a locking gas cap. (Madelyn had a locking gas cap on her own new car). Madelyn's co-workers always stopped what they were doing and chatted with "Doc" when he came into the office. However, it seemed that most of them did not feel so warmly toward Madelyn.

When she became an "empty nester," Madelyn had decided to join the workforce. Her first job had been as a teller at a bank just down the street from the G6PD office. Actually, she had worked there "twice." One night at a social gathering, Randy had learned about her stay at the bank from a bank vice-president. After several months on the teller job, Madelyn was fired by the bank for excessive absenteeism. Madelyn then contacted a state agency to file a complaint claiming that she had been discriminated against improperly; she was subsequently rehired by the bank. Realizing that bank management probably was unhappy with her, that the bank teller job was a dead-end position, and that the pay wasn't to her liking either, Madelyn decided to look for other employment. She took a position with the G6PD as a secretary at a higher salary.

Madelyn James excelled at her secretarial responsibilities. Because she held a B.S. degree in marketing management from a state university, about a year later she was offered the position of marketing representative when a marketing rep job came open. Madelyn was not given any training in her new position other than to accompany another experienced marketing rep for about a week or so in her contacts with area employers. However, in Randy Russell's mind, Madelyn James did not make a satisfactory transition from secretary to marketing rep.

Madelyn's problems in the job weren't because she wasn't bright enough. Randy Russell believed that Madelyn's problems were caused primarily by personality conflicts and by her negative reactions to suggestions about how to improve the situation. Only two days ago, one of the agency secretaries had filed a grievance because Madelyn was typing her own letters. Most secretaries would have been happy to have the marketing reps type their own letters. The real reason for the grievance was that Madelyn had been upset about the way the letter was first being typed by the secretary, and Madelyn had ripped the letter out of the secretary's typewriter.

Randy Russell had received several informal telephone complaints from area employers to the effect that Madelyn James didn't understand or recognize their needs to have competent, skilled employees. One employer told Randy that Madelyn was "preachy" and "dogmatic," and that she had "lectured" him that it was his moral obligation to hire some unemployed miners. Madelyn had been a marketing rep for about six months, and she had been successful in finding employment opportunities only for several individuals.

She told Randy that she was still "learning her job," and that her contacts with area employers would "pay off" in the near future.

Further, Randy Russell was not pleased with Madelyn James because Madelyn did not like to be told how she could improve her performance as a marketing rep. That's normal, Randy thought; very few people react well to being criticized. On the other hand, Madelyn was going to have to change the way she approached her job. She was taking psychotherapy courses at a local community college in order to more fully understand the nature of mental problems of those who were unemployed. That in itself was good, but it appeared that she was "going overboard" in trying to turn herself into a counselor. Her real job was the placement of unemployed workers.

DECISION TIME

Randy Russell knew that Madelyn James had become part of a group of women in town who were practicing assertiveness training and conducting seminars on "feeling good about yourself." He wasn't sure how this was influencing her job performance. However, he knew that he and his district manager had had several discussions with Madelyn about her attitudes toward people and the way she did her paperwork. Randy had decided that he was going to put Madelyn James on probationary status tomorrow and that she would be given ninety days to change or be terminated.

EXERCISE–9

Favoritism in the HR Department

You are Patricia Wiesley, director of human resources at a manufacturing plant of an international corporation. Your plant is located in a southern city, and it employs approximately five hundred people.

Four years ago, you were hired as an assistant manager in the HR department. You had just completed your B.S.B.A. degree from a local university, majoring in personnel and industrial relations. You were hired by Larry Presh, who at that time was director of human resources at the plant. You replaced his prior assistant who had resigned and left the firm. Presh delegated a large amount of staffing responsibilities to you, among these being the recruitment, interviewing, and screening of applicants for sales, clerical, and administrative positions. At the time, the plant was adding employees because of several major contracts, including a large government order. Presh was very supportive of you, and, with his guidance and assistance, you settled into your position rapidly.

During about the third month of your employment, Larry Presh came to you with a request. He wanted you to do "everything possible" to hire a young woman for one of the open accounting department positions. This young woman was Barbara Amoca, the daughter of George Amoca, who was chairperson of the local community's regional planning commission. Presh told you that George Amoca had considerable political and environmental influence in the local community and in the state legislature. The plant manager, William Grimsley, had called Presh urging him to give Barbara Amoca "every consideration," since George Amoca was an influential person and also a personal friend of Grimsley.

You decided to cooperate. You called Barbara Amoca in for an interview, and you carefully checked her credentials. She had compiled almost an A average in college, majoring in accounting from the same university business school that you had attended. You concluded that she was an excellent candidate, so you strongly recommended her to the manager of the accounting department, Lila Delmont. Delmont also interviewed Barbara Amoca, and Delmont agreed to hire Amoca for a staff accounting position. Subsequently you received a call from the plant manager, William Grimsley, who thanked you for your efforts. Larry Presh also told you, "Great job, Pat! This will help all of us."

All names are disguised.

Some four years have passed. About three months ago, Larry Presh was promoted to corporate vice president of human resources at the company's headquarters in New York, replacing the retiring individual. On Presh's recommendation, you were promoted to his former position of plant director of human resources. This morning, Larry Presh called you. Here is what he said to you:

> Pat, I need a favor. Our CEO is on the board of a company on the East Coast that is also one of our major customers. The daughter of that company's senior executive just graduated from college with an accounting degree. I want you to hire her into the accounting department just like you did for me four years ago when you hired Barbara Amoca. This is really important to me. I know there is an opening for an entry-level accountant in Barbara's area. You probably know that Barbara is now a supervisor in one of the sections of the accounting department, and I am sure that she will go along with this.

You told Larry Presh that you would check into the matter and get back to him as soon as possible.

You called Barbara Amoca. She acknowledged that she did have an opening in her section, but she already had interviewed several qualified applicants whose applications were on file. Two of these applicants were minority persons, and she previously had received a "confidential" memorandum from the corporate controller that urged that the plant's accounting department should give "major consideration" to hiring qualified minority individuals. In fact, said Amoca, she had been told several months ago by Larry Presh that the accounting department should make extraordinary efforts to hire qualified minority persons because of the company's affirmative action program, which was not meeting its current commitments. Barbara Amoca also told you that she felt it would not be proper to give preference to an unknown person just because she was the daughter of a prominent customer.

You are quite disturbed by all of this. You have worked hard to succeed in the company, and you are proud of the progress you have made. You are worried that if you submit to Larry Presh's request, there will be no end to this type of "insider favoritism."

EXERCISE–10

Calculating Effects of Labor Turnover

You are Bill Jones, human resources manager of the XYZ Division of the ABC Corporation. You have been studying the details of a research paper presented at a conference you have just attended. The research results pointed up in some detail the relationship between the length of service of the employees in a company and the labor turnover rate. Further, the research results indicated that (typically) in companies with 2.5 percent per month turnover rates, employees with zero to six months of service had work performance levels of only about 85 percent of the output norm for their jobs, and those with seven to twelve months of service had average performance levels of about 95 percent of the norm.

From reading an employer association's newsletter, you know that the average turnover for your industry has been about 1.7 percent per month, or about 20 percent per year. Further, your own XYZ Division, which had about three thousand employees, had a turnover rate of some 30 percent per year, the 2.5 percent per month rate mentioned in the research study.

Tables included in the research paper also gave the typical constellation of employees by length of service. After checking your records, you find that the research results agreed with data on seniority patterns in the XYZ Division. In companies with 30 percent annual turnover, 20 percent of the employees had an average of three months' service, and 10 percent an average of 9 months' service. On the other hand, companies with only 20 percent turnover had only 5 percent of their employees in the three-months' service category and 2.5 percent in the nine-months' service category.

You wonder whether you could use these data, along with the average hourly wage cost in the ABC Corporation of about $6.00 per hour, to make a case for budgetary support for a multipronged labor-turnover reduction program. Such a program would require more staff for exit interviewing and employment interviewing and processing for increased applicant traffic. You know that increased employment advertising would be required, and you would further need extra staff to better monitor the grievance system and to bring the job-evaluation system up to date and to keep it current. Additionally, you suspect that analysis of exit-interview results would indicate additional training was needed for many first-line supervisors and their managers, especially if turnover reduction were to be targeted as a priority effort.

This exercise was prepared by Professor James A. Lee of the College of Business Administration of Ohio University at Athens. All names are disguised. Used by permission.

EXERCISE–11

A Training and Development Problem at Sumerson Manufacturing

You began working for Sumerson Manufacturing Company as a human resource department trainee a few days after receiving your M.B.A. degree with a major in management from a large midwestern university. After a one-year training program, you served two years as assistant director of training and development in one of Sumerson's machining and assembly plants. You then were promoted to plant director of training and development, in which capacity you served for approximately four years. This assignment ended when you were transferred to corporate headquarters as staff assistant to the corporate director of training and development. The corporate director is scheduled for retirement in six months. You hope to become the next corporate director of training and development, but you know that this depends largely on how well you handle your next major assignment.

Sumerson is planning to open a new plant in sixteen months. The new plant is going to hire approximately one thousand employees. However, only one of eight production lines is to go into operation when the plant opens. The other seven production lines will be phased in over a period of three years from the date of the plant opening. Construction of the new plant has just started in a town of ten thousand people eighteen miles south of Memphis, Tennessee. The plant will be very similar to the plant in which you previously had been director of training and development. You have been asked by the corporate vice president of human resources and your boss to submit a plan for recruiting, selecting, and training the personnel for the new plant. You have been given four months in which to do the job. Four hundred and fifty new employees must be hired and trained prior to the plant opening date.

Top management has made the decision that forty-nine members of management from Sumerson's other twenty-one plants are to be transferred to fill all second- and higher-level management positions. For most of these managers, this will be a promotion. Also, many nonmanagement employees in the company will be offered jobs in the new plant, but few are expected to accept. All front-line management, such as foremen and supervisors, must be trained by Sumerson, not hired "off the street" as supervisors.

You are not sure what you should do, because this is the first time the company has ever built and staffed a new plant. There is no past experience

---

This exercise was prepared by Professor James C. Hodgetts of the Fogelman College of Business and Economics of the University of Memphis. The name of the company is disguised. Used by permission.

on which to draw. You have decided that you have two separate but related problems:

1. How to hire and train an entire staff of new employees below the second level of management in one year and have them ready to open the new plant; and
2. How to procure and train the balance of the thousand employees needed to staff the plant by the projected full-operations date.

The Exaggerated Self-Appraisal

You are Mark Delcor, associate store manager at a local outlet of a major discount department store chain. You are preparing yourself for a meeting with Shirley Guswelle, an employee who reports to you. You are somewhat apprehensive about this meeting.

Under the policies of your firm's human resources department, annual performance evaluations are required for all employees to be conducted by their managers. Although your firm has an appraisal form that may be used, the actual format of the performance evaluation and the appraisal interview are left up to each manager to follow according to his or her needs and preferences. Prior to this year, your approach has been to fill out in your office a company performance appraisal form on each employee. You then would meet individually with each employee, show the employee the evaluation that you had made, and discuss the evaluation and suggest future areas for improvement. You have had rather mixed results with this approach. In particular, Shirley Guswelle, who is a lead employee (or working supervisor) in one of your merchandise departments, has been very defensive about the appraisals that you gave her on the last two occasions. In fact, you felt that she had become somewhat hostile and resentful of any suggestions for improvement that you had offered.

About three months ago, you attended a supervisory training program that was offered by your company for store managers and associate managers. The seminar was conducted by a university professor who had been hired by the company to develop and present the seminar. One of the sessions dealt with performance appraisals. In that session, the professor advocated using the self-appraisal technique in which the employee is given an opportunity to rate himself or herself in advance of a meeting with the manager, who then compares and discusses the employee's self-appraisal with his or her own evaluation. The professor stated that much research had indicated that when employees were allowed to appraise themselves, they tended to be more critical of themselves than were their managers. According to the professor, with this aproach, employees also were usually more receptive to suggestions for improvement.

You decided to try this approach with Shirley Guswelle. About a week ago, you gave Ms. Guswelle a copy of the company's appraisal form and told her to fill it out as she evaluated her performance during the past year. You

---

All names are disguised.

asked that she give it back to you a day or two before a scheduled meeting when you would discuss her self-appraisal and your own evaluation of her. Shirley Guswelle filled out an appraisal form on herself and gave it to you yesterday. You were astonished to find that she had given herself a "superior" or "outstanding" rating in every category on the performance appraisal. Further, under the section entitled "Areas for Improvement," Shirley Guswelle had left this section entirely blank.

You realize that this was not the outcome you had hoped for, nor was it consistent with what the professor had stated in the seminar. Your own appraisal of Shirley Guswelle is that her performance has been generally average at best, with several areas of serious deficiencies that need major improvement. She is coming to your office this afternoon to have her performance appraisal interview.

Your Leadman Ed

You are a day-shift foreman on a three-shift operation. You have twenty-seven employees reporting to three leadmen[1] under you. Two of your lead-hands are really good on their jobs. They are both about thirty years of age, and, with a little more experience, either could be considered for a first-line supervisory job when one comes up. They have been with the company for about five years each. Your third leadhand is your oldest in point of service. He has fifteen years with the company and six years in your department. He has been a leadhand for the last four years. His name is Ed Hilliard.

Ed is one of the nicest people you have ever met. He is sincerely accommodating to people both inside and outside the department. He's as loyal as they come. He was elected president of the bowling league two years running. He served on the board of directors of the employees' credit union after being a member of its loan committee for three years.

Because he is so nice, Ed has made a lot of friends in the company, both inside the department and in neighboring departments. Ed wants to be a supervisor in the worst way, but he never comes right out and says so. He doesn't do the kinds of things people think of as "bucking for a promotion," but you know that he would only make a mediocre supervisor at best, even with a strong general foreman behind him. You have learned of his lack of potential the hard way.

You are the one who recommended him for the leadhand job—outside the departmental seniority at that. Ed's problem, you've finally discovered, is that he leans heavily on his "way with people" and his good nature. What hurts is that you know he really is sincere in his service-mindedness. His big problem is that he actually isn't very bright. His mental wheels just don't turn fast enough. Some things he just can't figure out at all, and others take him

---

This exercise was prepared by Professor James A. Lee of the College of Business Administration of Ohio University at Athens. All names are disguised. Used by permission.

[1]The position of "leadman" is sometimes called "lead person" in order to avoid an appearance of gender bias. Regardless of its designation, the position is somewhat ambiguous in that a leadman is not considered to be a member of management, yet performs certain activities associated with management. He or she usually makes routine job assignments, instructs new employees, and checks on the quality and quantity of output of employees in the department. On the other hand, a leadman usually does not discipline workers, make performance appraisals, reassign employees to permanent new jobs, or perform other duties usually associated with a manager's position. If there is a labor union in the company, the leadman is a member of the union.

forever, it seems. Also, he is especially poor—and slow—with paperwork, scheduling, and production and scrap reports.

For example, on several occasions, by either failing to read or to understand the weekly production schedules, Ed failed to adjust both the quantity of parts and the product mix specified in the schedules. As a consequence, his department produced either the wrong items or too many or too few items during his work shift. These errors resulted in delayed delivery of finished items to customers or the production of excess inventory.

On another occasion, a worker was injured on the job. Instead of following established procedures and summoning the first-aid attendant, Ed attempted to move the injured person to his office. As a consequence, the injury was aggravated. The employee lost several weeks of work, and the company's medical bills amounted to more than $8,000.

Ed has also had problems with several marginal workers whose quantity and quality of production were considerably below average over an extended period of time. Ed altered the production reports on two of them to make them appear satisfactory—until another employee reported his actions to you. Only then did you understand why several workers had been complaining about "favoritism" in the department.

Ed has big trouble with complicated schedules. He takes up twice as much of your time as both the other leadhands, and he really does need the help. Because you are naturally loyal to your people, you have never seriously complained to your general foreman about Ed. You have more or less covered for Ed on several occasions. Perhaps you do this because you are the one who originally recommended him, at a time when you were a fairly green supervisor yourself.

Your problem right now with Ed is this. The maintenance department needs a night-shift foreman and claims that none of its people has had enough experience on the different jobs. Ed has worked in both maintenance and one other production department before transferring into your department. Turnover has been fairly high in maintenance, and they have been moving toward more specialization. Anyway, they have asked specifically for Ed. They have gone to the plant superintendent (your general foreman's boss), and you feel that the superintendent may be expecting a release and transfer authorization for Ed's promotion with no problems.

You hesitate to open up about Ed's low brainpower, because you are sure they will think you are trying to hang onto a good leadhand. Except for you, the other leadhands, and a few of Ed's subordinates, everybody is fooled by Ed's sincere attitude, loyalty, willingness to work any job and any hours, and so on. You are also aware that a supervisor in maintenance is faced with many more situations calling for intelligence than Ed is in the straightforward production job he is doing now. The maintenance department is responsible for repairing all kinds of machines and equipment. The factory has milling machines, lathes, drill presses, power brakes, punch presses, grinders, overhead cranes, welding machines, forklifts, and a considerable amount of sophisticated testing equipment for metallurgical and chemical testing. The maintenance supervisor must know enough about each machine to help in the diagnosis of problems, determine parts and equipment needed to repair it, select the maintenance crews needed, and estimate the time required for the maintenance work on it. You are certain that Ed will be "found out" as quite inadequate for the job very soon after his promotion. You are sure that he will still be known as a really nice guy, but. ...

You now realize that Ed has become a problem both for you and the company. The plant superintendent and the plant maintenance manager have set up a meeting with you. You anticipate that they will want your assessment of Ed for the supervisory position in the maintenance department. Your meeting is scheduled for 3 P.M. It is now 2 P.M.

PART FOUR

Issues in Managing Diversity

CASES

EXPERIENTIAL EXERCISES

Discrimination in the employment, development, and promotion of people is as old as recorded history. It has been overtly and covertly incorporated into all economic, political, social, and religious institutions. Race, color, religion, nationality, disability, sex, and age have been the primary bases for various types of segregation and discrimination through the ages. However, in the United States during the past several decades, almost all major institutions and organizations have undertaken to bring their policies and practices into closer alignment with the professed ideals and values of a democratic society.

Racial discrimination against African Americans (blacks) occupied most of this country's attention during the 1960s, and this focus of attention was continued and expanded in the 1970s to include women and other minorities. The 1980s brought continued efforts to eradicate discrimination on the bases of race, sex, religion, color, national origin, and age. In the 1990s, considerable emphasis has been placed on eliminating bias against those with disabilities and on making public and work areas accessible to them. Increased emphasis also has been focused on eliminating discrimination in higher-level positions in organizations—that is, more attention has been devoted to questions of discrimination within managerial and professional positions.

The constantly changing composition of the workforce has brought both demands and opportunities for human resource management efforts to deal with the overall challenge of managing workforce diversity in better ways than in the past. These demands and opportunities require not only a commitment to ending discriminatory practices but also to utilizing the strengths of all members of our changing and diverse society.

A starting point for employers in eliminating discrimination and managing diversity in the workplace is to know the laws and to take positive steps to comply with laws and regulations that seek to remove considerations of race, color, sex, religion, national origin, age and disability from most human resource decisions. A partial listing of some of the major federal laws of equal employment opportunity is included at the end of this introductory section. Nondiscriminatory efforts must characterize the entire employment relationship from the initial recruitment steps to the conclusion of the relationship at retirement, resignation, or termination.

Another important step employers must take is the thorough assessment of the entire human resource management process to change, whenever necessary, policies, procedures, and methods that have been or can be discriminatory. Throughout this assessment, the organization's managers and human resource specialists should be seeking opportunities to take appropriate actions to recruit, hire, train, and advance those who may have been negatively affected by prior positions or actions of the organization.

In attempting to comply with legal requirements and to take affirmative action steps, organizations are faced with complicated problems and questions. One of these diversity issues is balancing certain affirmative action efforts with the desire to avoid discrimination against others—"reverse discrimination," as it sometimes is called. Another issue is how to define the proper representation of various groups, by race, gender, age or other criteria in an organization's workforce. Should national or local population characteristics be used as guides, or should criteria be more sharply focused on the organization itself, or on job and skill categories?

Another complicated problem is how to remedy the effects of past discrimination and promote diversity in the workforce while maintaining and improving productive efficiency to the levels demanded by global competition. An organization that fails to compete successfully may place the jobs of all of its workforce in jeopardy. Also, organizations themselves may not unilaterally set some criteria for employment. Professional groups and accrediting bodies may decide the standards which will govern hiring—for example, the Ph.D. in chemistry for the university; the board-certified specialist for the hospital; or the accounting certification for the accounting firm or financial executive's position. Another standard often used throughout human resource management decisions is seniority. Seniority may be used by management as a criterion, and it is often part of a negotiated union agreement. Wherever seniority plays a part in deciding lay offs, rehires, training, or promotional opportunities, its impact may fall most heavily on minorities or women who have been most recently employed, trained, or promoted.

Gender is a factor that affects many human resource decisions. Ideas of "men's work" or "women's work" have largely broken down; an organization needs to be certain its processes for job assignments are open and nondiscriminatory. Roles and behaviors have changed, requiring both male and female workers to make adjustments. These changes have accentuated other problems and tensions: sexual harassment; dual-career couples; women entering previously all-male departments and occupations and often supervising the men; and single parents with major responsibilities at home. All of these types of challenges require top management's awareness, support, and leadership. All organizational members must be offered learning opportunities and assignments that will effectively eliminate discrimination and promote diversity in the workplace. The cases and exercises in Part Four are representative of these types of issues and concerns and the challenges to human resource managers to make appropriate choices and decisions.

Laws of Equal Employment Opportunity
(Partial Listing)

1963   *Equal Pay Act.* Requires payment of equal wages to women and men who perform substantially equal work.

1964   *Title VII of the Civil Rights Act,* as amended. Prohibits discrimination in hiring, promotion, discharge, pay, benefits, and other aspects of employment on the basis of race, color, religion, sex, or national origin. Equal Employment Opportunity Commission (EEOC) has authority to bring lawsuits against employers in the federal courts.

1967   *Age Discrimination in Employment Act,* as amended. Prohibits discrimination in employment on the basis of age for most employees over age 40.

1972   *Equal Employment Opportunity Act.* Extended coverage of Title VII of the Civil Rights Act to government employees, local employers, and educational institutions.

1973   *Rehabilitation Act, Section 503.* Prohibits job discrimination because of a disability. Employers holding $2,500 or more in federal contracts or subcontracts must set up affirmative action program. Enforced by Office of Federal Contract Compliance Programs (OFCCP) in the U.S. Department of Labor.

1974   *Vietnam-era Veterans Readjustment Assistance Act.* Requires affirmative action among federal government subcontractors for military veterans.

1978   *Pregnancy Discrimination Act.* Requires employers to treat pregnancy, childbirth, or related medical conditions the same as any other medical disability.

1990   *Americans with Disabilities Act (ADA).* Prohibits discrimination based on physical or mental disabilities in places of employment and public accommodation. Modeled after the Rehabilitation Act of 1973 but applies to state and local governments, employment agencies, and labor unions, as well as private employers with 15 or more employees. In effect, employment discrimination is prohibited against "qualified individuals with disabilities."

1991   *Civil Rights Act.* Amended five existing civil rights laws to extend their coverage and protection in employment situations. Increased damage awards to victims of discrimination up to $300,000 for corporations with over 500 employees. Reversed or responded to nine U.S. Supreme Court decisions.

Adapted from a list included in Raymond L. Hilgert and Edwin C. Leonard, Jr., *Supervision: Concepts and Practices of Management* 6th ed. (Cincinnati: South-Western, 1995), pp. 635–636.

All in the Family

Louis Minardi, age fifty-four, was president and chief operating officer of Minardi Bakery, Inc. Minardi Bakery was begun almost twenty-four years ago by Louis Minardi, who built the enterprise from one to seventy-five employees through hard work and a dedication to customer satisfaction. Minardi had learned the bakery business when, for financial reasons, he was forced to leave high school and go to work in a local bakery. Even though he would have liked to finish high school, providing financial support for his family was more important to him. With the unexpected death of his father, Louis Minardi was expected to help his mother make ends meet for the two of them and three younger children. Louis often told people that those very hard times brought the family together and that "Close family ties are all that really matter."

Minardi Bakery was one of the finest bakeries in the local area. It had an excellent reputation for quality baked goods and customer service. Both retail and wholesale customers seemed to be very satisfied, and the organization was profitable. Employees were a happy and cohesive group, and they seemed to derive considerable satisfaction from social interaction both on and off the job. The employees had organized company-sponsored softball and bowling teams, and they often went out together to drink beer after work. Much of this cohesiveness was attributable to Minardi's human resource policy of internal recruiting. As the organization grew, personnel requirements were met primarily from referrals from current employees. Minardi often would say that the company is "just one big happy family."

A problem, however, had recently developed. Louis Minardi had just received notice from the regional office of the Equal Employment Opportunity Commission (EEOC) that the firm was being investigated on charges of employment discrimination. Takia Wilson, a twenty-two-year-old African American (black) female, who had applied for a supervisory position at Minardi Bakery about a month and a half ago, had charged that she was denied the job because of her race and gender.

Louis Minardi reflected on the events leading to this problem. Takia Wilson had seen an advertisement in the local newspaper that indicated that Minardi Bakery was seeking to fill a supervisory position (see Exhibit C–31A).

This case was prepared by Charles A. Rarick, Ph.D., Associate Professor and Director of Management at Transylvania University in Lexington, Kentucky. All names are disguised. Used by permission.

Exhibit C–31A   Employment Advertisement

*** SUPERVISORY ***

Minardi Bakery is looking for an energetic and highly motivated person to assume a front-line supervisory position. Ability to get along with others essential. Past supervisory experience or technical training required.

Call: Louis Minardi
      Minardi Bakery
      732-555-3456

Takia had recently graduated from a local community college with a two-year degree in business management. For the past four years, she had been working in a women's apparel shop; during the last two years, she was assistant manager. Takia had received good performance reviews. She provided Mr. Minardi with letters of recommendation that indicated she was a highly motivated and productive employee in her current position. During her four years of employment at the apparel shop, Takia received recognition for her ability to deal effectively with customers. In her position as assistant manager, she was praised for her skills in supervising sales associates.

After reading the discrimination charge, Louis commented to Harry Bruns, his production manager: "Yeah, I remember her. I just didn't think that she would fit in here." The position was later filled by Nick Pitino, a nephew of a supervisor at Minardi who had worked in the bakery during the summer months throughout high school and college. Although Nick Pitino did not have supervisory experience, he did have knowledge of the business, and Minardi had been able to assess Pitino's abilities during the six summers he was employed at the bakery.

Takia Wilson had called the telephone number in the advertisement and scheduled an interview with Mr. Minardi. When she arrived at the bakery, she was given an application form to fill out (see Exhibit C–31B). Upon completing the application form, she was granted an interview with Minardi. During the interview, he asked Takia about her work experience at the "dress shop." The interview process was interrupted several times by telephone calls and company personnel who needed Mr. Minardi's advice. During the interview, Louis Minardi asked Takia if she, or her boyfriend, would mind if she had to work the late shift. Takia responded that the late shift would present no problems; in fact, she often worked nights at the apparel shop. A major concern Mr. Minardi expressed during the interview was Takia's ability to supervise men. He told her that she would have to supervise the work of eight men, most of whom were older than Takia and who had worked in the bakery on

EXHIBIT C–31B

MINARDI BAKERY
APPLICATION FOR EMPLOYMENT

Name_____ Date_____

Address_____
     Street   City   State Zip

Telephone Number_____ Date of Birth_____

Social Security Number_____ Age_____

Education _____Grade School
     School Name   Dates

     _____ High School
     School Name   Dates

     _____ Other School
     School Name   Dates

Work Experience   Employer   Position   Dates

     _____

     _____

     _____

Do you smoke?   _____ YES _____ NO

Do you owe money?   _____ YES _____ NO

Have you ever been arrested? _____ YES _____ NO

Who do you know that works at Minardi Bakery? _____

I hereby affirm that my answers are true and correct to the best of my knowledge.

Signed_____ Date_____

average seven to ten years. Minardi said that he was concerned that Takia did not have previous experience supervising men. Takia told him that she had supervised the work of six part-time women in the apparel shop. Takia Wilson also mentioned to Mr. Minardi that she had taken a number of supervision courses in her studies at the community college and that these courses had prepared her to deal with any problems she would encounter at the bakery. Takia reiterated that even though she had no direct supervisory experience with men nor experience in the bakery business, she would be willing to work very hard to learn the business and to get along with everyone.

Louis Minardi ended the interview by stating that he would "let her know his decision in about a week or so." After two weeks had passed, Takia Wilson called Mr. Minardi to ask about his decision. He told her that the position had been filled by someone else. When pressed about his decision, Minardi responded that a young man had been hired because of his experience and education. "He will probably fit in here better since he has a four-year degree and has worked here before," were the words used by Minardi. He thanked Takia for her application and wished her luck in finding a position. As he put the telephone receiver down, he felt that he would never see Takia Wilson again.

Louis Minardi recognized that he had to respond to Takia Wilson's and the EEOC's charges of employment discrimination.

Atkins, Berry, and Jones vs.
The John Rogers Corporation

The situation facing the John Rogers Corporation seemed most unlikely—almost ironic, thought Dave Green, director of human resources, as he looked up from the report he was reading. Imagine, he thought, a company with an established reputation for fair dealing with employees was now confronted with a lawsuit charging employment discrimination in its Columbia, Tennessee, headquarters plant!

When company founder and CEO John Rogers had learned of the charges filed against the company a few weeks ago, he was both surprised and upset. He had called Dave Green immediately and directed him to take charge of an investigation of the allegations and to follow closely further developments in the case. Green had called on key personnel to study the situation and to prepare a report for him on their findings which he had received. He had hoped that the report would help vindicate the company in the discrimination case and corroborate the supervisor's position that she had not racially discriminated in completing the employee performance ratings.

BACKGROUND

The John Rogers Corporation, with headquarters in Columbia, Tennessee, was a manufacturer of automotive hardware and operated ten plants east of the Mississippi River. The company was founded in 1951 by John R. Rogers with the establishment of its first manufacturing facility in Cleveland, Ohio. The small company experienced considerable success, and the business grew substantially over the next quarter-century, expanding to nine plants in seven states. In 1977, Mr. Rogers, president and CEO, established the tenth plant in Columbia, Tennessee. Two years later, he moved the corporate headquarters from Cleveland to Columbia.

John Rogers had prided himself on the positive employee orientation of the management of the company he had built. Although there had been exceptions, morale of both employees and management had generally been good throughout the plants. Wages, salaries, and benefits were at least competitive in all labor markets and often exceeded the industry average. Furthermore, during the life of the company, there had been few substantive

This case was prepared by Professors Roy Williams, James Hodgetts, and Thomas Miller, all of the University of Memphis. All names are disguised. Used by permission.

grievances and only a few minor cases of discrimination, and these had usually been readily resolved. Mr. Rogers had actively promoted a management policy of fair treatment of employees, not only to discourage the formation of unions in the plants, but also as a matter of implementing his personal philosophy of management.

THE INVESTIGATION

On January 2, 1990, Claude Atkins, Kevin Berry, and Terri Jones filed employment discrimination cases against the John Rogers Corporation in the Circuit Court of Maury County in Columbia, Tennessee. The plaintiffs, all black and all production workers in the machining department at the Columbia plant, alleged "invidious racial discrimination and harassment" by their white supervisor, Sue Chambers. Because of their low performance ratings by Chambers; Atkins, Berry, and Jones charged that they had been unlawfully denied bonuses and promotions. The plaintiffs' primary complaints were based chiefly on the allegation that black employees systematically received lower performance evaluation scores than their white associates who held jobs with the same duties and responsibilities. In particular, they charged that Ms. Chambers consistently and persistently rated black employees lower than white workers.

When Dave Green had learned of the charges from Phil Hogan, plant personnel manager, he asked Hogan and Larry Stokes, corporate legal counsel, to meet with him to discuss the situation. Near the end of their lengthy conference, Stokes stated that he needed to have some detailed information about the employee performance appraisal system at the Columbia plant "as soon as possible." Although Stokes indicated he did not know if, or how, this information would ultimately be used if the case came to trial, he wanted to study the data in preparation of the company's defense to the plaintiffs' charges of discrimination. Green then directed Hogan to prepare a report on the Columbia plant performance evaluation system which showed the history of supervisors' performance ratings over the three-year period the system had been in operation.

Also, at Green's suggestion, it was decided to bring in Beth Nelson, manager of operations analysis, to assist in the investigation. Nelson headed up a relatively new staff group at John Rogers which was charged with the responsibility of general performance and productivity improvement within the total corporate structure. Green thought that the quantitative skills of the "number crunchers" on Nelson's staff would be helpful in determining the information needed and in processing and analyzing the data.

Although Green was aware that this project could be time consuming, he asked Hogan to have the report turned in to him in one week. He regretted the deadline, but explained that the matter deserved high priority given its importance to the company.

After the meeting, Dave Green wondered what the report of Hogan and Wilson would reveal about the employee rating system at the Columbia plant. Certainly he hoped that the data would help vindicate the company and corroborate the sound reputation of the John Rogers Corporation for favorable employee relations. He was well aware that the firm could suffer substantial financial loss and damage to its image if the lawsuit went to trial and was decided against the company.

THE REPORT

As he had requested, Dave Green received the report from Hogan and Nelson within the week. He was quite impressed with their work since it was evident that quite a lot of information had been gathered and analyzed on employee performance ratings within the Columbia plant. As he leafed through the document, he was particularly struck by the statistical tables documenting the characteristics of performance ratings and raters. Green wanted to study the report in some detail before he met again with Larry Stokes, corporate legal counsel. That afternoon he sat down to read the report.

Specifically, Green recalled that each plaintiff had charged that black employees systematically received lower performance evaluation scores than did white workers who held the same jobs with the same responsibilities. Performance evaluations at Columbia were made every six months for each employee. Each department manager was responsible for evaluation of about twenty-five to thirty-five employees. The Columbia plant employed approximately two hundred workers, resulting in about four hundred evaluations each year. Since the current evaluation system had been in operation for three years, it was determined to study performance ratings of this period.

In order to investigate if there was discrimination in the cases involving the three plaintiffs, Atkins, Berry, and Jones, the report analyzed all employee performance data for the Columbia, Tennessee, plant and paid particular attention to Sue Chambers's rating results. The analysis covered the three-year period from January 1987 through December 1990.

The average composite score for each employee, along with the (1) name of the employee evaluated, (2) name of the employee's manager, (3) employee's ID number, (4) employee's race, (5) date the evaluation was performed, (6) and the manager performing the evaluation, had been in each employee's file. The composite score was obtained by averaging individual scores for rating variables including quantity of work, quality of work, job knowledge, attitude, promptness, initiative, attendance, and safety practices. Each factor was given equal weight in computing the average, which was the reported score for each worker.

The report had summarized the collection and analysis of the performance information and presented a series of data tables. Table C–32A showed the overall plant evaluation scores and the scores by the race of employee.

Table C–32A   Columbia Plant 1987–90
Averages For the Plant, White, and Black

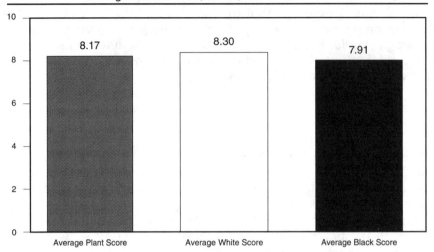

1. The average performance rating for the Columbia Plant as a whole was 8.17.
2. The average performance rating for white employees was 8.30.
3. The average performance rating for black employees was 7.91.

In Table C–32B performance evaluations were presented by the race of the rater.

Table C–32B   Columbia Plant 1987–90
Evaluation Scores by Race of Rater

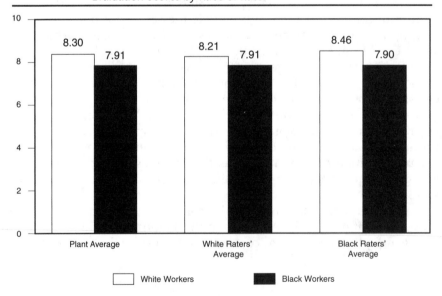

1. The average performance evaluations given by white managers to white employees was 8.21.
2. The average performance evaluations given by black managers to white employees was 8.46.
3. The average performance evaluations given by white managers to black employees was 7.91.
4. The average performance evaluations given by black managers to black employees was 7.90.

Table C–32C characterized the ratings of individual managers by their race.

1. Sue Chambers, evaluator and supervisor of the plaintiffs, had given average performance evaluations for both black and white employees of 7.77, which was 0.40 lower than the corresponding average for all managers.

In Table C–32D, the analysis revealed the pattern of individual manager evaluation for their white and their black employees.

1. Sue Chambers's average performance evaluations for white employees was 7.83, which was 0.47 lower than the average rating of all white employees by all managers.
2. Sue Chambers's average performance evaluations for black employees was 7.69, which was 0.22 lower than the corresponding average for all managers evaluating black employees.

Table C–32C   Columbia Plant 1987–90
Employee Scores by Each Rater's Race

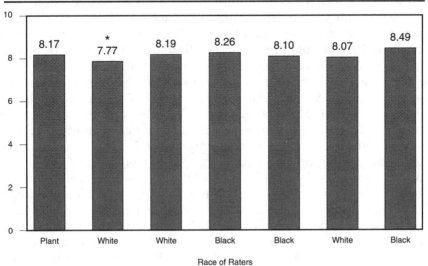

*2nd Column is Chambers

Table C–32D Columbia Plant 1987–90
Each Manager's Rating of Black/White Employees

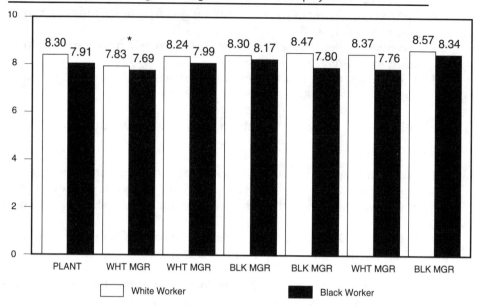

White Worker | Black Worker

*2nd Column is Chambers

After reading the report and studying the statistical tables, Dave Green felt somewhat relieved. He felt that the data collected from the Columbia plant were rather positive in supporting the company's position as he had especially noted the comparability of evaluations given by black managers and white managers for black and for white employees. Also, the report revealed that black managers evaluated black employees lower than white managers evaluated black employees. Although the number of evaluations performed by black managers was less than those completed by white managers, the numbers were large enough for statistical validity, according to the report. In addition, the difference in rating of white employees, compared to black employees (8.30 to 7.91, a difference of 0.39 evaluation points) could be associated with factors other than race. Although Sue Chambers's evaluation scores for black employees were 0.22 evaluation points lower than the plant's average evaluation of black employees (7.91 − 7.69), she also evaluated white employees lower than the plant average (8.30 − 7.83 = 0.47), and by a greater differential. The findings of the report indicated that Sue Chambers was the most rigorous evaluator of the department managers, but she was consistent with other supervisors in her rating of white employees and black employees. Green did not believe the results of the evaluation data suggested that Sue Chambers showed racial prejudice in her evaluations, and he was disinclined to think that Atkins, Jones, and Berry were victims of discrimination.

THE CONFERENCE

The next morning, Green sent a copy of the report to Larry Stokes, who had wanted to see it before they got together to discuss it. Attached to the report was a memo from Green indicating his satisfaction that the report supported the company's position in the dispute.

Late that afternoon, Green received a call from Stokes. "Dave, I finished reading the report this afternoon and I'm ready to get together with you about it. By the way, I have to say I'm not sure I agree with you that this data helps our defense in the discrimination case," Stokes remarked.

"Larry, I'm surprised to hear you say that since I didn't see it that way," Green replied. "We had better meet on this early tomorrow morning," he continued.

"OK, Dave, I'll see you at 9 o'clock in your office," Stokes agreed.

As Dave Green hung up the phone, he was a little puzzled by Larry Stokes's comments. Was there something in the report that he had missed?

CASE–33

The Board's Selection Dilemma

In early January, Dr. William Montgomery, executive director of large national professional association, announced his retirement, effective September 30. Dr. Montgomery, a black man, had been the executive director for the past ten years. The Association, with headquarters in Washington, D.C., was unique in that approximately 80 percent of its members and the profession's practitioners were women; however, all four executive directors in the association's history had been men.

THE SEARCH BEGINS

The Board of Directors of the Association decided that a new executive director should be sought who had these primary qualifications: (1) possess a graduate or professional degree from a nationally accredited university, (2) possess demonstrated managerial background and administrative skills, and (3) have at least ten years of professional and managerial experience.

A search committee was immediately appointed by the board of directors of the association and was assigned the task of searching for a new executive director. The Search Committee consisted of eleven members—seven women and four men. The committee selected Dr. Jane Morrison as its chairperson; she had been an active member of the association for twenty-five years. The search committee placed ads in all of the appropriate professional journals as well as in various publications that were anticipated to attract the attention of both minority and female candidates. Additionally, a number of women and minority candidates were specifically identified and invited to apply for the position. Over eight hundred letters were sent to influential members of the association and the profession soliciting nominations.

THE SCREENING PROCESS

Sixty-five individuals were nominated in response to the letters sent out by the search committee. However, only thirteen of these individuals—seven women and six men—ultimately sent in their resumes. Fourteen other applicants

---

This case was prepared by Dr. Benjamin Weeks of the Graham School of Management, St. Xavier University in Chicago. All names are disguised. Used by permission.

submitted resumes in reply to advertisements placed by the committee; six were women, eight were men. After careful consideration and screening of the twenty-seven applicants, eight candidates (four women and four men) were selected to be interviewed. Recognizing that all of the candidates had extensive professional qualifications and experience, the search committee hired a consultant to structure the interview process. The committee wanted to evaluate each candidate's written and oral communication skills, managerial abilities, and his or her personal and social "graces."

The following process was designed by the consultant and approved by the search committee. Each candidate was invited to fly to Washington, D.C., for a two-day interview at a hotel near the airport. Prior to the interview, each candidate was given a topic and was asked to write a position paper on the subject. At the interview session, each candidate met members of the search committee for dinner. The following morning, the candidates were given ninety minutes to prepare a brief speech on a topic of importance within the profession. Each candidate was videotaped delivering the speech, with members of the search committee serving as an audience. All candidates were asked to participate in an in-basket exercise that was based on actual memos and other correspondence that had been received by the retiring Executive Director in the previous eight months. Finally, each candidate met with the search committee for a group interview. After all the eight interviews were completed, the search committee met and identified five individuals—three men and two women—to be invited to participate in a second round of interviews.

The second round of interviews was conducted by the officers of the board of directors of the association. One week before the five candidates were to be interviewed, one of the two remaining women withdrew her name from consideration. Her husband was a partner in a large San Francisco law firm, and they had decided that it would be difficult for him to establish a law practice in the Washington, D.C. area. The remaining four candidates—three men and one woman—were interviewed over a two-day period. Three candidates were then recommended as finalists to be interviewed by the entire board of directors and the senior staff of the association. The three finalists were all white men.

PROTESTS AT DECISION TIME

As soon as their names had been announced in an association memorandum, two groups from within the association filed formal protests with the board over the fact that no women were included among the final three candidates. These protests came from the Committee for Equal Rights Among Professionals (CERAP) and the Social Responsibilities Feminist Task Force. CERAP wrote to the board of directors that although they felt that proper general procedures were apparently followed, an inadequate number of women and minority candidates were identified. They especially were concerned that the procedure did not do enough to identify and recommend qualified women candidates. They felt that the board of directors of the association should postpone any decision about filling the executive director's position and that new search procedures should be implemented.

It was now July 10, and Dr. Montgomery was due to leave in less than three months. The board of directors was scheduled to meet on this date to consider the recommendations of the search committee and the protests of the association's groups.

The Promotion of Melba Moore

The Global United Manufacturing Company employed some fifteen hundred people in its headquarters in Cleveland, Ohio. The company had several large government contracts and thus was subjected annually to an equal employment opportunity compliance review conducted by a federal agency, the Office of Federal Contracts Compliance Programs (OFCCP). As part of this, the company had formulated and submitted an affirmative action plan to implement its policies of equal employment opportunity. The government's compliance staff had found the company's affirmative action program to be comprehensive and the company to be serious in its attempts to correct any deficiencies uncovered by periodic reviews.

The purchasing department of Global United was responsible for ordering most manufacturing materials, office supplies, and services. The department was headed by the chief purchasing agent, Pete Wilson. Reporting to Pete were five supervisors, each having responsibility for purchasing different types of goods and services. Each supervisor had a staff of several buyers and two word processors.

Most of the buyers were college graduates or had a college background with equivalent experience. The buyers were considered semiprofessional employees and had considerable leeway in their purchasing decisions. The buyers were expected to exercise tact in dealing with the many salespersons who called on Global.

Under the provisions of the company's affirmative action plan (and as required by various governmental orders), major suppliers and subcontractors must certify that they are equal employment opportunity employers and that they have an affirmative action program. The purchasing department was responsible for seeing that the necessary certifications were received from each supplier and subcontractor.

However, over the years, the purchasing department itself had employed only a few minority employees. During an annual compliance review in February, the OFCCP compliance staff pointed out that Global was deficient in employment of African Americans (blacks) in the purchasing department. Pete Wilson and the five supervisors reporting to him agreed that they should make a special effort to employ buyers who were black.

This case was prepared by John R. Hundley, Director of Human Resources and Adjunct Instructor in Management at Indiana University–South Bend. All names are disguised. Used by permission.

In August, Melba Moore, a young African American woman, began her employment with Global as a word processor in the purchasing department. Melba had attended a junior college in Cleveland and had studied several courses in business administration. After a year and a half of college, Melba left school after getting married. Upon leaving college, Melba went to work as a clerk-typist in the accounting department of a chemical company headquartered in Cleveland. Melba worked for the chemical company for three years before leaving after becoming pregnant. After being out of the employed labor force when her son, Jeff, reached age one, Melba decided again to take a job in order to assist in earning the family income. Melba's husband, Bob, was employed as a marketing representative by a major oil company and was assigned to a territory in the Ohio area. Although Bob earned a fairly good income, both Bob and Melba wanted to save enough money to purchase a home. Both of their parents lived in Cleveland and were willing to "babysit" Jeff as needed.

During her first several months on the job, Melba performed in an outstanding manner. She learned her job quickly, and the quantity and quality of her work were high. Melba formed cordial relationships with the other employees in the purchasing department, and she was very pleasant with the salespersons who called on Global.

In January, one of the buyers under supervisor Tom Schmitt left Global to accept a position with another company. After discussion of possible ways to fill the vacant buyer's position, Pete Wilson and Tom Schmitt decided to offer the promotion to Melba. Melba accepted the promotion and was placed under Tom Schmitt's supervision. The company HR manager was pleased that purchasing had been able to promote a black woman to fill this semiprofessional position. Melba was given a week to observe and work along with one of the experienced buyers. She was then told by Tom Schmitt that she was "on her own," and that she would learn the job as she proceeded to do it along with the other buyers.

However, after several months as a buyer, Melba began to complain to Tom Schmitt about discriminatory actions on the part of other members of the department. Melba cited examples of not receiving phone messages or copies of departmental memoranda on several occasions. Melba mentioned an incident in which one of the word processors refused to do some of Melba's important work because another buyer had already given her some work. Melba further stated that she felt certain supervisors both in purchasing and in other departments were biased.

Tom talked with Melba for several hours, advising her that these incidents should "be taken for what they are and no more—irritations that cannot be avoided in the business world." Tom advised Melba that even Pete Wilson didn't receive all of his phone messages, and that this was not necessarily a subtle form of discrimination on the part of her co-workers. Melba told Tom that these incidents were attempts "to remind me that I'm the least important person in the department." Melba further stated, "I'm not important here, so if I'm out a day or so, my work won't suffer—someone else will do it or it'll wait."

After Melba became a buyer, her attendance began to slip. During a six-month period, Melba missed fifteen days. On each occasion, Melba had seemingly good reasons for being absent, but this amount of absence was far more than was customary in the purchasing department.

Melba was shaken by the following incident. She invited several of her co-workers to a "home-decorating" party over a weekend. A representative of a home decorating firm planned to display merchandise and provide Melba with a commission on any merchandise sold as a result of the party. None of the men or women working for Tom Schmitt whom Melba had invited attended the party. One of the buyers said he planned a trip on that date. Another buyer said he became ill several days prior to the party and was unable to attend. A word processor said she decided not to attend because she did not know anyone else attending the party. Even though several employees of the company did attend the party, Melba was disturbed that no one from the purchasing department had attended. She made it a point to tell Tom Schmitt about this experience on Monday morning, and she commented, "This shows again that the whites in this department are against me and don't care about my feelings."

In previous discussions of problems in relationships with co-workers, Melba usually had reacted negatively to Tom's advice. No amount of reassurance or personal counseling had convinced Melba that her beliefs were without foundation. Tom Schmitt was concerned if he should take any action regarding the latest incident and Melba Moore's job situation.

CASE–35

A Problem of Tardiness

Lloyd Dauten was foreman of the assembly department of a manufacturing company. Most of the time Dauten supervised about fifteen assembly line workers. All of the employees in the department were white, with the exception of George Douglas.

Douglas was black, thirty-six years old, and a widower with six small children. He had worked in the company for about two years since he had changed jobs and moved to the city following the death of his wife. Douglas was considered a very good worker, one of the best in the department, but he was perennially tardy for work in the morning. Lloyd Dauten had discussed the problem of tardiness with Douglas numerous times. Dauten had pointed out to Douglas that his tardiness was detrimental to the departmental operation, but Douglas nevertheless consistently was tardy, often several times a week. Douglas stated that he made every effort to be at work on time, but he just didn't seem to be able to make it because of the problem of his children. Douglas stated that getting six children off to school and to the baby sitter made it impossible for him to get to work by 7:30 A.M.

Douglas had stated to Dauten that he worked harder than anyone else in the department and that he stayed over late in the afternoon and early evening to make up whatever time he lost in the mornings. There was little question in Dauten's mind that George Douglas did work as hard as anyone else in the department. Since the assembly operation was on an individual rather than a group process basis, the actual departmental production usually did not suffer too much from this situation. However, Lloyd Dauten was becoming concerned about Douglas's tardiness because it did create occasional problems with rush orders, and there were some rumblings of discontent among the white employees in the department.

One Tuesday morning, George Douglas's tardiness was holding up a specific assembly job that was supposed to be finished by noon of that day. It was already 8:45 A.M., and regardless of how Douglas might work later during the morning, it would be difficult to finish the job by noon, since the production material had to dry out for several hours before leaving the department. Dauten might have assigned this particular assembly operation to some other worker in the department, but he felt that Douglas was the most quali-

---

This case was originally developed by the late Professor Theo Haimann of the School of Business and Administration of St. Louis University. All names are disguised. Used by prior permission.

fied person to do this particular job. Dauten also was worried that if Douglas did not come in at all or came in quite late, the entire production schedule of the department might be in a difficult situation for the day.

As this was going through Dauten's mind, he overheard a conversation among several workers at one of the work stations. Since the discussion was quite loud and the workers made no effort to conceal it, Dauten felt sure that the workers were deliberately trying to have him hear what they had on their minds. The general nature of the conversation focused around statements such as the following: "Why should a black guy like Douglas get any preferred treatment around here? He's always late, and the boss doesn't do anything about it. Just because he's black, he's getting favors like he's something special."

At 9:30 A.M., Douglas arrived on the job and reported to Lloyd Dauten. Said Douglas: "I'm sorry, boss, but I had a special sickness problem with my three-year-old daughter that had to be taken care of. I should have called you, but I forgot about it in all the turmoil at home. I'll work extra hard to make up the time, even through my lunch hour, and I'll make up the rest at the end of the day. You can always count on me." With that, Douglas headed toward his work station. Foreman Dauten knew that he had to do something to correct this situation.

CASE–36

"Mentoring" the Sales Force, or Sexual Harassment?

Biff LaFourche, president of Provincial Insurance Company of Jackson, returned from lunch to find the human resources manager, Frank Anderson, waiting to see him.

"I think we've got a problem with Bob Snowden and Sally Ambrose," Anderson said, after he closed the door to LaFourche's office.

Bob Snowden, thirty-two, was one of Provincial's three vice presidents and had supervised the company's three regional offices for about five years. Snowden had received excellent performance evaluations ever since he joined the company and was thought to be one of the company's rising stars. Aside from improving bottom-line results, Snowden was known to have taken a personal interest in developing agents who sometimes had problems with their work. Without exception, these "problem" agents were attractive women in their twenties.

Recently, Snowden had been spending a great deal of time attempting to improve the performance of Sally Ambrose. Sally, twenty-five, had been employed as a marketing representative (salesperson) in the company's Meridian branch office for less than two years. About three months earlier, Sally had come to the Jackson headquarters to discuss her job performance and future career goals with Snowden as part of a formal company program of job enrichment for marketing representatives. After work that day, LaFourche had run into Sally and Bob at a local bar where they were having a few drinks. LaFourche talked with them for a few minutes about the company and about their job-improvement discussion.

From that chance encounter, it appeared to LaFourche that Snowden was going to take Sally under his wing and develop her abilities in sales, just as he had with several other young women. Before their meeting, Sally's sales performance had been lagging, and it appeared that she might have to be terminated not too far down the road unless she showed dramatic improvement. In the last two months, however, it appeared to LaFourche that Sally Ambrose was making the improvements that were necessary for her to stay with the company.

This case was prepared by Professor Roland E. Kidwell, Jr. and Professor Amy Laura Oakes, both of the College of Business at Louisiana State University in Shreveport. The case is based upon an actual incident, but all names, locations, and some details have been disguised. Used by permission.

LaFourche recognized that Snowden's effort to improve the performance of these marketing reps was sometimes a tricky matter because the reps did not directly report to Snowden. For example, Sally Ambrose's direct supervisor was Estelle Landry, manager of the Meridian office. Estelle, in turn, reported to Bob Snowden (See Exhibit C–36A).

"What seems to be the problem?" LaFourche asked Anderson.

Anderson explained that a company employee had come to him in confidence a few days earlier. The employee had been in the Atlanta airport two Fridays ago on a business trip when the employee saw Bob Snowden and Sally Ambrose walking down the concourse, holding hands. The employee noticed the pair enter the boarding area for a flight to Orlando.

EXHIBIT C–36A Provincial Insurance Company—Organizational Chart

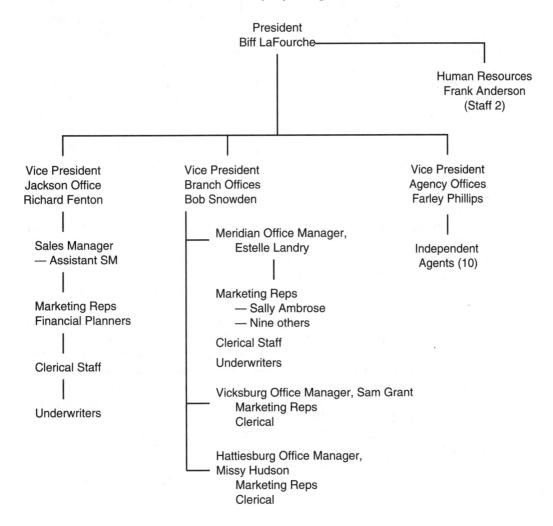

The employee expressed concern that there appeared to be a romantic relationship between the manager and the marketing rep and was worried about how that might affect the treatment of other employees at the company. Anderson said he checked company records and found that both Snowden and Ambrose had taken that Friday and the following Monday off from work.

"The employee asked not to be identified," Anderson concluded. "I hope you understand."

"Certainly," LaFourche replied. "I assume you believe that the employee was telling the truth?" Anderson nodded.

Briefly, LaFourche tried to figure out if the employee was one of the twenty people who worked in the Meridian office, one of the fifty employed at the Jackson headquarters, or someone at another branch office of the company. Was the employee a woman, perhaps someone Snowden had jilted? Was the employee a man, upset at possible favoritism toward a woman agent? Or was the employee genuinely concerned the company could be harmed if the apparent relationship between Snowden and Sally Ambrose turned sour, and Sally filed harassment charges?

"What do you think we should do about this, Frank?"

Anderson shook his head. "I'm not really certain there is anything we can do. I'm worried, though, that if this gets out it could affect Snowden's work with other people, particularly Estelle. It certainly puts her in a difficult position."

"Yes, and if we don't do anything, what do you think the employee will do? Spread gossip about what might or might not be going on?"

"I'm not sure. But I do know that the sexual harassment policy we wrote last year doesn't deal directly with this sort of thing," Anderson said. (See Exhibit C–36B).

Anderson continued, "You know, there seemed to be a lot of concern on the part of the employee who told me about this. Coming to me like that about one of the top managers around here certainly could put that person out on a limb. That's why I think the story is true."

"Thanks, Frank," LaFourche said. "Let me think about this a bit."

As president of a medium-sized insurance company, Biff LaFourche had other matters to consider that afternoon. Yet his thoughts kept returning to what Frank Anderson had told him about Bob Snowden and Sally Ambrose. Had it been just a coincidence that the marketing reps whose performance had improved after Snowden's help were all attractive, young women? Were Snowden's nonwork activities any of LaFourche's business? Could these activities be considered non-work-related now that another employee was involved? Should he contact the company's lawyer and get some advice?

The next morning, after LaFourche finished his morning coffee, he dialed 283.

"Bob Snowden speaking."

"Bob, this is Biff. Can you step into my office for a couple of minutes?"

EXHIBIT C–36B

Provincial Life Insurance Company of Jackson
Policy Statement on Sexual Harassment

Provincial Life Insurance Company of Jackson strongly opposes any act of sexual harassment. It is illegal and against our policy for any person to make unwelcome sexual advances, requests for sexual favors, or verbal or physical conduct of a sexual nature to an employee when

1. The employee's submission to the conduct is made a condition of employment.
2. The employee's submission to such conduct is used as the basis of an employment decision affecting the employee.
3. Such conduct creates an intimidating, hostile or offensive environment.

All such conduct is strictly prohibited.

We encourage employees to raise questions or seek advice regarding the sexual harassment policy from their supervisors or the Human Resources Department. All employees have the right to make a confidential complaint if they feel they have been sexually harassed.

Buford LaFourche, President
Frank Anderson, Director of Human Resources

CASE–37

General Physical Condition
As an Occupational Qualification

John Jones recently had purchased an old warehouse with the intent of converting it to a lumber yard. Jones had little experience in managing a private business, but had good knowledge concerning all phases of building and lumber requirements. Jones had limited capital so he had to keep his starting expenses to a minimum. After the building was converted and he had his inventory in stock, Jones went through the process of hiring his personnel.

Jones's intention was to manage and supervise the whole operation himself so he could keep expenses to a minimum. His primary objective was to hire people to stock lumber and assist customers in loading their vehicles with their purchases. Jones ran the following advertisement in the local newspaper:

> HELP WANTED—young men needed in lumber yard to load lumber and assist customers in their purchases. Much heavy lifting is involved.

Jones was careful to word his company's application forms so as to avoid any problems of racial discrimination. One applicant, Jim Smith, had experience in the lumber business and impressed Jones with his knowledge, but Jones was hesitant in hiring him because of his physical condition and age. Jones conducted an employment interview with Smith and made the following written comments on Smith's application: "Is qualified, but appears to be out of physical shape."

During his interview with Jim Smith, John Jones explained to Smith that he was looking for young men to fill his positions, and that Smith's age (forty-five) was a cause for concern. Jones went on to explain that there was a lot of heavy lifting involved, and he wanted younger men who had the stamina needed for a lumber yard. Jones did tell Smith that if he were to get a haircut and improve his physical appearance, there might be a position at the customer service counter where he would be dealing with the public. According to Jones, although this position paid slightly less, it would be more reasonable for a man of Smith's condition and age. Smith left without making a decision.

John Jones felt confident that he had given Smith a reasonable opportunity to accept a position and felt justified in not allowing a person in obvi-

---

This case was prepared by Professor Kenneth A. Kovach, Ph.D., of George Mason University in Fairfax, Virginia. All names are disguised. Used by permission.

ously poor physical condition to take a job that involved strenuous physical activity and exertion. Further, Jones was insistent in wanting his employees to look presentable to the buying public.

Several days later, John Jones received a notice from the local office of the Equal Employment Opportunity Commission that a Mr. James Smith had filed age-discrimination charges against Jones for not hiring him in the lumber yard.

CASE–38

Unintentional Prejudice

Richard Wayne, owner and manager of a family-owned business that manufactured and distributed religious articles, was faced with a dilemma. A small but well-organized religious group had commenced picketing in front of his shop and was well on the way toward boycotting his products. The founder and president of Citizens for Morality, Jane Edwards, had informed Wayne that two of his employees were making a mockery of morals and religion by shamelessly cohabiting and by publicly announcing the impending birth of their child out of wedlock. The Citizens for Morality, Mr. Wayne was told, felt that employees of a religiously oriented shop should be above reproach and that Mr. Wayne had a moral obligation to terminate their employment.

John Willet and Sheila Harper, the employees in question, had been with the business for several years. John's performance had been marginal, but Sheila had proved to be an astute businesswoman, so Richard Wayne had chosen to ignore the rumors that had been circulating. Additionally, he had believed the demonstrations organized by Jane Edwards and her Citizens would soon end.

The group's fervor did not wane. Instead, Wayne found the Citizens for Morality attracting other religious groups, and their combined activities had begun receiving local news coverage. It was not until local church fundraising organizations began cancelling orders for merchandise that Wayne felt obliged to act. It was no longer in his best interest to keep both employees, so he compromised by attempting to force John's resignation. Sheila Harper was an asset to his business, and he felt that the Citizens for Morality would be appeased with John's resignation.

John Willet was neither overly ambitious nor unusually bright, and Richard Wayne easily convinced him he would be better off accepting a job offer he had received from a discount store closer to his school and home.

The Citizens for Morality were not satisfied. In the ensuing weeks, they continued their demonstrations and their boycotts. Jane Edwards appeared on a local TV program denouncing Mr. Wayne as a hypocrite who continued to condone Sheila Harper's behavior. Wayne's business deteriorated, and even Sheila's sales and managerial skills could not sufficiently offset the shop's losses.

Wayne had no options left—he either had to fire Sheila or go bankrupt, so he sent for her immediately. When she entered his office, Wayne could see

---

This case was prepared by Professor Kenneth A. Kovach, Ph.D., of George Mason University in Fairfax, Virginia. All names are disguised. Used by permission.

she had been crying. John Willet, Sheila told him, had left her. She was distraught because her baby was due within the month, and now she had no way of supporting herself in the months that would follow the baby's birth. She felt helpless because she realized Wayne's business was suffering because of her. However, her need for income was imperative.

Richard Wayne proposed to Sheila that he discharge her for "lack of work." That way she could be eligible for unemployment compensation before the baby's birth and during the months following her recovery. He assured her that she would have no trouble getting another job when she was ready, because he would gladly give her a good recommendation.

Since Wayne's suggestion looked like the only possible solution for both of them, Sheila reluctantly accepted it. She thanked him, and she left with his recommendation in her possession.

It was not until about a year later that Wayne heard from Sheila once again. She wanted her job back, she said, because she had been unable to find employment anywhere, despite his recommendation. Wayne, who had replaced both John and Sheila with two bright young men, told Sheila he could not help her.

A few days later, Richard Wayne received a letter from the law firm of Richards, Jones, and Spencer. He was shocked to find that he was going to be sued for unlawfully firing a pregnant woman, for practicing discrimination against a single woman with a small child, and for failing to help Sheila find a new job. Sheila wanted to be reinstated in her old job and demanded payment of back wages.

CASE–39

The Sexist Remark

Dr. John Marshall, professor of human resource management at Sherwood University, was serving as chairperson of an all-day conference in a major city attended by about a hundred HR professionals. The conference was being held in a local hotel and was devoted to the general theme "Contemporary Issues in Human Resource Management." It was approximately 3 P.M., and a major speaker had just completed his presentation. Dr. Marshall stood up to announce, "Ladies and gentlemen, we will take a fifteen-minute break, and then we will reassemble to hear a discussion of the topic, 'The Glass Ceiling and Diversity Issues in Business,' presented by a three-member panel of HR professional women who hold prominent positions in our city." Dr. Marshall noticed that there were empty seats available at the front tables of the conference room and that some members of the audience were standing in the rear of the room. Dr. Marshall then added, "Incidentally, there are plenty of seats in the front of the room. I'd suggest that some of you in the back move up to these front tables so that you'll better be able to hear what our informed, attractive panelists have to say."

With that comment, Dr. Marshall moved away from the speaker's microphone to greet the three women who were at that point taking their places for the panel presentation. One of the women, Alberta Cook, approached him. Marshall said, "May I help you in any way to get ready for your presentation?" Ms. Cook replied, "No, Dr. Marshall, but I'd like to tell you that your comment about us was sexist, and I resent it." Dr. Marshall replied, "What do you mean? I don't know what you're talking about." Ms. Cook stated, "You referred to us as attractive panelists. Do you introduce male panelists by calling them handsome?" Dr. Marshall replied, "I get your point, but I didn't realize that what I was saying was sexist. I meant it as a sincere compliment."

With that, Dr. Marshall walked away from Ms. Cook and from the speakers' area. Marshall felt rather angry about this incident. But at the same time, he was concerned about other remarks and terms he customarily used that could offend certain women or others. He also wondered if any members of the conference audience had "picked up" on his use of the word "attractive," and, if so, whether they found it to be sexist or offensive.

All names are disguised.

CASE–40

The Disabled Student

This case involved a situation that developed on the campus of Sherwood University, which was located in a midwestern urban setting.

Early in July, Dean Ernest Jordan of the School of Business informed Professor Alex White, professor of accounting, that a problem had presented itself in conjunction with his 1–2 P.M. Monday, Wednesday, Friday section of the Accounting 201 class. Raymond Pyle, a 180-pound paraplegic in a 60-pound wheelchair, had signed up for the section, scheduled to be taught in Waite Hall, Room 211. This room, like all the rooms in Waite Hall, was only accessible after navigating more than twenty steps, and it was therefore impossible for a wheelchair-bound student to get in and out of this classroom without help. The building was some eighty years old, and there were no elevators in this three-story structure.

Professor White agreed that this posed a serious problem, but nothing more was said or done about it, since Professor White and his wife left for a European vacation on July 21.

Upon Professor White's return to the campus on Monday, August 7, he was informed orally by Dean Jordan that the class in question had been moved to Atkinson Hall, Room 100. That same day, he received a written communication from Dr. Jane Eason, the university's coordinator for disabled students, to the effect that the Rehabilitation Act of 1973 and the 1990 Americans with Disabilities Act (ADA) had required this move. The action had to be taken in Professor White's absence, because the fall semester was rapidly nearing its start. Professor White was concerned, since he anticipated that his course would have seventy or more students enrolled. Further, because of the size of the class, visual aids had to be used extensively. He decided that he would take a survey of the assigned room.

Atkinson Hall was located on the opposite side of the campus, several hundred yards from Waite Hall. It was a relatively new building, having been constructed about fifteen years ago. For the most part, it was occupied by the economics and political science departments. When Professor White arrived to investigate Atkinson Hall, he found that neither the economics nor the political science department had a key to Room 100, so campus security was summoned. When the security officer unlocked the door to Room 100 and turned on the light, it revealed a windowless, chairless, concrete area, apparently built

This case was prepared by Professor Arthur E. Carlson of the John M. Olin School of Business of Washington University. All names are disguised. Used by permission.

as a large storeroom but never used. Recognizing that Atkinson 100 was completely unsuitable, Professor White decided to telephone Raymond Pyle and inform him of his predicament. He asked Pyle whether, under the circumstances, he would agree to being carried in and out of Waite 211 three times a week. Pyle replied that, although he was reluctant to agree to such an arrangement, he might do so in the interest of preserving quality instruction. Professor White said that in years past, he had observed that the commercial airlines sometimes employed three people to carry wheelchair-bound patients up and down portable airline steps—two on the back and one on the front. This appeared to Professor White to be a way to accommodate Raymond Pyle. He told Pyle that two or three members of the varsity football team would be in this section of the course, and they could receive nominal compensation for this service. Mr. Pyle said, "I consider this to be undignified, but if it's the only way, I suppose I'll have to accept it."

Professor White next called Dr. Eason to propose this solution to the problem. However, she expressed immediate concern about the idea itself and the liability of the university in the event of accidental injury either to Mr. Pyle or to the students who might perform "Operation Chairlift." Dr. Eason therefore arranged a meeting for Thursday morning, August 10, to discuss the problem with the university's legal counsel. Present at this meeting were Dr. Eason; Ellen Ginsburg, the assistant general counsel of the university; Nancy Kolar of the university research office; Dean Jordan of the Business School; and Professor White.

The discussion at this meeting revealed that the problem was much larger than what to do about Raymond Pyle. It was conceivable that Waite Hall and other older university buildings in their present condition could be declared unsuitable for holding classes because of lack of elevators, ramps, or lifts. Major capital expenditures were needed to rectify this situation.

Dr. Eason reported that she had located only one other available classroom on campus of the size and accommodations needed by Professor White for his Monday, Wednesday, Friday 1–2 P.M. class that was properly accessible for a wheelchair-bound student. This was Room 115 in Alexander Hall, which housed the Graduate School of Social Work. However, Alexander Hall was located at the extreme east end of campus, about one-third mile from the main body of classroom buildings, including Waite Hall. Dr. Eason commented, "It will be quite difficult for Mr. Pyle to move this far between his classes in a wheelchair. If we move the class there, we may have to pay someone to assist him across campus."

Ms. Ginsburg explained the federal statutes[1] that were applicable to Sherwood University. By law, the university was under obligation to make

---

[1]Recommended sources for information about the Rehabilitation Act of 1973 and the Americans with Disabilities Act of 1990 and compliance with these laws are: *Accommodating Disabilities: Business Management Guide*, (Chicago: Commerce Clearing House, 1991): and Raymond L. Hilgert and Edwin C. Leonard, Jr., *Supervision: Concepts and Practices of Management*, 6th ed., (Cincinnati: South-Western, 1995), pp. 492–495.

"reasonable accommodation" to disabled students and employees. She commented that the university's executive administration was extremely concerned about this problem, because the university received about $20 million annually in government contracts and grants. Yet there were no university plans at this time to spend tens of millions of dollars on all of the old buildings on campus to make them totally accessible and adaptable to all disabled people.

Professor White asked the question, "How reasonable is it to make a class of seventy students go far across campus to a less desirable room so that one wheelchair-bound student can be accommodated? Mr. Pyle is only a sophomore; will this have to be done for all of his classes while he's here at Sherwood, and for every disabled student in the future?"

Dr. Eason commented, "Part of the problem is that we didn't find out about this earlier. We had scheduled all of Mr. Pyle's other classes in suitable rooms, but he didn't decide to enroll in Accounting 201 until midsummer."

In this regard, Nancy Kolar asked, "Could we still juggle some other classroom assignments around campus in order to make a better room available for Raymond Pyle and Professor White?"

Dr. Eason replied, "Probably so, but we'll probably alienate many students and faculty and the room-scheduling office in the process."

After considerable discussion, Dean Jordan commented, "It seems that we've got several alternatives before us. We've got to reach a decision that is academically, legally, and practically sound."

CASE–41

The Resignation—or Termination— of Mrs. Snow

CAST OF CHARACTERS

Paulette Snow had been a first-grade teacher for twenty-nine years in the Lambright Elementary School located in Newton. Newton is located in a midwestern state; at the time of this case, it had a population of four thousand. Combined with the rural area, the Newton R-I School System had approximately nine hundred students in several schools, kindergarten through high school. Many of the people in the area had been in Mrs. Snow's first-grade classes or had relatives in her classes. She had been recognized as an innovative, dedicated teacher who was highly respected by former students, parents of former students, and persons in the community. To some, she had become something of an "institution" in the area. Since Mrs. Snow had prior teaching experience, she needed only one more year of teaching to be eligible to retire with full public school retirement pay and benefits.

John Tinker, superintendent of schools for the Newton R-I School System, had been with the district for eight years. He had a reputation for an authoritarian style of management, although he would not agree with that assessment. He described himself as being "benevolently paternalistic" to a faculty that needed his concern and guidance. Tinker had excellent interpersonal skills when he wished to utilize them. He was particularly adept at communicating with those in authority above him and with other influential persons—for example, with the Board of Education of Newton, the local Chamber of Commerce, and the Rotary Club.

Barbara McCalley, president of the Newton Community Teachers Association, had been in the district nine years. She knew Mrs. Snow quite well as they attended the same church and were involved in many of the same community and civic activities. Mrs. McCalley was a high school teacher; therefore, she had never been in the same building with Mrs. Snow to know firsthand of Mrs. Snow's abilities as a teacher.

Gretta George, vice-president of the local Community Teachers Association, was a teacher at the junior high school. Mrs. George Knew Paulette Snow only on a casual basis.

This case was prepared by Professor Fran Waller of the Department of Business Administration of Central Missouri State University at Warrensburg. All names and locations are disguised. Used by permission.

Louis Snow, husband of the first-grade teacher, was a "native" of Newton and very supportive of his wife and her teaching career. Mr. Snow was employed as a maintenance worker in a local factory. However, he served on several community citizen boards, and he was well known and respected by many Newton citizens.

MRS. SNOW'S PROBLEMS

Paulette Snow had asked for performance evaluations for the past three years, but her current principal, Wilfred James, had not completed these on her. Her last performance evaluation four years ago gave her a "superior" rating, but the principal who completed that appraisal, Ms. Jane Laclede, had retired and was now deceased. Mrs. Snow was perplexed that her new principal, Mr. James, would not evaluate her teaching performance. She realized that she was having some "health problems," but she did not consider these to be serious.

However, to other teachers at Lambright, the reluctance of Principal James to complete a performance evaluation on Mrs. Snow was obvious. To them, Mrs. Snow often seemed disoriented and confused. She taped paper over the window of her classroom door so that people from the hall could not view what was occurring in her classroom, but the noise level gave some indication for concern. When people did enter Mrs. Snow's room, she was often seen lying down on a divan or doing other things while her students were playing, visiting, or scuffling. Some parents had voiced their concerns to Mr. James, but he had defended Mrs. Snow citing her past reputation and years of service.

Paulette Snow was under a doctor's care, and the doctor had prescribed medication for "nerves and tension." Mrs. Snow openly told her fellow-teachers that she was going through menopause. She said that she and her husband did not consider her condition to be unusual, because "many females experience similar problems during this age period."

As the school year continued, more concerns were expressed by parents of her students and by fellow teachers. Consequently, Mr. Tinker and Mr. James had a conference with Mrs. Snow. Tinker suggested that she "take a year's leave to rest and recuperate." Shortly thereafter, Mrs. Snow and her husband agreed to this, and Mrs. Snow signed a letter indicating that she would go on a paid medical leave for up to one year. Mrs. Snow was on leave from November through May, that is, the remainder of the school year.

NO POSITION FOR MRS. SNOW

In late May, Paulette Snow made an appointment to see Mr. Tinker to discuss resuming her teaching the next fall. She told Tinker that she was again able to teach. To her surprise, Tinker indicated that she had no contract. He stated that the letter she had signed specifically indicated that she only would be given "consideration" for another contract if a position was available. Tinker told her that no teaching vacancy now existed in the district; in fact, several teachers had been laid off because of budget problems and declining student enrollments.

Mrs. Snow became quite upset about this, and her husband was outraged when he was so informed.

Mrs. Snow contacted Mrs. Barbara McCalley and asked that the local Community Teachers Association aid her in reestablishing her teaching position. McCalley and Mrs. Gretta George immediately arranged an appointment with Tinker to gain more information concerning Mrs. Snow's situation. McCalley had had difficulties in the past with Tinker's "misquoting her" or giving inaccurate reports of conversations or agreements between them; she took Mrs. George with her when issues were discussed so that a witness existed if needed.

Mrs. Snow had made many telephone calls to Mrs. McCalley. McCalley became increasingly concerned, because sometimes Mrs. Snow called at 10 P.M. and talked for forty-five minutes, with Mrs. McCalley saying little or nothing during the conversations. Mrs. Snow had placed a few similar calls to Mrs. George. Both were concerned about the mental health of Mrs. Snow, who appeared to be obsessed with the "treatment" that she was being given by Mr. Tinker, her being "lied to," and her need of having only one more year of teaching to qualify for full retirement pay and benefits.

When McCalley and George met with Tinker, he was quite cordial. He gave them copies of the letter that Mrs. Snow had signed, which indicated that Mrs. Snow only would only be given "consideration" for another contract—not that a contract would be offered. While they were in Tinker's office, one of the school board members called to discuss Mrs. Snow. Tinker indicated that this board member had been in his office when Mrs. Snow had called earlier, and that he had had the board member "listen in" on an extension telephone to the conversation so he would know of Mrs. Snow's mental condition. He said that Mrs. Snow had been calling him and "talking nonstop" to him as she had to Mrs. McCalley. McCalley asked if there was a possibility that Mrs. Snow could be placed on early disability retirement through the public retirement system. This way Mrs. Snow would not lose any of her full retirement pay and other benefits. Tinker responded that it had not been discussed the previous year. He added that he did not think Mrs. Snow would now consider it, since she was adamant about returning to teaching.

McCalley and George left Tinker's office in confusion. What should be done? Should this be presented to the Community Teachers' Association and a vote taken concerning giving or not giving support for Mrs. Snow's regaining a contract? Should Mrs. Snow's physical or mental condition be discussed publicly in this small town where everyone knew everyone? What would Tinker's reaction be if his authority were challenged? Could they argue to have Mrs. Snow back in the classroom influencing young lives if she did have mental problems? How would they react if their children were first-graders in Mrs. Snow's room? Why had no attempt been made to have Mrs. Snow take a disability retirement? What would happen to Mrs. Snow if she did not teach again? Why should a person with twenty-nine years of teaching experience now be unemployed and ineligible for full retirement benefits?

Mrs. Snow was perplexed when seemingly no support came from the teachers who had been her colleagues. She was equally perplexed when no support came from the students and relatives of students whom she had known for years. Her doctor had told her that she should be able to teach, and her doctor sent a letter to Mr. Tinker to this effect. Tinker received this letter, and yet he again told Mrs. Snow that she had "resigned" and would not be reinstated. Mrs. Snow felt betrayed, and she decided that her only recourse appeared to be the legal system. Supported by her husband and her family in her decision, she decided to retain an attorney to file discrimination and other charges against the Newton District in an effort to regain her position.

WHAT SHOULD THE BOARD DECIDE?

When John Tinker received formal notice of Mrs. Snow's charges and lawsuit, he immediately called a meeting of the board members of the Newton R-I School System and the board's attorney to discuss what should be done next.

EXERCISE–14

Ms. Geiger: Please Respond (B)

You are Elizabeth Geiger, director of human resources for the Wiersma Corporation. The Wiersma Corporation produces and sells glass and glassware products and is located in a medium-sized city in a southern state.

You recently received several memos from individuals within the company that require your immediate attention. You are concerned about these inquiries, because you believe that all of them have implications that could present problems for the company's nondiscrimination policies and affirmative action program.

You have decided, therefore, to write and send memos to each of the individuals in which you will: (a) respond to their questions, and (b) explain your position concerning what should and what should not be done in each situation.

The memos that you have received are as follows:

Memo Number One

To: Liz Geiger, Director of HRM

From: George Viener, Manager of Manufacturing

Subject: Summer Employment for My Daughter

My daughter, who is a junior in college and majoring in math, is looking for summer work. I told her that I could use her to cover for people going on vacation. There are a lot of unskilled and semiskilled jobs that she could easily perform. The summer work would help her earn tuition for the next school year. As you know we've been in compliance with our targets for minority employment.

I hope to get her started on June 10. Let me know if you object.

This exercise was developed by Professor Patrick A. Kroll of the General College of the University of Minnesota at Minneapolis. All names are disguised. Used by permission.

Memo Number Two

To: Elizabeth Geiger, Director of Human Resources

From: Jane Liebe, Receptionist

Subject: John Hart's Requests to Date Me

John Hart, the accounting office supervisor, is sort of becoming a nuisance. He has asked me out for a date for the fourth time in the last four days. When I'm receiving outsiders, I find it awkward to see John waiting in the hall to get his chance to talk to me again when I'm not with a customer or on the phone. It looks kind of silly to see him out in the hall with his sheepish grin.

My first response to his date request was a distinct, polite, "No thanks." After the fourth date request, I said "No, and don't bother me again." However, I have the feeling he is going to come back. John is a nice guy, but I'm not interested in a social relationship with him! What should I do?

Memo Number Three

To: Ms. Elizabeth Geiger, Human Resources Department

From: Arthur Katz, Sales Manager

Subject: New Personality Profile Test to Select Sales People

As you know, my department will have quite a few sales people retiring this year, and we're likely to have quite a flurry of recruitment and selection activity. Finding good potential sales people is no easy task, as you know. At a recent sales conference, I was talking to an old college friend who is a sales manager with a firm on the West Coast. He said that he just discovered a new personality profile test that seems to be helpful in selecting sales people. In his last three selection decisions, he has used this profile test and it seems to work.

I would like to use this personality profile test in our salesperson selection procedures, and start using it next month. Let me know what you think.

Memo Number Four

To: Elizabeth Geiger, Director of Human Resource Management

From: Helen Hughes, Manager of Administrative Services

Subject: Maternity Benefits for Unwed Mother

One of the women in our secretarial pool approached me about maternity benefits. She is planning to have a child, but she is not married. Does our regular maternity benefits plan for women employees cover her? Let me know as soon as possible.

Memo Number Five

To: Elizabeth Geiger, Director of Human Resource Management

From: Melanie Weber, Supervisor—Accounts Payable Section

Subject: Question Regarding Why the Employment Interview Is Problematic as a Selection Tool

During our recent meeting of managers, supervisors and other administrative staff, you advised us that we shouldn't make selection decisions based entirely or primarily on our interviews. I don't understand. I think I'm an excellent communicator! Why did you go out of your way to warn us about an overreliance on the employment interview in making selection choices? It's really the only way to learn about a job applicant's qualifications and motivations. Please advise.

Affirmative Action and Whom to Hire

You are Alice Green, vice-president of human resources at the Hackney Paper Box Company. You must make a decision concerning whom to select as personnel manager for a 125-employee unionized Hackney Paper Box plant in Philadelphia, Pennsylvania. At this time, Hackney Paper Box Company has forty-seven small plants at various locations throughout the country. Most of the plant personnel managers are white, and only five of them are women.

The company's corporate affirmative action officer has strongly advised you to hire a young black woman, June Triss, who has applied. However, you believe a young white male applicant, Bob Young, is better qualified for this position. You have narrowed the field to these two.

Your evaluation and summary of the qualifications of two applicants are as follows:

June Triss

1. Is very intelligent but seems to lack good business sense.
2. Has a Master's degree in industrial relations from Corning University, from which she graduated in the top 10 percent of her class.
3. Has three years' experience as an assistant personnel manager at a leading nonunion department store. No union relations experience.
4. Supplied fair references from Corning University and the department store.
5. Is very ambitious—told the plant manager she would have his job in three years.
6. Has aggressive personality—informed you that she was interviewing Hackney, not Hackney interviewing her.
7. The members of the management group at Philadelphia did not seem to like her.
8. Stated that she might sue the company for discrimination if she was not offered the job.

This exercise was prepared by Professor James C. Hodgetts of the Fogelman College of Business and Economics of the University of Memphis. All names are disguised. Used by permission.

Bob Young

1. Has three years as a human resource management major at a state university, but in his senior year had to transfer for economic reasons to a small liberal arts college in his home town. Received a B.A. degree and graduated in the middle third of his class.
2. Has five years' experience as assistant personnel manager in a three-person department in a 500-employee unionized paper box plant.
3. Supplied good references from his college and excellent references from the paper box plant.
4. Has an excellent personality—you and all members of management with whom he talked at Philadelphia liked him.
5. Is not very aggressive—you doubt that he would progress very far in the company but believe he would be an excellent plant personnel manager.

Both Triss and Young answered an advertisement in *The New York Times*. The advertisement set minimum qualifications of a college degree and three years' experience as an assistant personnel manager. The advertisement did not say what kind of experience as an assistant personnel manager was expected and did not say that union relations experience was necessary.

All members of top management at the Philadelphia plant are white men. The HR department at the Philadelphia plant consists of the personnel manager and a secretarial assistant. The plant manager and production superintendent have some experience dealing with the union, but this is primarily the job of the personnel manager.

You must make a decision this week so that the new personnel manager can spend some time with the retiring personnel manager before he leaves.

Union Influence on Construction Company Hiring Practices

Brown Bros. Construction Company operated in the suburban areas just south of a large northern industrial city. The city proper had a 55 percent nonwhite population, but the bulk of Brown Bros. construction work involved large housing subdivisions in predominantly white communities.

The company had been in existence since 1948. For many years, the electricians employed by Brown Bros. were represented by Local 444 of the Brotherhood of Electrical Workers, which had its headquarters in the largest of the suburban communities that surround the city. Local 444 remained the bargaining unit for electricians employed by Brown Bros., which had been an all-union construction company; therefore, all of its electricians belonged to Local 444.

Aside from Local 444, there was another union local, Local 432 of the Brotherhood of Electrical Workers, that represented electrical workers who lived within the city limits. Because of the different structures of the two electrician labor markets represented by the two locals, there was a corresponding difference between the labor pools of Local 444 and Local 432, as indicated in Exhibit E–16. The data included in Exhibit E–16 had been obtained from a report published in a local electrical contractors' association bulletin.

THE PRESIDENT'S CONCERN

You are Courtney Brown, the current president of the company. Brown Bros. recently won a large federal contract to renovate a local federal administrative office building. You are apprehensive about Brown Bros.' compliance with Title VII of the Civil Rights Act and Executive Order 11246 as interpreted by the Office of Federal Contract Compliance Programs (OFCCP). You have the following additional information available to you:

1. The electricians currently employed by Brown Bros. had the following racial distribution: Of the seventeen electricians, fifteen were white (88 percent) and two were black (12 percent).
2. The economic conditions were such that industries in the area employing electricians had fewer jobs open than there were unemployed electricians in the labor market.

This exercise was prepared by Professor Kenneth A. Kovach, Ph.D., of George Mason University in Fairfax, Virginia. All names are disguised. Used by permission.

3. The Local 444 contract with Brown Bros. required that employment priority be given to electricians furnished by the local's hiring hall. Among the members of Local 444, the unemployment rate had averaged 10 percent over the past twelve-month period.

What steps, if any, should you take in order to determine whether your company will be in compliance with applicable law and federal regulations if you continue to employ only electricians represented by Local 444?

EXHIBIT E–16 Racial Composition of Electricians within a 50-Mile Radius of Brown Bros. Headquarters

	WHITE		NONWHITE		
	NO.	%	NO.	%	TOTAL
Local 432 (city)	267	58	193	42	460
Local 444 (suburbs)	420	92	35	8	455
Nonunion electricians	165	72	65	28	230
Entire labor market	852	74	293	26	1145

EXERCISE–17

The Alleged Discriminatory Note

You are Dan Lander, owner of several state-licensed child day-care centers located in a midwestern metropolitan area. Upon opening your business mail one morning, you discover a letter and forms from the local office of the Equal Employment Opportunity Commission (EEOC). A former employee, Brenda Baker, has filed a sex- and race-discrimination suit against your firm, alleging that she has been discriminated against because she was a pregnant woman. The EEOC notice requests that you submit copies of her personnel files to the EEOC for review and that you answer numerous questions regarding Ms. Baker's employment record and termination.

You reflect on the circumstances surrounding Ms. Baker. She worked at one of your centers for about two and one-half years. You remember terminating her employment about a month ago because of her erratic attendance, poor attitudes, and insubordination. In fact, on two occasions, Ms. Baker made disturbing phone calls in the middle of the night to your home residence and also to her supervisor's (the day-care center's director) residence. Ms. Baker usually displayed a negative attitude on the job, and she was "crabby" with the children. She was often late to work and at times she did not arrive at all without notifying her supervisor of the situation. The state licensing agency requires that strict staff-child ratios be adhered to at all times. This makes it extremely difficult if an employee does not arrive at work on a regular and timely basis. You and the child-care business require dependable employees.

When you terminated her, Ms. Baker, an African American, was unmarried and pregnant with her second child. You wrote a note to her supervisor, Ms. Fran Costien, which included this statement: "We cannot tolerate unreliable employees who are not of good moral character and who do not demonstrate decent family values." Of course, this note had not been intended for Ms. Baker to see, nor was it to be placed in any permanent record file. However, somehow Ms. Baker had obtained a copy of this note. Ms. Baker based her EEOC claim of sex and race discrimination largely on this note, which Ms. Baker asserted had been "found" in her personnel file by "another employee."

All names are disguised.

EXERCISE–18

The Manager Offers an Opportunity

You are William "Buddy" Moore. You work in the internal customer service department of the McLean Distribution Services Company; this department is part of the headquarters offices located in a large midwestern city. Seven employees currently are in the department—the manager and six technical representatives, or "techs." All six techs have been hired within the past two years. The department had begun as a one-person operation comprised of Edward "Eddie" Jenner, the present manager; it then grew very quickly. The responsibility of the department is to take care of any customer needs that can be handled internally by the company. This primarily means solving problems by telephone and fax and coordinating field repair work done in-house by customers or by subcontractors. The company does no external service work other than for a few major local accounts.

All the other techs have left for the day. Eddie asks you to come to his office. Eddie shuts the door and tells you to sit down. Eddie stares at you and says, "This conversation never took place. Am I clear?"

"Absolutely," you answer, and stare right back.

Eddie: Here's the deal. (Eddie is never big on small talk.) I got an idea that will do both of us a lot of good, career-wise. I want to put a tech in the field who'll travel all around the country to our accounts. What this tech will do is to stop by and see how things are going. Get to know the people face-to-face. Build relationships. No pressure. "Hey, I'm just here to help." The real point is that after a visit or three, everybody is feeling warm and fuzzy about each other. The tech will get to know the customer's needs—some that the customer might not even know about himself or herself. And then we start to build the sales and service. We can use our own stuff and also work deals with other suppliers and service people. I don't know any of our direct competitors who are doing this.

You: What does management think about the idea?

Eddie: Nobody knows about it yet except you and me. I have to put a few things in place before I can make a move. But there's no doubt in

This exercise was prepared by Professor Martin R. Moser of the College of Management of the University of Massachusetts at Lowell. All names are disguised. Used by permission.

my mind that it will sell. I know how these top managers think. (Eddie smiles).

You: So what's the big deal with all this secrecy? You afraid I'm going to steal your idea?

Eddie: No. (Eddie has a serious look on his face.) Here's how I see the play. There are six techs in the department, but there are only two who have what it takes to do the job—you and Gerri. (Geraldine Morris is a black woman.) The problem is that it won't work with Gerri. To be perfectly honest, in some ways she is stronger than you. All things being equal, its neck and neck who could do the job better. But given the circumstances, the job won't work with her doing it.

(Pause.)

Eddie: Look, I'll spell it out for you. (Eddie stands up). This is not real comfortable to say, and I don't consider myself a prejudiced guy or a racist, but reality is reality. I've been working these accounts for a lot of years and I know the customers. They are going to be more comfortable with you than with Gerri. Facts are facts. In this job, a guy is usually going to do better than a gal, and a white person will do better than a black. That is just the way it is. Maybe I don't agree with it, but there is nothing I can do about it. And what I want to do is build business, not make the world a better place. I got my own problems.

(Pause.)

Eddie: OK, here's what needs to happen. (Eddie sits down.) You need to write me a proposal about the idea. Not too well developed, just the basics. Then I take it and develop it a little and then bring it to top management. Since it was your idea, you get to do it. Since I brought it to management, I get to run it. We both win, because I know it's going to work.

You: This is a lot to digest. I got to think.

Eddie: Fine, but just remember this. These kinds of opportunities don't come around very often. This is the way the real world works. You got to do what you got to do to survive and get ahead. Your college professors didn't teach you about this kind of stuff. But it happens every day in business. It isn't always fair, but that's the way it is. I need your answer by not later than noon tomorrow.

You leave and return to your office to decide how to respond.

PART FIVE

Compensation Management

CASES

EXPERIENTIAL EXERCISES

Compensation management is one of the most important areas of any organization's total human resource management program. Since compensation expenditures often constitute a major part of a firm's total costs, compensation must be administered properly for a firm to maintain a competitive position. At the same time, employee compensation concerns fundamental needs and goals of people. Compensation is necessary to meet the economic needs and expectations of employees, and it is also a factor in meeting such needs as self-respect and recognition. While compensation management has become an increasingly specialized area, it nonetheless is closely related to other areas of human resource management.

A well-managed compensation program can enable an organization to meet successfully a number of challenges. First, the general level of compensation must be high enough to attract the talents the organization needs, but not so high as to cause operating costs to become noncompetitive. Second, the compensation program must provide a structure of wages and salaries which reflects the responsibilities and difficulties of the jobs to which they relate. This structure and its underlying methodology should be understandable and explainable to members of the organization. Job evaluation processes are typically the tools used to determine levels of skills and responsibilities and to provide a rational basis for explaining the logic of the pay system.

A third dimension of a firm's compensation program is the necessity that pay clearly reflects the criteria the organization deems most important and can be adjusted according to those criteria. Performance and seniority are two major criteria used in determining specific pay levels for individuals and for adjusting those levels. Compensation programs also should provide mechanisms for adjusting job rates or individual pay in response to external market forces.

A fourth facet of compensation is the method (or basis) used to actually determine pay—that is, how to respond to the question of, "What are we paying for?" Essentially, organizations pay for time, or performance, or some combination of these. At lower levels of the organization, employees may be paid for output and/or for hours worked. At the top levels, executive compensation usually will include a base component plus a bonus or share in profits which may be the major part of an executive's compensation.

Fifth, compensation will generally include both a wage/salary component as well as a nonwage component. The non-wage portions are commonly called *benefits*, and they include all of the nonwage remuneration received by the employee. Among these are pay for time not worked (sick days, vacations); insurance (life, hospital coverage); deferred compensation (bonuses); and retirement plans or pension funds. Benefit packages are not only an important part of the firm's attractiveness as an employer, but they have become a large portion of the firm's total compensation expenditures, frequently amounting to one-third or more of total compensation.

Finally, and probably the greatest challenge of all, is the attempt to relate compensation to the stimulation of work performance. Some research suggests that pay alone does not motivate top work performance. Many managers, however, believe that if pay levels are sufficient and adjustments are large enough to make some difference in a person's life, then pay can be the prime motivating factor in improving performance. It should be noted, however, that whenever pay is to be used as a motivator of performance, careful attention is needed to the identification of the performance behavior desired and to its measurement. These are among the complex, interrelated challenges that constitute the focus of the cases and exercises of Part Five.

CASE–42

Petri Chemical Company (A): Tom Moxley

COMPANY BACKGROUND

Petri Chemical Company was a major manufacturer of industrial and pharmaceutical chemicals. Principal operations were at the Lafayette and Cartier plants, both of which were located in a large midwestern city. At the time of this case, Petri employed approximately nine hundred production personnel, eighty-five maintenance workers, and two hundred office, sales, engineering, R&D, and other personnel at the two plants that were situated about 1 mile apart.

The company had the reputation of being an excellent employer. The company selected employees carefully. Managers devoted considerable attention to encouraging and aiding individuals to seek to advance to the highest levels consistent with their ability and interests. Further, management prided itself in its policies and practices of fair treatment for everyone from the president to housekeeping services!

Production and maintenance workers belonged to an independent plant union with which the company had enjoyed a good working relationship for many years. The company had not had a strike during the last thirty years of negotiations for the collective bargaining agreement.

THE DISSATISFIED TECHNICIAN

Tom Moxley was nineteen years old and had worked for Petri Chemical Company for nine months as a laboratory technician at the Cartier plant. Tom was considered by his supervisor to be intelligent and dependable. He looked for additional work when he completed assignments given him, and his work was satisfactory in almost every way. His supervisor stated that Tom's only real fault was that he worked too rapidly on occasion, which sometimes led to errors. However, these had never been serious, and the supervisor thought of Tom as an outstanding employee.

In general, Tom liked his work, and he was enthusiastic about it. He felt that his job might serve as a steppingstone to promotion. To prepare himself for such an eventuality, Tom had enrolled in the night division at Sherwood

---

All names and certain wage and other data are disguised.

University. At this time, Tom was taking two courses paid for at his own expense—algebra and chemistry.

Previously, Tom Moxley had been employed on a part-time basis at a supermarket, where he had he had averaged $300 per week. His starting salary as a laboratory technician at Petri was $1,500 per month Tom took the position because it was full-time, had far better benefits, and had opportunities for advancement. But after only six months, Tom complained to his supervisor that his salary was very inadequate and that he should receive an increase in salary. His supervisor recommended that Tom be given an increase. After due consideration by the plant superintendent, Tom was granted an increase of $75 per month. Tom was dissatisfied with the size of the increase, feeling that it should have been at least $100. Shortly thereafter, he received a $60 per month "adjustment," as did all other laboratory technicians (in line with an "across-the-board" company increase in wages and salaries). Tom was dissatisfied with this increase also. He felt that his outstanding work was not being taken into account by the company and considered it unfair that several other laboratory technicians, who were not nearly so industrious and competent, had received the same increase.

Tom was very unhappy about his salary and had several discussions with his supervisor about the matter. On one occasion, he told his supervisor that other firms were paying $100 to $200 per month more for comparable work. When the supervisor expressed disbelief, Tom claimed that he had seen these salary figures in a local business newspaper's report of a wage and salary survey it had taken. Tom's supervisor suggested that salary surveys were usually unreliable, because other positions often involved night work or very undesirable working conditions. On another occasion, Tom told his supervisor that his fiancée was prodding him to look for a higher-paying job and that she was earning more in her office position at a local financial institution than he was at Petri Chemical Company.

The supervisor was very fond of Tom Moxley and tried to soothe his feelings about salary as much as possible. He told Tom to be patient and that "sooner or later" he would "take care of him." He even offered to help Tom with his studies should he run into difficulties.

Tom was also irritated by the fact that overtime in the lab was virtually nonexistent (usually only a few hours per month at time-and-a-half). Further, Tom expected to be transferred to a new lab facility away from both plants when it was completed in several months, and his transportation costs to the new location would be higher because it was farther from his home. In addition, Tom realized that the unionized plant chemical operators and machine attendants made more money than he did, even without the considerable overtime hours they worked. Most of them were paid in the range of $10 to $13 per hour for relatively unskilled work.

Tom's supervisor knew that the salary classification for laboratory technicians currently ranged from $1,560 to $2,100 per month, but this was confidential information for supervisors only. These ranges had been adjusted upward each year after a contract was settled with the plant union (which represented hourly paid production and maintenance workers). Whenever hourly wage rates were increased, across-the-board increases were granted to laboratory technicians, nonexempt salaried employees, and supervisors who were not in the union. The amounts were usually the monthly equivalent of the cents-per-hour increase negotiated with the union.

Tom's supervisor decided that he should discuss the matter with the plant superintendent again. He told the superintendent that Tom Moxley could perform about three-fourths of the work normally performed by a college-trained chemist and that the group of which Tom was a part was short-handed. Further, he stated that the company should make every effort not to lose Tom and that unless something could be done, Tom would quit shortly after the move to the new lab location.

After consultation with the plant human resource manager for her advice, the plant superintendent told the supervisor to talk to Tom, to point out to him the long-run advantages of working for Petri, and to promise Tom that management would consider a fair adjustment of his salary "at the appropriate time."

Salary Discrimination
among the Library Staff

Art Tipton, human resources director of Pierce University, had just finished reading and signing a letter he was sending to an employee on campus. As he sealed the letter, he recalled the events that had brought about this situation.

THE LETTER COMPLAINT

On June 7, 1990, Tipton had received the following letter from Carol Parker, a departmental supervisor in the main campus library.[1]

June 6, 1990

Mr. Art Tipton
Human Resources Director
Pierce University

Dear Sir:

I, Carol Parker, a black supervisor at Main Campus Library in the card preparation division, have a serious problem. I have approached my chief, Ms. Smith; the library administrative assistant, Ms. Caldwell; and the associate director of the library, Mr. Peebles, with no satisfactory results.

My problem is that I feel there is salary discrimination at Main Campus Library. One of my employees, Jean Rohs (white), has been employed by Pierce University for seven months and has received twice as much for this year in raises as I have. She also presently makes $140 per month more than Annie Waldron, a black employee in the same division who had been employed eleven months at one time and left to have a baby. She

All names, dates, and certain wage data are disguised.

[1]Most departmental supervisors in this library are considered to be "working supervisors," and they are not included as part of management for legal and wage and hour considerations. Pierce University is a private university located in a large urban city.

returned to work on July 1, 1989, almost four months before Ms. Rohs, who began on October 28, 1989.

Ms. Waldron has also had occasion to take over when I was out on vacation several times. Mary Laclede, junior cataloger, assisted her on several occasions, but there were times Annie kept things going alone. Yet Annie Waldron was never considered for a promotion.

I have been under the impression that raises were granted for merit. Merit as defined by Mr. Webster is "something deserving reward, praise, or gratitude; a reward of honor given for praiseworthy qualities or conduct." In my opinion, merit consists of dependability and the quantity and quality of work produced. If statistics mean anything, Jean Rohs's quantity and quality of work do not surpass mine.

When I approached the management people at Main Campus Library with the situation, I asked only for justification for this large raise, which I did not receive. I never brought race into the issue. Ms. Caldwell said that raises were based on merit, but no one attempted to show me where Jean merited any more than Annie Waldron or me. Mr. Peebles's reply was that there was nothing he could do at this time. Ms. Caldwell stated that she could neither admit nor deny the raises, but I know that Jean received an $80 raise in January (I received $60), and she received $160 in her June check, and my raise for July is $60. I asked for an explanation, and I got none.

I, myself, could think of no justification for the differences in raises, when I am supervisor and she is under my supervision.

The only conclusion that I could draw after receiving no answer from my superiors was that I am black and she is white. Maybe I am wrong, but as long as I receive no clear-cut answer, I will believe this.

I had thought of approaching the NAACP or the EEOC with this matter to see what they thought, but I felt I should approach the personnel office before I go to outsiders.

I would appreciate your looking into this matter, and I'm sure Annie Waldron would also.

Respectfully submitted,
Carol Parker

THE HR DIRECTOR'S REPLY

After investigating the situation thoroughly, Art Tipton invited Carol Parker to his office for a discussion of the complaint. His letter to Ms. Parker summarized the essence of that conversation.

Personal and confidential

June 13, 1990

Ms. Carol Parker
Main Campus
Box 1123

Subject: Your letter of June 6, 1990

Dear Carol:

Thanks again for coming over and talking with me yesterday afternoon. I think it helped both of us to better understand the total situation.

As promised, I have analyzed the salary patterns for you and Jean Rohs; see graph enclosed [Exhibit C–43]. Let me make some observations based on what I think the graph shows:

1. You have made unusually rapid progress since joining the library staff. I complimented you on this yesterday. Going from $1,100 per month to $1,780 per month in three years is a 62 percent improvement, an average of more than 20 percent in raises per year.
2. You and Jean both showed fast-learning ability (you mentioned to me that Jean had caught on quickly), and this showed up early in the graph. Notice that you received a 19 percent raise in one six-month period. Perhaps you did not realize this, since it occurred in your case back in the first half of 1988.
3. Salary increases for clerical personnel in the metropolitan area have been going up, on the average, between 3-1/2 and 5-1/2 percent per *year* in the past three years. The increases given *all* members of your department have considerably exceeded these averages, reflecting our concerted effort to upgrade our rates to competitive levels and thereby help to attract and retain good employees.
4. Our general policy is to maintain about 10–15 percent salary differential between our working supervisors and the *best* employee salary in the group. Your salary exceeds Jean Rohs's salary by $280 a month, or about 18 percent.

As mentioned in our talk, I am not particularly "happy" about your knowing detailed salary information on someone else; not because I think there are awkward or unjustifiable rates, but because a sharing of each other's salary information can easily lead to misunderstanding without knowing all the factors that management tries to consider in setting salaries at equitable levels.

Anyway, I encouraged you to stay in your present position at least until the operational changes taking place in your department are completed. You said you will think about it—and I'm assuming that means "yes" for now.

Your openness in letting me know of your concerns after you discussed them with library management was much appreciated by me. If I might be able to help further, I hope you will let me know.

> Sincerely,
> Arthur Tipton
> Director of Human Resources

Encl. graph included

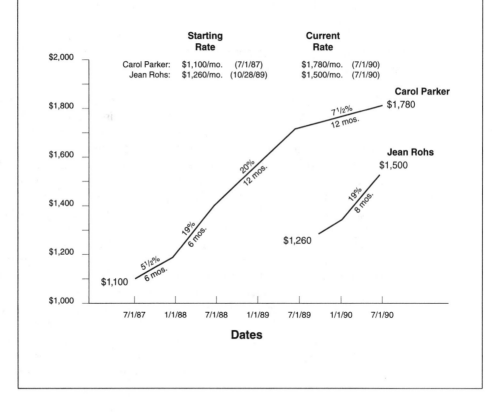

UNIVERSITY POLICIES AND THE FUTURE

Art Tipton decided to review the university policy statements concerning employee complaints and discrimination. The following statements were included in *Pierce University's Policies and Procedures Manual for Non-Academic Employees.*

Item 19b: Problem Handling

Employees who wish to question some treatment, procedure, or policy are encouraged to speak up. A procedure for handling such questions is available and in use, as follows:

1. Discuss with immediate supervisor.
2. If more satisfaction is desired, discuss with the department head.
3. Further appeal may be made to the director of human resources for a final reply. The "problem" should be explained in writing at this stage, and a formal reply in writing will be given after thorough study of all facts. The human resources office is available at any time to discuss with any employee questions or misunderstandings he or she may have.

Item 20: Equal Job Opportunity

Pierce University believes that the selection, training, and advancement of employees should be based on merit. The university is committed to a policy of nondiscrimination in the treatment of employees or applicants as regards age, race, color, religion, sex, disability, or national origin.

Art Tipton wondered whether his letter to Carol Parker would close this particular incident. But he also wondered what actions, if any, he could take to prevent similar problems. As a staff HR director, Tipton had no direct authority over the management people in other divisions of Pierce University. Yet Tipton knew that university employee policies were poorly administered by some line supervisors. Further, there was no labor union on the campus, but several rumors had been circulating recently that a representative of the Office Employees' Union had been distributing literature among the library employees.

CASE–44

Salary Inequities
at Acme Manufacturing

Joe Blackenship was trying to figure out what to do about a problem salary situation he he had in his plant. Blackenship recently took over as president of Acme Manufacturing from the founder and president for thirty-five years, Bill George. The company was family owned and located in a small eastern Arkansas town. It had approximately two hundred and fifty employees and was the largest employer in the community. Blackenship was a member of the family that owned Acme, but he had never worked for the company prior to becoming president. He had an M.B.A. and a law degree, plus fifteen years of management experience with a large manufacturing organization where he was senior vice president for human resources when he made his move to Acme.

A short time after joining Acme, Joe Blackenship started to reognize that there was considerable inequity in the pay structure for salaried employees. A discussion with the personnel director led him to believe that salaried employees' pay was very much a matter of individual bargaining with the past president. Hourly paid factory employees were not part of the problem, since they were unionized and their wages were set by collective bargaining. An examination of the salaried payroll showed that there were twenty-five employees, ranging in pay from that of the president to that of the receptionist. A closer examination showed that fourteen of the salaried employees were female. Three of these were front-line factory supervisors and one was the personnel director. The other ten were nonmanagement.

This examination also showed that the personnel director appeared to be underpaid, and that the three female supervisors were paid somewhat below any of the male supervisors. However, there were no similar supervisory jobs in which there were both male and female job incumbents. When asked, the personnel director said she thought the female supervisors may have been paid at a lower rate mainly because they were women, and perhaps Mr. George did not think that women needed as much money because they had working husbands. However, she added the thought that they were paid less because they supervised less-skilled employees than the male supervisors. Joe Blackenship was not sure that this was true.

The company from which Blackenship had moved had a good job-evaluation system. Although he was thoroughly familiar and capable with this

This case was prepared by Professor James C. Hodgetts of the Fogelman College of Business and Economics of the University of Memphis. All names are disguised. Used by permission.

compensation tool, Blackenship did not have time to make a job evaluation study at Acme. Therefore, he decided to hire a compensation consultant from a nearby university to help him. Together, they decided that all twenty-five salaried jobs should be in the job-evaluation unit, that a modified ranking method of job evaluation should be used, and that the job descriptions recently completed by the personnel director were current, accurate, and usable in the study.

The job evaluation showed that there was no evidence of serious inequities or discrimination in the nonmanagement jobs, but that the personnel director and the three female supervisors were being underpaid relative to comparable male salaried employees.

Joe Blackenship was not sure what to do. He knew that if the underpaid female supervisors took the case to the local EEOC office, the company could be found guilty of gender discrimination and then have to pay considerable back wages. He was afraid that if he gave these women an immediate salary increase large enough to bring them up to where they should be, the male supervisors would be upset and the female supervisors might comprehend the total situation and want back pay. The personnel director told Blackenship that the female supervisors had never complained about pay differences, and they probably did not know the law to any extent.

The personnel director agreed to take a sizable salary increase with no back pay, so this part of the problem was "solved." Joe Blackenship believed he had four choices relative to the female supervisors:

1. To do nothing;
2. To gradually increase the female supervisors' salaries;
3. To increase their salaries immediately;
4. To call the three supervisors into his office, discuss the situation with them, and jointly decide what to do.

C–45

Salary Administration in the Engineering Department

INTRODUCTION

Majestic Corporation was a major chemical company with many plant locations. The Rockville plant was one of the company's largest, and it produced a wide variety of chemical products. As part of its complex, the plant also housed Majestic's applied and developmental research laboratories and an engineering department.

The engineering department performed engineering services not only for Rockville but also for many other Majestic Corporation plant facilities. At this time, the department consisted of approximately one hundred personnel who were supervised by seven engineering supervisors reporting to the chief engineer. Engineers in the department were organized in functional groups such as mechanical design, instrument and electrical design, corrosion, pollution abatement and environmental quality, materials handling, and computer technology. Other engineers specialized in various production processes, performing chemical engineering work to improve existing processes and drawing upon functional groups as projects demanded. Approximately one-half of the engineers had less than five years' experience at Rockville; the other half had up to thirty-five years' experience with the company. Some seventy engineers performed professional engineering work in the department; the remainder were supervisors, computer specialists, technicians, secretaries, and word processors.

SALARY ADMINISTRATION POLICY

Majestic had a well-formulated salary administration plan. Each year, corporate headquarters allocated a "raise budget" to each plant, and the plant human resources department coordinated allocation of available raise funds. Each raise budget was expressed as a percentage of existing salaries, which was thus a constraint on the total amount of raises granted in one year. At the time of this case, company policy stated that any raise to be granted an engineering employee depended on the following factors:

All names are disguised.

1. *Present performance level.*[1]
   a. Excellent—maximum of 10 percent.
   b. Above adequate plus—maximum of 8 percent.
   c. Above adequate—maximum of 7 percent.
   d. Above adequate minus—maximum of 6 percent.
   e. Adequate—maximum of 5 percent.
   f. Below adequate—no raise permitted.
2. *Employee's present salary in relation to the guide-rate for job level.* For engineering positions (for which progressive job titles existed, such as assistant engineer, engineer, senior engineer, etc.) there was a single curve as a guide-rate at each performance level relative to the number of years since the employee received the baccalaureate degree. The curves sloped upward from zero years' experience to twenty years' experience and then leveled out. (Exhibit C–45A shows the salary curves for "engineers." Similar curves were developed for each of the other engineering job categories in the company. These curves were periodically revised and updated to reflect current conditions.)
3. *Availability of raise budget.* This was expressed as a percentage of total plant salaries at the beginning of the year.
4. *Raise frequency.* Newly hired employees could be given a raise after six months with Majestic, and thereafter no more frequently than every eleven months. The policy guideline for raise frequency was:
   a. Excellent—eleven to twelve months.
   b. Above adequate plus—twelve to thirteen months.
   c. Above adequate—twelve to fourteen months.
   d. Above adequate minus—thirteen to fifteen months.
   e. Adequate—fifteen to eighteen months.
5. *Promotional adjustment.* On promotion to a higher-level job, a person could be given an additional raise of up to 15 percent if necessary to bring his or her salary in line with the higher-level salary curve. This was not usually applied to the promotion from assistant engineer to engineer or to senior engineer.

Deviation from these policy guidelines could be granted if a supervisor made a very strong case for doing so. Seldom, however, was permission granted by higher management for deviation from the guidelines.

In addition, each year supervisors had to furnish a "potential-for-promotion" rating to the HR department for each employee. The scale here was excellent, good, fair, and limited.[2] These ratings were forwarded to the

---

[1]The performance ratings of "excellent," "above adequate plus," and so on were overall annual ratings given by each supervisor to subordinates as part of a systematic companywide merit-rating system.

[2]To be discussed in more detail later in the case.

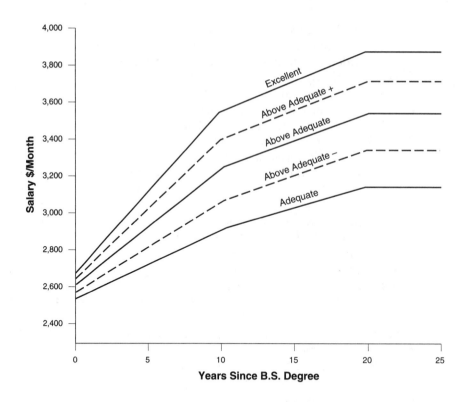

EXHIBIT C–45 A Salary Curves for Engineers

salary administrator in the HR department. However, according to policy, the potential-for-promotion rating was not supposed to influence salary administration. The potential ratings were supposedly used in organizational planning and for developing training programs.

MECHANICS OF SALARY ADMINISTRATION

About March of each year, each engineering department supervisor prepared a salary raise plan for employees for the following year. Each individual plan was reviewed with the salary administrator in the human resources department who negotiated some adjustments in order to:

1. Ensure equity among various plant groups;
2. Ensure that planned increases were within the plant raise budget;
3. Ensure that no one was overlooked.

The engineering supervisors also reviewed their raise plans with the chief engineer to be sure that the department head concurred with their decisions. The salary administrator usually "kept" a small reserve of raise money to cover exceptional performance improvements and new employees not on the plan. There was seldom any major problem using up the entire plant raise budget. A few January raises could be moved up to December or vice versa to do the fine tuning.

THE SITUATION

Tom Green, one of the engineering department supervisors, had just returned from a review of his next year's salary plan with the HR salary administrator. Green went into John Benson's office; Benson was a fellow engineering supervisor. Tom closed the door.

Tom: You know those personnel types are a real slippery bunch of so and so's.

John: Oh, what have they done now?

Tom: I've just returned from reviewing next year's salary plan with Fran Hays (the HR department salary administrator), and she wants to pass out the raises based on the ratings I assigned my engineers for potential rather than on the ratings I assigned them for present job performance.

John: Did Hays really say that?

Tom: No, I just concluded that from the adjustments she recommended. She was constantly pushing raises up for the new kids we've hired out of college the past few years whom we have rated excellent on potential but only so-so on present performance. Fran says we don't have to worry about our people getting too high on the salary curve because they mostly will be promoted to higher-level jobs in a few years anyway. Of course, this doesn't leave much raise budget for our real good performers that have reached their top level of advancement.

John: I know what you mean. Mike Jones just transferred into my group last year, and he is about $400 below where his excellent performance and thirty years' experience should put him. I don't know what we would do around here without engineers such as Mike. The sad part is that Mike will be retiring in about seven or eight years, and his pension will be based on his last five years' salary. I feel I've got to get his salary in line within a year or two.

Tom: Too bad his former bosses didn't go to bat for Mike.

John: I really think that the HR office is working pretty hard to do a good job of salary administration. Generally, I think they are fair. The trouble is that there is just not enough raise money to do everything we would like to do.

During their discussion, Tom Green and John Benson reached the conclusion that an employee's present performance was measured reasonably by the annual performance-appraisal system but that the potential rating was extremely subjective. HR staff had never really defined what it meant by "excellent potential" for advancement, and company policy was supposed to be that the potential ratings were not to influence salary administration anyway. The chief engineer had attempted to fill the definitional vacuum by providing the guidelines shown in Exhibit C–45B to the engineering supervisors.

EXHIBIT C–45 B   Chief Engineer's Guidelines for Potential Rating

POTENTIAL RATING	CRITERIA
Excellent	Expect person to advance two job levels in five years
Good	Expect person to advance one level in five years
Fair	Person may or may not advance one level in the next five years
Limited	Expect person definitely will not move beyond present level

Majestic Corporation had the dual-advancement route, whereby individuals could move up the managerial ladder, or advance by the technological route from "engineeer" to "senior engineer" to "engineering specialist," "senior engineering specialist," "technologist," and "advanced technologist." Majestic tried to make pay and status for top technological jobs "equal" to top managerial jobs. The above criteria were applied to either managerial or technical advancement. Both Green and Benson concluded that the potential rating was still too highly subjective.

Don Moran and the New Sales Compensation Plan

On July 1, 1992, Avery Industries, a medium-sized pharmaceutical research and manufacturing firm, announced a major change in compensation policy for its sales staff of fourteen salespersons. The Avery salespersons, officially known as "medical sales representatives," called mainly on physicians. Their selling efforts consisted primarily of what has been referred to as "detailing"— that is, making physicians aware of what Avery had to offer that physicians might prescribe for patients when appropriate, including for research testing.

Prior to July 1, all Avery salespersons had received a salary plus a semi-annual bonus. The bonus was determined solely by management on the basis of the company's economic situation as shown on the semiannual financial reports as well as management's evaluation of a salesperson's performance.

Although top management realized that certain problems would arise as a result of this change, each salesperson was to receive an adjustment in base salary to compensate for the loss of the bonus. Adjustments varied in amount. In some instances they were less, in others more, than the amounts that salespersons had been averaging.

Don Moran, a salesman with the firm for nearly six years, was earning a base salary of $32,500 per year at the time the policy change was announced. His bonuses during the previous two years were in the following amounts:

1990, second six months: $4,506

1991, first six months: $4,212

1991, second six months: $3,846

1992, first six months: $4,145

In addition to salary and incentive bonuses, salespersons also participated in a year-end profit-sharing plan, which for the last three years had amounted to 15 percent of base salary. The policy change did not alter their participation in this plan in any way, other than to increase their future payments due to the increase in base salary resulting from the adjustment.

On July 23, Hank Logan, the division manager, sent the following letter to Don Moran. Other salespersons received similar letters, except that the salaries varied according to the individual.

This case is based on a case originally developed by the late Professor Emeritus Charles L. Lapp of the John M. Olin School of Business of Washington University; the case was subsequently revised. All names and certain data are disguised. Used by prior permission.

Dear Don:

It has always been one of your company's objectives to provide you with one of the best—if not the best—compensation plans in the pharmaceutical industry. To continually meet this objective, we have, over the years, made changes and adjustments in our medical sales representatives' compensation policy.

After months of careful study, I am happy to announce that we have been successful in instituting a new compensation plan for our field staff. This straight-salary plan has been made effective July 1, 1992. Many of its features are derived from those previously suggested by members of our field staff.

All adjustments are retroactive and will appear in August salary checks. Your salary has been adjusted to $42,000 per annum. Let me assure you that the opportunity to further increase your total compensation has never been greater. However, sales performance will be more critically evaluated in the future to determine equitable and deserving salary increases.

We are confident that our new compensation plan will effectively motivate our field staff to accomplish future objectives.

Kind regards,
Hank Logan

When Hank Logan entered his office on the morning of July 27, his secretary handed him a telegram that read:

Hank Logan
Avery Industries, New York, NY

Thank you for the confidence you have expressed in me through the recent sorry adjustment. Your support will continue to be justified.

Don Moran

Dismayed, Hank Logan dropped the telegram on his desk; wondered what, if anything, he should do to respond to the sarcastic telegram.

The Bonus Committee

The five members of the materials handling (MH) department of Westover Metal Fabrication Company entered the company human resources director's office. They had requested this meeting with the HR director, Jim Harrison, because they were concerned about the outcome of bonus allocations following the second year of the company's cash bonus plan. The plan had been developed and instituted by Harrison two years ago at the company president's request.

The basic idea was to reward those employees who achieved better-than-average performance in hopes that all employees would work harder if they could see that they would benefit financially. Each of the company's seven departments selected five employees to serve on departmental bonus committees. Each of these committees decided on several appropriate performance standards. In addition, these committees reviewed the performance of each employee at the end of each year and made a recommendation to the department head. Then each employee was placed into one of four categories or levels of performance, each of which coincided with a level of bonus pay. The department heads compared the committees' recommendations with each employee's self-appraisal and then made their recommendation for each individual. Finally, the president reviewed all these recommendations for the company's 100 employees. The president's approval of these recommendations—subject to changes he might make—was the final step in determining the bonus each individual received.

To make this process as fair and equitable possible, Jim Harrison had requested at the outset of the program that each department establish good, challenging performance criteria by which to judge each employee. He then reviewed and approved each department's criteria when the program was initiated two years ago.

The members of the MH Department Bonus Committee, headed by its chairperson Jerry Evans, were meeting with Jim Harrison because of their concern about perceived inequities in this year's bonus allocations. They had sent a memo to Harrison one week ago expressing the concern that other departments were receiving larger bonuses, primarily because their performance standards were lower and thus easier to attain. They expressed the

This case was developed by Professor Charles Boyd and Professor D. Keith Denton, both of the Department of Management of Southwest Missouri State University in Springfield. All names are disguised. Used by permission.

concern that when the bonus recommendations reached the president, he rarely made any changes in them. The committee had hoped that Jim Harrison would either reduce bonus recommendations for other departments or raise them for MH before sending the bonus recommendations to the president; however, Harrison did neither.

After Jerry Evans briefly restated the committee's position at the beginning of the meeting, the committee members waited for Jim Harrison's response.

Harrison: First, let me say that I agree with you that your performance standards are higher than those of the other departments, and I want to commend you for them. I also want to encourage you to stick with them. I hope and believe that as time goes by other departments will rise to your level.

Evans: But, Mr. Harrison, if we maintain our standards and other departments aren't made to conform to similar standards, we are beating ourselves over the head. We are needlessly forfeiting bonus money that could be ours if we would simply rewrite our standards more loosely, as the other departments have done. Unless you are willing either to reduce the bonus payments to other departments or tell them to get more serious about setting realistic performance standards, it would be absurd to maintain our high standards.

Harrison: I understand how you feel. But I can't do what you are asking, because I approved the standards submitted to me by those other departments; they seemed reasonable. I cannot now tell those departments that they must change the standards I have already approved. If you will just be patient, I think you will find that these other departments will see you as a role model. I think they will want to raise their standards to your level, and I am confident that they will in fact do so. When that occurs, the whole company will perform better and we'll all benefit.

Seeing that Harrison was unwilling to make any adjustment in the bonus plan's performance standards, the conversation drew to a close and the meeting ended. After the committee left the HR director's office, Jerry Evans told the other committee members that he would send them a memo in the next few days that would set up a meeting to discuss how the committee should proceed.

Neglected Management

For several years, the Smith City Police Department had encouraged police officers to pursue formal education through local community and state colleges. The primary incentive provided by the city was reimbursement for tuition and books for approved job-related courses, plus a departmental attempt at preferential shift scheduling whenever possible.

A survey was conducted to determine the educational level of all officers within the Smith City Police Department. The survey established that of 195 officers, one held a graduate degree, four held bachelor's degrees, nine held associate's degrees, and twenty-nine had at least one year of college. It also established that some 20 percent of the department had one or more years of college. Based on the premise that an investment in knowledge would pay for itself in the long run, the administration of the police department established a goal that within three years, 60 percent of the sworn personnel of the department would have completed at least one year of college.

THE EDUCATIONAL PAY INCENTIVE PROPOSAL

The following year, the administration of the police department of Smith City presented to the city administrator's labor-relations representative a proposal for educational pay incentives for all police officers. The educational pay incentive proposal had been discussed by the chief of police's staff in preliminary meetings with the department's bargaining representatives. However, this particular proposal, either through negligence or inadvertence, had not been included in the list of demands presented to the city by the police bargaining representatives. The proposal, therefore, was included as an alternative administrative offer.

The educational pay incentive proposal was structured to provide a 5 percent increase over base pay for officers who had been awarded either an associate of arts degree or an intermediate certificate awarded by the state's commission on Peace Officers Standards and Training (P.O.S.T.). The proposal

This case was prepared by Professor J. David Hunger of the College of Business Administration of Iowa State University, Professor Thomas L. Wheelen of the College of Business Administration of the University of South Florida at Tampa, and Richard M. Ayres of the FBI Academy (Quantico, VA). Although the case is an actual situation, all names are disguised. Used by permission.

further provided an additional 5 percent increase over base pay for officers who had been awarded either a bachelor of arts degree or an advanced certificate from P.O.S.T. The awarding of the intermediate and advanced certificates by P.O.S.T. was to be predicated upon completing a specific number of years of service, accumulating a combination of specific training points, and acquiring a specific number of academic credits from a college.

Negotiations were concluded. Among the benefits granted by the city was the educational pay incentive proposal. However, the resolution ratifying the agreement, as passed by the mayor and city council, limited the educational pay incentives to patrol officers, investigators, sergeants, and lieutenants. The reason given for this limitation was that the public bargaining unit did not represent management. Therefore, it was felt that the pay incentive proposal should not be applied to management. At that time, management was defined as anyone holding the position of department head, assistant department head, or division head. To further complicate matters, management was not represented for bargaining purposes on the theory that the city administration would provide adequately for the managers. A department heads' organization already had formed to discuss management problems. This group, however, had never engaged in bargaining.

THE CAPTAIN'S REQUEST FOR A DEMOTION

After adoption of the resolution that implemented the educational pay incentive proposal, the division commander of the uniform division, a captain, submitted a request for a voluntary demotion to the rank of lieutenant. The reasons he gave for this requested reduction in rank were:

1. The existing pay differential between a captain and a lieutenant was only 10 percent.
2. Within two months, the captain would fulfill the requirements for an advanced certificate from P.O.S.T.
3. The educational pay incentive limitation excluding management was "not equitable."
4. In returning to a field command level, the captain would give up the stress of divisional responsibilities. He would be able to avoid a subsequent reduction in pay, since as a lieutenant he would qualify for the 10 percent additional pay incentive.

When the chief of police received this request, he was beside himself concerning how to respond. The captain was one of his best commanding officers and a close personal friend.

The Superintendent's Vacation Pay

The telephone rang in the office of Dr. John Marshall, professor of management at Sherwood University.

Marshall: Hello, this is Professor Marshall.

Peterman: Dr. Marshall, this is Bill Peterman. You and I met last year at the Public School Educators' Conference at the university. If you remember, I'm chairman of the board of education of our city's public school system.

Marshall: Oh, yes, Mr. Peterman. It's nice to hear from you again. What can I do for you?

Peterman: Well, Professor, I've really got a problem, and I thought you might be able to give me some advice. You see, George Whitaker, our superintendent of schools, recently resigned, and we discussed the problem at the meeting of our board of education last night.

Marshall: I doubt that I know any likely candidates to help you out, Mr. Peterman.

Peterman: Oh, no, that's not our immediate problem, Professor. What we've got is something directly concerned with Dr. Whitaker, and our board has to reach a decision on it as soon as possible.

Let me give you the background of what we're concerned about. Dr. Whitaker has been our superintendent of schools for about eight years. He is one of the finest men I have ever known. He is well respected as an educational administrator, and he did an outstanding job as our superintendent. His salary was $84,000 annually, and he was worth every penny of it.

Well, he was just appointed to the presidency of Bay State University, which is quite an honor, and it reflects well on our school system. We were happy to release him from his contract with us so that he could accept the appointment effective March 1.

Dr. Whitaker's contract with our school system was a twelve-month contract, which allowed for thirty days of vacation and extended from August 1 of last year to July 30 of this year. What puzzles us is what we should do about a payment request Whitaker turned in to the treasurer of our school system. Whitaker wants us to pay him seven-twelfths of one month's pay to cover the vacation time he feels he has earned since last August. He's turned in a request for seven-twelfths of $7,000, or about $4,100.

Last night at the meeting of the board of education, several members were extremely unhappy that Whitaker would turn in such a payment request. They felt that it was ridiculous for Whitaker to expect us to pick up the tab for his vacation when he hadn't fulfilled the conditions of his contract. But other members thought that the board should pay the $4,100 on the grounds that Whitaker had "earned" and was entitled to seven-twelfths of a year's vacation, even if he did resign in the middle of his contract.

Regardless, all members of the board were unhappy that Whitaker, as a top-salaried school official, would even turn in such a request.

They didn't think it was fitting for a superintendent at his salary level to be so mercenary under the circumstances of his leaving.

Marshall: Have you any policy with respect to such matters?

Peterman: Not to cover such a unique circumstance. We just weren't prepared for this. However, last year we discharged a manager in our supplies department for major cash shortages. We first did not pay her any accumulated vacation allowance. We didn't have any definite proof that she had embezzled any funds. Because there was a lot of discussion about this case in the media—and because we wanted to avoid a possible legal hassle—we finally paid her the equivalent of ten days' pay for the six months she worked into the annual vacation period.

Marshall: You still haven't told me what you would like me to do, Mr. Peterman. Do you want me to advise you on what action you should take?

Peterman: Well, yes and no, Dr. Marshall. When the problem came to a vote last night, the board voted 5–4 to turn down the vacation pay request. But right after the vote was taken, some of the board members began having second thoughts about the decision. We don't want to be accused of being penny pinchers if Whitaker really is entitled to the vacation money. I suggested that we should contact several authorities in industry and at the university to get their opinions, and then reconsider the matter at the next board meeting. So, that's why I called you today, Professor; would you be willing to offer your view as to what we should do?

Marshall: Well, frankly, Mr. Peterman, I'm not exactly sure myself. Let me think the problem over a little while, and I'll call you back later today.

Family Values or Abuse of Benefits?

Jim Colburn sat at his desk quietly staring at the phone. He could not believe what he had just heard. Sarah Conrad just had called to tell him that she would not be coming back to work. She was to have returned that morning from her six-week paid maternity leave. Jim was Sarah's supervisor at Birch & Green P.C., a small accounting partnership with a total of eight employees. Sarah had joined the firm three years ago as a staff accountant.

Birch & Green P.C. was formed five years ago by Mike Birch and Dale Green. The firm was located in a community of approximately fifty thousand people in the Midwest. Anticipating the growth of their clientele, Birch & Green hired Jim Colburn as a staff accountant/supervisor. Along with his accounting duties, Jim was responsible for the hiring, training, and supervising of all additional staff. Sarah was the first person that Jim hired after joining the firm.

Sarah Conrad had graduated with a 3.92 grade point average from a state university in December of 1990. The following May, Sarah took and passed all sections of the Uniform CPA Examination. That summer, she married a young man whom she had dated during her senior year at the university. Although Sarah was much sought after by several of the "Big Six" accounting firms, Sarah chose to accept the offer from Birch & Green. Sarah was impressed with the firm's vision for future growth as well as the personable atmosphere of the office and the "family orientation" of the partners and Jim Colburn. Jim had told her during the employment selection interview that the firm believed that "the family should come first, work second." Sarah also liked the idea of getting in on the "ground floor" of a growing firm. She believed that the opportunity to reach the level of partner would come more quickly at a small firm.

Sarah had been a model employee for the past three years. Jim could still remember how happy everyone in the office was when Sarah announced she was pregnant. Because the firm had never dealt with a maternity situation before, Jim met with the partners to discuss the firm's policies concerning maternity leave and benefits. The partners reviewed the requirements of the 1978 Pregnancy Discrimination Act and the Family and Medical Leave Act of 1993.

This case was prepared by Charles St. Clair, Marketing and Management Instructor at Moberly (Missouri) Area Community College, and Ron Stephens, Professor of Management and Management Department Chair at Central Missouri State University at Warrensburg. Used by permission.
The names of the organization, individuals, and locations are disguised.

The 1978 Pregnancy Discrimination Act had amended Title VII of the Civil Rights Act of 1964. Under this Act, employers are not required to provide specific benefits to employees; however, if the employer does offer health insurance and temporary disability plans to employees, the employer cannot discriminate on the basis of pregnancy. Title VII of the Civil Rights Act of 1964, as amended, prohibits discrimination on the basis of race, color, religion, sex, or national origin with respect to compensation and terms, conditions or privileges of employment. Federal, state and local governments are covered by these statutes, as are private employers with fifteen or more employees.

The Family and Medical Leave Act of 1993 was the first federal mandate requiring employers to provide family benefits. This Act mandates that employers with more than fifty employees provide up to twelve weeks of unpaid job-protected leave per year for the birth or adoption of a child or the serious illness of the employee or an immediate family member. The Act also allows employers to recapture health insurance premiums paid during the leave if the employee does not return to work.

After reviewing the legislation on family benefits and maternity leave, the firm decided to offer Sarah a benefits package that would include six weeks of paid maternity leave, would allow her to take an additional six weeks of unpaid leave with continued health and medical insurance coverage, and would offer her the option to return as either a full- or part-time employee. The partners decided to offer these benefits despite the fact that they were exempt—because of size—from the Family and Medical Leave Act. Birch and Green firmly believed that "the family should come first," and they wanted to help their employees where possible. Jim Colburn also pointed out that the policy would help the firm to remain competitive in recruiting top accounting prospects.

Sarah Conrad was elated when Jim Colburn presented the benefits package to her. After discussing it with her husband, Sarah informed Jim that she planned to take the six weeks of paid leave and then return to work on a full-time basis. She had confirmed this decision several times during her pregnancy, including just before she left on maternity leave. This was the reason that Jim Colburn was so surprised when Sarah called to say that she would not be returning to work. Sarah had been in every other week, including last Friday, for the past six weeks to pick up her check, and she had never mentioned the possibility of not returning to work.

When Jim Colburn brought this news to Mike Birch and Dale Green, they all felt that Sarah Conrad had acted in bad faith. They discussed whether the company should pursue any legal or other efforts to demand that Sarah repay the income and health care premiums that she had received during the past six weeks.

The Markham Company

The Markham Company is a food-processing company with main offices in Chicago and several processing plants located in agricultural communities throughout the southwest. The processing plants operate seasonally, usually employing some two hundred people from the local community during off seasons and up to eight hundred town, country, and other temporary workers during peak periods.

You are Tom Clark, vice president in charge of human resource management at the main office in Chicago. At the processing plants, each plant superintendent has responsibility for employee and personnel matters. Each plant usually has an employment office with one or more employment clerks who interview job applicants and process necessary paperwork. The employment office also may have one or more clerks who handle payroll and other routine matters.

Costs had been high and efficiency low for several seasons at the Billings, Texas, plant. Consequently, the plant superintendent was removed, and Charlie Shire, one of the company's production vice presidents, was sent to the Billings plant to improve its record.

About a month after this change, you (Tom Clark) receive the following letter from Charlie Shire, who had taken over the Billings plant:

Dear Tom:

The company really handed me a lemon when they gave me the Billings plant here in Southern Texas. I am writing you not for the purpose of crying on your shoulder but to get some real advice as to what I should do about some of these complaints that are piling up.

As you know, this plant does not have a union, so each gripe is an individual one. If there were only a few, I'm sure that I could handle them, but everybody seems to have at least one gripe and many of the employees have several. Most of the gripes are about pay, although our rates here are generally in line with what other companies in this area are paying. In

---

All names and certain data are disguised.

fact, we're somewhat above what the local merchants and farmers pay for their help. Some of the complaints seem senseless; I can't understand them. Maybe if I give you some typical examples you can tell me what I ought to do. Compensation rates make up a substantial part of our costs, so I have been reviewing our policies and procedures very carefully.

Tim Smithies is a hopper operator. He only has one arm, but that doesn't incapacitate him for his job; it's all he needs for this position. His foreman says he was hired as a sort of favor because he can't do farm work. We pay him $.35 per hour less than other operators. He is bawling that he ought to get the same rate—feels no gratitude just to have the job. Should I boost his rate?

Luis Gomez, one of the Hispanic truck loaders, is complaining that he ought to get more than the current federal minimum wage of $4.25 per hour. Nobody here pays Hispanics more than the minimum wage of $4.25 per hour. A lot of them are probably illegal aliens anyway who are lucky to get this much in this country. Before Luis started complaining, I was thinking about hiring more and more Hispanics, since I could get them at the minimum wage rate and reduce our labor costs considerably. Do you think this would be advisable?

One of the maintenance men, Steve Stankowski, says he'll quit if I don't give him $.45 per hour more. He's already getting $.35 per hour more than the other maintenance men now, and he's not the best of the bunch. But we need him so badly right now that I may have to give it to him. I hope that the other men don't hear about it. I'll caution him to be quiet about it. If I have to make too many deals like this, I know that some of them will leak the information, and then I'll be in bad with the rest of the workers. Can you tell me any way to ensure that they don't find out?

George Chambers really presents a tough problem. He operates the large tomato canning machine, which I always thought was a fairly easy job. He claims he ought to get $.30 to $.40 per hour more because the job is so strenuous, and I don't know whether it is really a hard job or whether he just "talks a hard job." How in the devil am I supposed to know whether a job is tough or easy and how much it ought to pay? This is the only plant where we can tomatoes on this sort of machine, so I know you can't give me any comparative rates.

Mary White presents another lulu of a problem. She was peeling tomatoes at $5.35 hour last June. Her husband ran away, leaving her with four children to take care of, and my predecessor gave her a raise to $6.05 an hour. I hate to cut her back to $5.35 per hour; but if I don't, I'll probably have to pay all of the other peelers $6.05, which is too much. What do you think I ought to do? The worst of it is that she has been with the plant about 10 years now, off and on. If I had my choice I would never have hired her in the first place, because she is definitely a submarginal worker at best.

There are some indications that my predecessor here had very little "sales resistance." I know that some workers who are not too productive but very demanding are rated higher in pay than some others who do a good job but don't ask for so much. I'm afraid that some day some of these timid souls will rebel and up will go my costs. What can I do to forestall this?

As a result of a policy of giving some employees a small raise every year, I have a few old cronies here who are getting more than they are worth. Some of the other employees are complaining that they do twice as much work as these older hangers-on, but they get the same or less pay. It is a bad situation. Should I fire the old ones, reduce their pay, or what?

One of my foremen, Pete Jackson, is at my desk twice a day with a request for pay increases for one or more of his workers. I can't seem to discourage him; I wish that he were more like Mary Somers, who never bothers me but who does a good job. The trouble is, Mary's workers are grumbling because Pete got a lot of raises out of my predecessor for his workers and Mary's group didn't get any. Pete is too good a man to get rid of, or even offend. How can I discourage him in these requests—and tactfully?

These are just a few of my problems, chum! Please give me some practical suggestions by return mail about what I can do to clear the air and get people thinking about their jobs instead of about their so-called wage inequities.

As ever,
Charlie

After studying this letter, you recognize that you must write Charlie Shire a letter right away to advise him concerning how to handle the specific wage problems and the overall compensation situation at the Billings plant.

EXERCISE–20

What Is the Proper Chauffeur's Rate?

Assignment: You are the impartial arbitrator selected by the company and the union to render a final and binding decision in this matter. Your decision should include a thorough presentation of the reasoning that you used in making your determination.

BACKGROUND

The Sharon Confections Company, located in a large midwestern city, and the United Confection Workers, Local Union No. 622, had resolved all issues pertaining to a new two-year labor agreement except for one very thorny problem: the rate to be paid to "chauffeurs." The company and the union agreed to submit this one remaining issue to an impartial arbitrator, whose decision would be final and binding upon both parties.

At the time of this case, the company was primarily involved in the production and sales of quality candy and related products. The company employed some 150 persons and distributed many of its products through its own stores and other outlets in the city and its suburbs. Many of these outlets were franchise locations in shopping malls. Local 622 of the United Confection Workers (hereafter referred to as "the union") represented some 100 bargaining unit employees, mostly in the plant but also including those in the job classification of "chauffeur."

The job classification of chauffeur included only employees who were delivery truck drivers. Ordinarily, the company employed not more than one full-time and one part-time employee in this category, but at the time of the arbitration hearing, seasonal needs—just prior to the year-end holidays—required the services of two full-time and one part-time employee in this job category.

The chauffeur operated a 2 1/2-ton truck; his principal duty was the cartage of products from the employer's plant and storage areas to various retail outlets. At the factory, he loaded his truck with or without help and arranged the loads on the truck according to destination. At the retail stores, he unloaded either with or without the aid of a porter. The individual freight bundles that he handled weighed from 10 to 70 pounds. At times, he hauled items such as peanuts and oil from cold storage to the factory. The job involved not only the necessity of knowing the metropolitan area and its dif-

---

All names and certain data are disguised.

fering traffic conditions and regulations but also care in arranging the order of deliveries and arrivals of goods at proper destinations to meet business necessities of the retail outlets. The ordinary care of the delivery truck was a garage operation in which the driver had no part.

The new two-year contract provided in the first year that all other bargaining unit employees would receive a flat $.30-per-hour increase of wages over the previous rates; a further increase of $.25 per hour was to be paid in the second year. The company insisted that the chauffeur's increase should be limited to these figures. The union contended that the chauffeur's increase should be much greater.

THE COMPANY'S POSITION

In support of its position, the company furnished historical evidence of the wage rates established for the chauffeur and for certain production employees in the factory, showing a differential of $.40 per hour in favor of the chauffeur. The company showed that as wages increased over the years, the same differential was maintained in three successive contracts.

In other words, in each instance, the chauffeur received the same flat increase in hourly wage rates as did the production workers. The company's position was that this showed an industrial pattern settled and established by the parties in successive contracts.

The company further contended that to grant the chauffeur an increase of more than $.30 per hour in the first year of the contract would create inequities within its organization or within the bargaining unit. Under the company's proposal, for the first year of the contract, the chauffeur's rate would be $9.42 per hour. The parties had previously agreed upon rates of $9.02 for production workers, $9.82 for stock clerk, and $9.92 for shipping clerk. The company pointed out that stock clerks and shipping clerks usually advanced to these positions from that of chauffeur, and they enjoyed a higher wage rate in those positions because they carried more responsibility than did driving a truck. Hence, an increase of much more than $.30 for a chauffeur could almost entirely eliminate an already well-established differential favorable to jobs of more skill and responsibility and so place a junior-level job on practically the same wage level as a higher-level job. The company regarded the whole matter as a type of job evaluation already established by the prior conduct of the parties and justified on the basis of its own business knowledge as to the relative worth of the several jobs.

THE UNION'S POSITION

The union took the position that a rate of $9.42 per hour was not enough for a truck driver in a metropolitan area. Other companies in the area paid much more for their truck drivers in positions similar to that of the chauffeur. For example, the Sunshine Candy Company rate was $10.50, and Sweetheart Confections, Inc., paid $10.95. The union claimed that in the case of the Sunshine Candy Company, negotiations for an increase were now pending. In addition, the union pointed out that the prevailing wage rates of truck drivers in the metropolitan area generally were much above $9.42. Truck drivers belonging to Teamsters Union Local 873 were paid, on average, in various industries, as follows:

Grocery	$11.96
Intercity	12.85
Diesel operators	12.10
Fuel oil	12.40

In rebuttal, the company differentiated its position from that of the other candy manufacturers by pointing out that the products of the other companies primarily were machine-made and involved mass production and distribution. The average sale of the Sharon Candy Company was less than 2 pounds per item.

EXERCISE–21

Jones Manufacturing Company

BACKGROUND

Jones Manufacturing Company had a large, non union plant located outside of a small, rural city in a southern state. The company was a wholly-owned subsidiary of a major national corporation. At the time of this case, management of the Jones Company had decided to and was in the process of implementing a job-evaluation program in its plant and machine shops, based upon a widely published job-rating plan. This program was an attempt to establish more consistent relationships between hourly rates for the various jobs and, generally, to improve the company's overall wage structure.

Current job descriptions were prepared for the different jobs to be evaluated, and an "evaluation committee" assigned point ratings to them in accordance with the rating plan.[1] The evaluation committee consisted of several knowledgeable supervisors plus a staff person from the company's HR department. It then became necessary to establish a point-to-money conversion curve for determining the actual monetary job values or labor-grade rate ranges. Out of all the jobs evaluated, the actual hourly rates for thirteen were considered by the committee as properly representing current and undisputed hourly rates. It was decided, therefore, to base the intraplant wage survey on these thirteen *key* jobs, and to establish the conversion curve from this survey. After this conversion curve had been established, the hourly rates for the balance of the jobs could be determined from the various point values assigned by the committee. As a result of the survey, the table on the following page shows the job names, the point ratings assigned by the committee, and the actual hourly rates being paid at the time for these various occupations (see Exhibit E–21A).

The original version of this exercise was prepared by the late Professor H. Barrett Rogers of the Kellogg Graduate School of Management, Northwestern University. All names and certain data are disguised. Used by prior permission.

[1] For an expanded discussion of job evaluation, point rating, and conversion of point evaluations to wage scales, see Donald DeCenzo and Stephen Robbins, *Human Resource Management-4th ed.*, (New York: John Wiley & Sons, 1993), pp. 418–424.

EXHIBIT E–21A   Job Ratings

JOB NO.	JOB	POINT RATING	ACTUAL HOURLY RATE
1	Automatic screw machine operator	275	$7.50
2	Bench lathe operator	241	7.08
3	Bench work—filing and assembly	164	5.34
4	Casting grinder and polisher	209	7.26
5	Drill press operator	224	5.92
6	Milling machine operator	311	7.76
7	Machine operator (tool room)	311	8.88
8	Punch press operator	271	7.44
9	Soldering	216	5.70
10	Stores clerk	205	5.66
11	Tool crib attendant	246	7.08
12	Tool maker	381	8.82
13	Turret lathe operator	331	8.28

INSTRUCTIONS TO STUDENTS
TO SOLVE THIS PROBLEM

1. On regular linear coordinate paper (8 1/2 × 11), plot the point ratings as the independent (X) variable along the 11-inch side of the paper, and the corresponding hourly rates as the dependent (Y) variable along the 8 1/2-inch side of the paper. Start both scales from zero in the lower left-hand corner and allow one-half inch for each 25 points and each $1.00. Since the money values are "actual" hourly rates, the points will not fall on a smooth curve; therefore, a "line of average relationship" must be determined.

   If this wage curve were to include the entire range of wages and salaries, from the lowest grade of common labor to high executive salaries, the line of average relationship would take the form of an upward curve with a gradually increasing slope as the point values increased. The actual direct labor wages in the typical factory represent only a relatively small range, and for this smaller range, a linear or straight line approximation is satisfactory for practical application. The general equation for a straight line is:

$$Y = a + bX$$

where Y is the monetary hourly rate that corresponds to any specific point value X. The method of least squares should be used in finding the mathematical equation of this line. To do this, Exhibit E–21B should be filled in first.

   The table values then should be substituted into the following equations, which are to be solved simultaneously to find the values (a) and (b):

Equation (1): $(\Sigma Y) = aN + b(\Sigma X)$

Equation (2): $(\Sigma XY) = a(\Sigma X) + b(\Sigma X^2)$

Submit your calculations with this problem.

EXHIBIT E–21B

JOB NO.	(X) POINT RATE	(Y) HOURLY RATE	(X × Y)	(X²)
1	275	$7.50	( )	( )
2	241	7.08	( )	( )
3	164	5.34	( )	( )
4	209	7.26	( )	( )
5	224	5.92	( )	( )
6	311	7.76	( )	( )
7	311	8.88	( )	( )
8	271	7.44	( )	( )
9	216	5.70	( )	( )
10	205	5.66	( )	( )
11	246	7.08	( )	( )
12	381	8.82	( )	( )
13	331	8.28	( )	( )
Totals (N = 13)	( ) (ΣX)	( ) (ΣY)	( ) (ΣXY)	( ) (ΣX²)

Using the values of (a) and (b) thus calculated, write the equation for the straight-line wage curve:

Equation (3):   Hourly Rates = (a) + (b) × Point Value,

showing your calculated values in place of (a) and (b).

Substitute point values of (100) and (300) into Equation (3) and calculate the corresponding hourly rates. Plot these two points on the graph and draw a straight line through them, extending the line until it intersects the (Y) axis. This intersection should agree with the (a) value. Show Equation (3) on the graph.

2. Using this equation, determine the rate range for each labor grade by calculating the minimum and maximum monetary hourly rates (see Exhibit E–21C) for the corresponding minimum and maximum point values for each of the ten labor grades, and fill in the table, showing the hourly rates to the nearest cent.

3. Calculate equations for rate range "limit" lines. The upper limit line should be 10 percent above the "mean" line represented by Equation (3), and this limit line equation may be calculated from the (a) and (b) values in Equation (3).

Upper Limit Rate = 1.10(a) + 1.10(b) Point Value.

The lower limit line should be 10 percent below the "mean" line, and its equation may be calculated as

Lower Limit Rate = .90(a) + .90(b) Point Value.

EXHIBIT E–21C

| GRADE | POINT RANGE | | HOURLY RATE RANGE | |
	MINIMUM	MAXIMUM	MINIMUM*	MAXIMUM*
10	162	183	( )	( )
9	184	205	( )	( )
8	206	227	( )	( )
7	228	249	( )	( )
6	250	271	( )	( )
5	272	293	( )	( )
4	294	315	( )	( )
3	316	337	( )	( )
2	338	359	( )	( )
1	360	381	( )	( )

*Since the least squares equation describes an "average" trend-line through the scatter diagram of actual rates, this trend-line is equivalent to an "arithmetic mean." The calculated minimum and maximum rates are thus "minimum-mean rates" and "maximum-mean rates" for the respective labor grades.

Draw these limit lines (dotted) on the graph and show their equations.

Next, construct "rectangles" on the graph to show the entire rate range for each of the labor grades. To construct the "rectangles," do the following: Starting from the lowest rate on the lower limit line, corresponding to the minimum point value of a grade, draw a horizontal line across the grade, *left* to *right*. This lowest rate (below the lower limit line) becomes the "base" rate for the grade. Starting from the highest rate on the upper limit line, corresponding to the maximum point value of the grade, draw a horizontal line across the grade, *right* to *left*. Although varying with differing point spreads for the several grades, this method of constructing the rectangles automatically gives roughly two-thirds overlap of the rate ranges for consecutive grades. (Smaller overlaps can be achieved through arbitrary policy decisions.) Each labor grade thus will have a rate range in which the maximum rate is roughly 25 percent to 30 percent higher than the minimum (or base) rate.

4. In Exhibit E–21D, for each occupational number, check whether the present rate is inside or outside the established rate range as indicated by the rectangles. Calculate the theoretically correct hourly rate for each job by substituting the job point rating into the hourly rate equation (3). Then show the differences between the theoretically correct rate and the actual rate now being paid, and in front of each "difference" indicate by a (+) or (–), respectively, whether the present base rate should be raised or lowered to bring it into line.

5. Write up an outline of instructions for making any adjustments that you consider necessary at the present time or that may develop in the future in regard to base rates that are, or may become, out of line. Submit your outline with the rest of the problem.

JOB NO.	RATE WITHIN RATE RANGE	RATE OUTSIDE RATE RANGE	POINT RATING	PRESENT ACTUAL RATE	THEORETICALLY CORRECT RATE FROM EQUATION	AMOUNT DIFFERENCE (+) OR (−)
1	( )	( )	275	$7.50	( )	( )
2	( )	( )	241	7.08	( )	( )
3	( )	( )	164	5.34	( )	( )
4	( )	( )	209	7.26	( )	( )
5	( )	( )	224	5.92	( )	( )
6	( )	( )	311	7.76	( )	( )
7	( )	( )	311	8.88	( )	( )
8	( )	( )	271	7.44	( )	( )
9	( )	( )	216	5.70	( )	( )
10	( )	( )	205	5.66	( )	( )
11	( )	( )	246	7.08	( )	( )
12	( )	( )	381	8.82	( )	( )
13	( )	( )	331	8.28	( )	( )

WAREHOUSE APPLICATION?

Soon after the job evaluation program was installed, the warehouse foreman, Al Raymond, called at the human resources office asking for help about a report he had received from the evaluation committee. The evaluation committee also had studied jobs in the warehouse department along with Al Raymond and had assigned point values to various warehouse jobs as a first step in bringing these jobs into alignment with the overall company compensation program.

Raymond stated that in the past he had received numerous complaints about wage rates in his department. "It's not my fault these rates are all fouled up. I've only been foreman for two years—and we've always had this mess!" With this comment, Raymond presented to the HR director the data that he had received from the evaluation committee (see Exhibit E–21E).

"Okay," said Raymond, "I know something should be done to get some of these rates in line, but what? Frankly, I don't trust these point values any more than I do the whole job evaluation program!"

EXHIBIT E–21E Warehouse Department

JOBS	POINT VALUES	AVERAGE PRESENT WAGE
Foreman (management)		$1,650 per month
Assistant foreman (nonmanagement)	400	9.50 per hour
Lift truck operator	206	7.70 per hour
Shipping clerk	315	6.20 per hour
Stocker	246	5.20 per hour
Loaders	175	4.60 per hour

EXERCISE–22

The Salary Equity Question at Midwest Valley University

You are Dr. Jordan Temple, an assistant professor of marketing research and statistics at the College of Business of Midwest Valley University. You have just met in your office with Dr. Mildred Carrie, an assistant professor of accounting at your school. Dr. Carrie is one of five women professors in the school who are planning to meet in the near future with the dean of the College of Business in order to discuss their concerns; their primary concern is salary inequity.

In preparation for their discussion with the dean, Dr. Carrie has asked you to conduct some statistical tests on the salary and personnel data that are shown in Table E–22, along with some additional information. Dr. Carrie told you that since Midwest Valley University is a state public university, salary data were available in the university library reference section as part of the state's annual budget report. This state budget report included recent merit pay increases, which were reflected in the listed salaries. A separate salary data publication by the university was used to obtain information about the ranks of the full-time faculty (assistant, associate, or full professor) and the number of years each professor had been at the university. Data were based on when each professor joined the university and were not adjusted for sabbaticals and other leaves of absence. (Since salaries in this university publication did not reflect recent merit increases, they were not used in the analysis.) Information regarding the possession of a doctorate or not was gathered from a recent university catalog that listed professors, degrees earned, schools earned from, and the dates earned.

Dr. Carrie further indicated that the remaining data were collected via her personal observation. Gender, race, minority, and department data were collected on the professors in the College of Business. *Race* referred to Caucasian or non-Caucasian, whereas *minority* referred to women and/or non-Caucasians or Caucasian men. Professors were identified as belonging to one of four departments (accounting, finance/law, information sciences, or management/marketing).

In your meeting with her, Dr. Carrie cited a recent publication of the American Assembly of Collegiate Schools of Business (AACSB), which included a survey report on gender and business school faculty pay. The AACSB

This case was prepared by Dr. Jeff W. Totten, Food Marketing Specialist at the Food Processing Center of the University of Nebraska at Grand Island. The names of all individuals and the locations are disguised. Used by permission.

TABLE E–22 Business School Data for Analyses

SALARY	GENDER	RACE	DEGREE	RANK	MINORITY	YEARS
Accounting Department						
$51,400	Male	Caucasian	Masters	Associate	No	29
66,000	Male	Caucasian	Doctorate	Full	No	28
51,800	Female	Caucasian	Doctorate	Associate	Yes	13
54,900	Male	Non-Cauc.	Doctorate	Assistant	Yes	4
42,500	Male	Caucasian	Masters	Associate	No	24
55,400	Male	Caucasian	Doctorate	Associate	No	17
62,700	Female	Non-Cauc.	Doctorate	Full	Yes	15
49,600	Male	Caucasian	Doctorate	Associate	No	23
44,000	Male	Caucasian	Masters	Associate	No	27
Information Systems Department						
$69,900	Male	Caucasian	Doctorate	Full	No	22
51,500	Male	Caucasian	Doctorate	Assistant	No	9
56,500	Male	Caucasian	Doctorate	Assistant	No	2
54,500	Male	Caucasian	Doctorate	Assistant	No	6
54,000	Female	Caucasian	Doctorate	Associate	Yes	8
57,900	Male	Caucasian	Doctorate	Assistant	No	3
59,000	Male	Non-Cauc.	Doctorate	Full	Yes	12
51,200	Female	Caucasian	Doctorate	Assistant	Yes	7
64,000	Male	Caucasian	Doctorate	Full	No	31
65,200	Male	Non-Cauc.	Doctorate	Full	Yes	15
Finance/Law Department						
$68,400	Male	Caucasian	Doctorate	Full	No	17
64,800	Male	Caucasian	Doctorate	Full	No	23
36,700	Male	Caucasian	J.D./Mast.	Assistant	No	7
55,700	Male	Caucasian	Doctorate	Associate	No	6
44,800	Male	Caucasian	J.D./Mast.	Associate	No	9
60,500	Male	Caucasian	Doctorate	Assistant	No	3
64,600	Male	Caucasian	Doctorate	Full	No	21
35,600	Female	Caucasian	J.D./Mast.	Assistant	Yes	7
64,000	Male	Caucasian	Doctorate	Full	No	24
60,000	Male	Caucasian	Doctorate	Associate	No	4
Management/Marketing Department						
$74,000	Male	Caucasian	Doctorate	Full	No	22
55,000	Male	Caucasian	Doctorate	Assistant	No	3
49,500	Male	Caucasian	Doctorate	Assistant	No	6
58,400	Male	Caucasian	Doctorate	Associate	No	10
51,600	Female	Caucasian	Doctorate	Assistant	Yes	3
65,700	Male	Caucasian	Doctorate	Full	No	17
52,600	Male	Caucasian	Doctorate	Associate	No	8
66,300	Male	Caucasian	Doctorate	Full	No	24
48,000	Male	Caucasian	ABD/Mast.	Assistant	No	2
65,000	Male	Caucasian	Doctorate	Full	No	19
53,900	Male	Non-Cauc.	Doctorate	Associate	Yes	4
49,600	Male	Non-Cauc.	Doctorate	Assistant	Yes	6
49,900	Male	Caucasian	Doctorate	Assistant	No	7
63,200	Male	Caucasian	Doctorate	Associate	No	16

salary survey showed that women professors, associate professors, and assistant professors earned 87.9 percent, 96.4 percent, and 96.3 percent, respectively, of the salaries as a whole for each rank.[1]

Dr. Carrie has requested that you statistically analyze the data she has provided you and to let her know your findings within the next ten days.

---

[1]"Gender and Faculty Pay: Mixed Progress Toward Equity," *AACSB Newsline*, (Winter 1993), pp. 4–5.

PART SIX

Employee Representation and Labor Relations

Cases

EXPERIENTIAL EXERCISES

An important aspect of human resource management involves employees and employers having agreements and understandings about the wide array of matters affecting conditions and accomplishment of the organization's work. Among these, for example, are: how work is to be assigned, how jobs are to be filled, how employees are to be disciplined and rewarded, and how disagreements should be handled. All organizations necessarily face these questions, and, for a segment of the workforce, they are worked out through a representational system—employee representatives who meet with employer representatives to resolve issues that are significant to both parties.

For about one-sixth of the U.S. workforce, employee-employer issues are handled under agreements negotiated by labor unions (or employee associations) and management representatives. Union/management relationships are often reported about in the newspapers or on television. It is noteworthy that union-management confrontations and problems of unionized companies still receive considerable attention, even though union membership as a percentage of the labor force has declined significantly since the 1960s.

As of the mid-1990s, union membership in the United States comprised approximately 16 million workers. Complex events have combined to limit the power and influence of unions. Recessions, rising costs, and global competition have resulted in layoffs and downsizing. In many manufacturing industries, such pressures have meant lost jobs and lost union membership. Occupations and industries experiencing gains in recent years are those employing higher numbers of white-collar, technically trained people, service employees, and women—all categories that unions have had difficulty organizing. Further, as economic pressures have mounted, nonunion employers have been more aggressive in resisting union organizing efforts. Unionized employers have been willing to grant union employees only modest or few gains at the negotiating table, and many have negotiated concessions particularly in reducing certain employee benefits.

These recent pressures and trends have brought about reorientation in some labor-management relationships. Competition and productivity have begun to play a more important part in negotiations. Management is focusing more on work-rule simplification, and unions seek better job-security provisions. Strikes have generally lost their effectiveness as a means for conflict resolution. Cooperative labor-management efforts such as total quality management (TQM) and quality-of-work-life programs appear to be spreading, and emphasis on work teams appears to be gaining acceptance. While adversarial-type bargaining will not disappear, adaptation and accommodation seem to characterize more and more labor-management relationships.

Some nonunion firms pay wages and salaries and pursue employee relations policies comparable to or exceeding those of unionized firms. Many have developed effective problem-solving, communication, and grievance-handling processes. In both union and nonunion settings, more emphasis is being devoted to training supervisors and managers in applications of behavioral research to foster communication, improve teamwork, and develop better interpersonal relationships. This is a recognition that people at work want a voice in their work life, desire open communication, wish to be respected, and prefer a positive working environment. These will be over-riding considerations in the years ahead, in both nonunion and unionized firms alike.

The cases and exercises of Part Six primarily focus on varied aspects of employer-employee relationships in unionized firms and attempts by unions to organize employees in nonunion settings. Nevertheless, the human aspects of the case situations presented in Part Six are usually applicable to most nonunionized organizations as well.

CASE–51

McGrath Hospital: The Organizing Committee

McGrath Hospital was a large, private, nonprofit hospital in New York City. It had a national reputation as a medical center. In the past four years, there had been three serious but unsuccessful attempts to unionize the hourly employees of the hospital. These attempts had been made by outside union organizers attempting to obtain signatures for an election.

Recently, five employees from the laundry and six from the kitchen formed a committee to organize a union for the hospital. They felt that most of the hourly employees wanted and needed union representation for collective bargaining of wages, hours of work, work conditions, and shift assignments. The committee wasn't sure if it should form its own union or affiliate with a national one. The local business representative for a national union, Harry Brown, was contacted. He had previously attempted to unionize the hospital. He presented the pros and cons of a local hospital union and of an affiliation with a national union. He offered his services "with no strings attached." After several meetings, the committee decided it was better to affiliate with the national union because of the organizational backing it could provide. Members of the committee actively solicited the comments of most of the employees they contacted concerning the unionization question. Many favored the idea of a union, and the other people contacted were noncommittal.

Initially, three members of the committee orally notified the personnel director, Pete Watson, of their intent to unionize the hospital. He requested a formal meeting with the entire committee in his office on a Friday to discuss the reasons for unionization. Watson tried to persuade the committee through discussion against this unionization attempt. He emphasized that it was for the good of the hospital and the patients not to have a union. The committee members concluded the meeting with the understanding that they were going to attempt to unionize the hospital and contact the employees at the main entrances at shift changes.

On Monday, committee members, with the support of other employees, began handing out unionization literature to all employees at the three main entrances to the hospital at the beginning of the first and second shifts and at the close of the third shift. Several of the older hourly employees complained to their supervisors that these individuals, and they named them, had asked

This case was prepared by Professor Thomas L. Wheelen of the College of Business Administration of the University of South Florida in Tampa. All names are disguised. Used by permission.

them to sign cards to hold an election for a union. They said they weren't sure what this meant, and they weren't about to read the literature. Other staff members complained to the personnel office that they were slowed up in leaving or reporting to their jobs because of the congestion around the main entrance. The personnel manager, after receiving complaints for a week, issued the following letter to all employees.

To: All Hospital Employees
From: Peter Watson, Personnel Director
Subject: Unionization Activities

During the past few days, several of our employees have come to us and complained about being pestered on their way to work by people passing out union handbooks and other union propaganda and asking for their signatures on union cards.

We are sorry that our people are being subjected to this kind of annoyance at this time. However, we want to make our position absolutely clear. We sincerely believe that it is in the best interest of all our employees, as well as the patients under our care, to keep this union out of our hospital. Our hospital is not perfect—no hospital is—but we believe that any problems we have can be worked out between ourselves, face to face, on a fair and honest basis, without the disruption and bickering that this union could bring on the scene.

During the coming weeks you can expect to see more union propaganda, more campaign promises, and more attempts by union organizers to get you to sign a union card. We ask you to think very carefully before putting your signature on any union card. These cards have been used by unions to gain representation.

Why do they want your signature? Why sign a blank check for a bunch of strangers?

If you have any questions on this or any other matter, please contact your supervisor.

The committee members were working when they read the letter. One member said, "Who does he think he is? I am no stranger, and I don't try to mislead my friends." Dave Burns, chairman of the committee, called Pete Watson and asked for an immediate meeting concerning the letter. Watson replied, "I can't meet you today since I will be tied up in a meeting in town until 5 o'clock, so let's meet tomorrow in my office at 3 o'clock." Dave Burns said he felt the issue was important enough that the committee would stay and meet with Watson after 5 P.M., even though most of the members worked on the first shift. Watson said, "I am not sure when the meeting will end, and we can handle it tomorrow without any problem." Burns said he felt the letter was unfair and uncalled for. In total, the members of the committee had 157 years service to the hospital; they felt being called "strangers" was underhanded. Pete Watson interrupted and said, "Let's discuss this in my office tomorrow when we have time and can see each other face to face." Dave Burns concurred and hung up the phone.

When Dave Burns communicated this to the other members of the organizing committee, they all felt insulted that Watson would not meet with them that day. One said, "He did the damage and now he hides. What do you want to bet that he will postpone our meeting." Another said, "He chooses 3 o'clock so that we can't be out at the entrance trying to talk with our fellow employees. That was a cute trick to choose the end of the first shift as a meeting time." They contacted Harry Brown, the national union business representative. Brown told them to "hold their ground," and he would attend the meeting if they so desired. They asked him to be at the personnel manager's office for the meeting.

On the next day at 3 P.M., the committee members, along with Harry Brown, appeared at the personnel manager's outer office. His secretary announced them and opened the door to Pete Watson's office. Watson recognized Brown and said, "What is Mr. Brown doing here? You didn't mention he was going to attend. You asked for a meeting with me and your committee. I don't see why we need his services."

Management Persuasion of Potential Union Members

Cahen Mills, a large textile corporation in the southeastern portion of the United States, was interviewing applicants for an open position of machine operator. The company had thirty machine operators in its plant.

The company had in recent months been hearing rumors that the machine operators wanted to form a union because of inadequate pay for the jobs they performed. (This job was a specialized type position in the industry.) When Wesley Hall, president of the company, was informed of this rumor, he quickly put out the word to all supervisors to try to squash this effort. He also stated to his human resources director, Arthur Jones, that the vacant position should be filled by an applicant "with no prior record of union membership."

Art Jones tried to recruit a candidate who would comply with Hall's request. But after several weeks, the only job applicant to possess all other necessary qualifications had prior union affiliations. Jones was very upset about this, because he had a candidate who was suitable except for his union past. This man's name was Bill Swigart.

Art Jones, in a worried state, went to Mr. Hall and described the circumstances. Hall flatly refused to consider hiring an individual with prior union affiliation, even if it meant hiring one with less ability and experience.

Art Jones continued to advertise for several more weeks without success. Bill Swigart—the earlier candidate with prior union experience—noticed in a newspaper ad that the company was still in need of help. Swigart called Jones to ask why he had not been awarded the position. Swigart knew that he had all the qualifications and that because of the unique required skills for this position, not too many candidates could be recruited. Jones told Swigart that he wanted to talk to him about the possibility of hiring him for the job; however, he wanted to clear up some matters first.

Bill Swigart came in the next day. Art Jones proceeded to say that Swigart could have the job on the condition that he would not try to organize or bring in a union. Jones said that the company president was very anti-union, and that he would hire no new employees with prior union backgrounds. Art Jones then stated that he would pay Swigart a higher wage than any of his counterparts if Swigart would refrain from any union activities. Swigart readily agreed to the terms, since he had just moved into town and he needed a job.

This case was prepared by Professor Kenneth A. Kovach Ph.D., of the School of Business Administration of George Mason University in Fairfax, Virginia. All names are disguised. Used by permission.

Art Jones was very happy that Swigart willingly accepted his terms. Jones thought that because of this, Mr. Hall would agree with what he had done. Since Hall was out of town temporarily, Jones went ahead and hired Swigart at the higher rate.

Several weeks later, Wesley Hall happened to be going over the payroll computer printout sheet when he came across the machine operators' payroll and noticed a discrepancy in the operators' pay rates. He immediately called the accounting department and asked what was going on. Hall was told that Art Jones had sanctioned a higher pay rate for Bill Swigart. Wesley Hall immediately called Jones and asked him why he had done this without prior approval. Jones explained the circumstances surrounding the higher wages and said that his scheme was working well. Mr. Hall, still very unhappy with the whole situation, called the accounting department and told them that as of now Bill Swigart would earn the same wage as the other machine operators.

When Swigart learned of this, he requested a meeting with Mr. Hall. Hall refused and instructed his supervisors to start writing up Swigart for any and everything they could think of. As a result of this, Bill Swigart later told Art Jones that he no longer was obligated to keep his agreement about not attempting to organize a union among the machine operators. Swigart also told Jones that unless his higher wage rate was restored, he would immediately begin to organize a union.

Filmore Electric Company (B):
The Assembly Department

At the time of this case, the assembly department of Filmore Electric Company was divided into three major sections. The largest was Section A—known as the "line"—where approximately seventy-five employees assembled standard sizes of fractional horsepower motors. Several units within Section A produced subassemblies, and others completed the final assemblies of various standard motors produced for stock. The other two sections each employed about twenty-five workers. Section B produced small motors from 1/500 to 1/3000 horsepower in size, and Section C handled special and custom-made motors. Because of the delicate nature of the work and the large number of manual operations in small-motor assembly, only the "line" had been able to adopt modified production-line techniques. About two-thirds of the employees were women, and this ratio was approximately the same in each section. About 15 percent of the employees were African American.

THE INCENTIVES PROGRAM

John Bosch, an industrial engineer assigned to the department, had completed job descriptions and job evaluations for all the regular positions in the department. The jobs were evaluated and base wage rates were established in accordance with the company's point-rating system of job evaluation. It required about one day per week for John to maintain and operate the job-evaluation program because of changes in operations and innovations in products and procedures. With the assistance of a time-study clerk who usually worked in other departments, John also had standardized a number of operations in the assembly work and had instituted a wage-incentive program. Using a 100-percent time-premium incentive plan, individual standards and incentive rates were established for approximately 60 percent of the jobs in the "line" section and 20 to 30 percent of the operations in Sections B and C.

Only a few employees in the department were able to work full-time on wage-incentive jobs. Most of the assemblers could work on incentive jobs for part of each day, but several employees spent full time on tasks that had not been standardized and for which no incentive rates had been established. Most of these day-work jobs, without opportunities for earning incentive pay,

---

All names and places are disguised. See Case–10 for background information.

were in Sections B and C where the work was highly specialized and did not lend itself to standardization. The wage-incentive plan had been in operation for only a few months, but already John Bosch and the departmental foreman, Henry Freitel, had received many complaints from employees who felt that it was unfair for them to be on jobs that did not permit incentive earnings. In general, base rates for assemblers in Sections B and C were 10 to 20 percent above those of assemblers on the "line." Even with these differentials, most Section A assemblers with lower base rates and incentive jobs received more take-home pay than those with higher base rates and no opportunities to earn bonuses.

John Bosch believed it was not feasible to significantly increase the percentage of operations in the department that were standardized and on the wage-incentive program. The frequent changes in styles, sizes, and speeds of the smaller motors assembled in Section B and the custom-order nature of operations in Section C made it practically impossible to put many of the jobs in these sections on standards.

In an attempt to reduce some of the employee complaints, John began to work toward establishing standard operations for certain subassembly work in Sections B and C, with standard times varying with the sizes of materials. John's objective was to make it possible for more of the assemblers to spend at least part of their time on incentive operations. One of John's first attempts in this direction was to improve and standardize a soldering operation in Section B. A job the assemblers referred to as "pig-tailing" involved soldering a small spiral wire to a very small motor brush. After reviewing the method used by the assemblers—the operation seldom had runs of more than two or three hours in length,—John developed a fixture for the soldering iron so that it would be mounted vertically and directly in front of the operator. He developed another fixture consisting of two small bins that delivered the spiral wires and the brushes or metal parts to which the wires were soldered. Another improvement in this operation was the development of a drop delivery chute for the completed "pig-tailing" assembly. The chute permitted the operator to slide the finished part off the table into a delivery chute with minimum effort.

After training Mary Horton in the new method for this soldering job, John timed the operation carefully and established a standard time and an incentive rate. About a month later, John learned that only two or three assemblers had performed the new operation, and then for only about eight to ten hours per week. In discussing his problems with the chief engineer, John pointed out that the standards on the "pig-tailing" job permitted a few women to earn a bonus of several dollars, but from the company's point of view it was a marginal incentive job. John's comment was, "It is doubtful if the cost savings will ever pay for the time and trouble we've spent in studying the job."

A CONVERSATION WITH MARY HORTON

As John Bosch was walking through Section B one morning, he stopped at Mary Horton's bench and asked, "How's the pig-tailing job this morning, Mary?" The following conversation took place.

Horton: "Hi, John. I've only been at it for two hours, and I don't have much left to do. We all like this new stand you fixed up for the soldering iron, but we're not sure that these wooden fixtures are so good. Maybe we'll get used to them."

Bosch: "See how it works, Mary, and let me know if you have any trouble. And let me give you a tip. When you put that soldering paste on with that little paddle, you could save some time if you just used your little finger. Just daub the paste on with your finger and never bother with the paddle."

Horton: "What? You want me to put my finger in that old pot of grease? That's terrible! This job is dirty enough without making us handle that stuff."

Bosch: "It's up to you, Mary. We wouldn't reduce the time standard and expect you to put the paste on with your finger. But I'm just suggesting you could go a little faster, make a little more bonus, if you used your finger."

Horton: "Not me, John. I could get dermatitis from that stuff. Besides, what's the big hurry, anyway? It isn't worth it for what we get for it."

Bosch: "I see you have that new woman, Georgia, on pig-tailing now."

Horton: "Yes, we call her Peaches, and she likes this job. She used to be a beauty operator, and she says these pig-tails remind her of pinning up curls. She's a lot of fun and she's really fast. Henry says she's made standard faster than anyone he's seen in a long time."

Bosch: "I thought Henry said some of the women around here didn't like Georgia."

Horton: "Oh, he's probably talking about those "baby boomers" over there on the 'line.' We call those gals at the bench by the wall baby boomers. They never wear hose to work and the things they do are terrible! They're not so young either—in fact, one's a grandmother. They don't really like any of us here in Section B because we dress well and we put on aprons at work. Those kids wear terrible clothes and never use aprons. It's too bad, but right now they're picking on Peaches."

Bosch: "What have they got against her?"

Horton: "Oh, Jean over there thinks she can get Peaches into the union. They really go after her."

Bosch: "Doesn't anyone at this bench belong to the union?"

Horton: "No, only Marge—and she only joined because her husband is shop steward at some plant and practically made her. She's really against the union just like the rest of us back here."

Bosch: "It's none of my business—but I don't see how they can bother someone like Georgia."

Horton: "Oh, they try all right. The other day Jean and two other organizers had Peaches in the cafeteria trying to get her to sign a union card. They work on all the new women that way—promising them everything and filling them with everything imaginable. They're really giving us the works these days about the money we should be making over here. But Peaches swears that she won't join a union and she'll quit her job first. Apparently she had some trouble with another union when she had her own beauty parlor."

Bosch: "Well, I can be thankful for one thing. This union business is none of my worry. I've got enough to do with time standards around here."

With that remark, John Bosch left Mary Horton and walked down the aisle.

A CONVERSATION WITH HENRY FREITEL

Later in the afternoon, John Bosch was talking with Henry Freitel, the senior departmental foreman.

Bosch: "Mary Horton tells me you have a hot organizing campaign going on for the union now, Hank."

Freitel: "Yeah—it's getting to be a mess. Every time some new woman goes to the washroom, Jean and a couple of others take off after her, and no telling what goes on behind those closed doors. Sometimes the women complain about the trouble they have. And I know a lot of them sign the union cards just to get Jean off their backs."

Bosch: "But Mary tells me that the new woman, Georgia, in Section B and some of the others don't really want to join up. How many members do you figure the union has now?"

Freitel: "I'm not sure, but I think they've got almost three-fourths of the people on the line, and I just don't know how many in Sections B and C. You know, John, I think they're using this incentive plan of yours as an excuse for raising hell. The people on the line are complaining that we're not paying enough bonus money and that more jobs should be put on incentive. They're riding the workers in B and C about the fact that assemblers on the line make more money, and then they're saying that a union would see to it that this whole thing would be straightened out.

"I really think that much of the trouble is just a plain difference in people. Those jobs on the line are dirty and monotonous. But those women back there in B and C are ladylike. They don't want to get their hands too dirty, and they don't want to join a union. Actually, they add a little class to our department. They're always neat and clean. I'd hate to see them forced into the union if they don't want to join. On the other hand, it may not be long before the union could win an election."

Bosch: "Well, how much time can this Jean spend running around the department trying to get people to join the union?"

Freitel: "I don't really know. But I talked to her and the women at her bench the other day—and they just don't like Mary and the women over in B and C. I told them flatly that they weren't supposed to sign up people for the union on company time. They know I'm watching them all the time, but apparently they don't care. If I tried to fire someone for trying to organize a union, I'd probably get into trouble. Besides, most of the organizing seems to be done in the washroom. I can't stop her from doing whatever she wants to in there!"

Bosch: "Does Jean get paid for all this work she does for the union?"

Freitel: "I think they've told her that if the union is recognized, she can be the shop steward. I suppose she would get her own dues paid for collecting from the others. Jean has a lot of enthusiasm, and that whole gang at the benches along the wall are all hepped up about the union. Sometimes I think it would be better if we just accepted the union and got rid of all this wrangling and organizing business. The Electrical Union is really not so bad. The men in the machine shop have their union, and I don't see that they have as much trouble with it as we do without it."

Bosch: "I'll tell you one thing, Hank. If the union gets in this department, the old man and the brass in the front office aren't going to like it. It's pretty well known that the boss thinks we can operate better and cheaper without a union."

Freitel: "Who knows? As it is now, I have employees fussing at each other, bickering and scrapping among themselves—all because of this. Maybe a union could settle this place down. You know, I met the union agent the other day outside the plant handing out literature. I talked with him, and he's really not a bad fellow. But, of course, he tries to make our people think that they're going to get their pay doubled by joing the union. And then some of the stuff his hand-outs say about the management is just foolishness. He says we're trying to run a sweatshop, bleeding every last ounce of energy out of people without paying them in return. Frankly, it's a hell of a situation. I don't know why anyone wants to be a foreman in a place like this, and I've been here for twenty-five years."

Bosch: "Hank, I've got to get back to my own work—all I can say is that I sympathize with you."

Filmore Electric Company (C): Communications during a Union Organizational Campaign

The following notices were among those distributed to employees by both the Filmore Electric Company and the International Electrical Workers Union during the organizational campaign conducted by the union.

Company Letter

February 18, 19XX

To Our Employees:

We have been asked by some of our employees to advise them as to their rights concerning labor unions and other matters of employment. The following statement is sent to each employee to clear up any misunderstandings concerning our policies pertaining to these subjects. These policies, which have been the same for many years and which are based on sound principles, will not be changed.

1. The company has paid wages as high as those prevailing for our industry in our locality. Wage rates are being reviewed periodically and revisions made based on merit and existing conditions. Hours of work have been given careful consideration at all times and are in full compliance with any laws regulating same.
2. Our endeavor has been to give continuous employment whenever conditions warranted. Our record in this respect speaks for itself.
3. It has been the policy of the company, as far as it is feasible, to make promotions from the ranks based on ability, loyalty, and seniority.
4. All employees have the privilege to present any suggestions or grievances to the management and can expect them to be given careful consideration.
5. You are protected by law as to your right to join or refuse to join a labor union. No employee or group of employees belonging to a union will receive any added benefits or preferences over nonunion employees. The solicitation

---

All names and places are disguised. See Cases C–10 and C–53 for background information.

of labor-union memberships or the collection of dues or fees on company time or property is prohibited.

6. It has been and will continue to be the policy of this company in dealing with its employees to act without any discrimination because of the employee's affiliation or nonaffiliation with any labor union. Membership in any organization—religious, fraternal, or labor—has not been and will not be a requisite of employment by this company. In other words, the plant will continue to be operated as a plant where any person can work as long as he or she applies himself or herself to his or her job, and there is work to do.

As a business institution, we have always sought the good will of our employees and have requested their cooperation to the end that the business may be successful and thereby benefit all. In the past we have received your wholehearted cooperation with the result that at the end of the year, for the last five years, it has been possible to give each employee a substantial bonus. Your cooperation has enabled us to do this. Let us continue this fine teamwork.

Sincerely,
Filmore Electric Company
C. J. Filmore
President

Union Letter

February 25, 19XX

To All Employees of the Filmore Electric Company:

To have the following questions answered to your satisfaction by competent representatives of the International Electrical Workers Union, attend the
MASS MEETING
Tuesday, March 5, 19XX
2:30 P.M. for night workers and 6:30 P.M. for day workers at 225 South Market Boulevard.

1. How does the company figure your piece work?
2. After the rate is set, does it remain as is?
3. If you can't make out, what does the time-study department do for you?
4. When you make a set-up, how are you paid?

5. Have your rates been cut?
6. Have you a guaranteed piece-work rate?
7. Does the time-study person lay the watch down while he or she is timing you?
8. Are the jobs timed from floor to floor or bench to bench?
9. Do you have anything to say about your rate?
10. What is done when you claim your rate is not fair?
11. When a rate is put on a job, has the operator anything to say if it isn't satisfactory?
12. What pay do you receive when time is lost due to no fault of your own?

These and many more questions can be answered at these meetings and *can be eliminated* by an agreement under the banner of the International Electrical Workers Union.

Remember: You will approve this agreement before it is submitted to the company—and a committee selected by you will sit in on all these conferences.

Remember: The International Electrical Workers Union would never have lived for seventy-five years and have a membership of 750,000 with thousands of *written and signed agreements* if we were not doing our job to the *satisfaction of the membership.*

Remember: The International Electrical Workers Union is a democratic organization, and the membership has absolute control of it.

Remember: It is your duty to join these organizations and help protect your rights and the rights of all men and women who work.

It is our goal to have an election in the plant in which you will have an opportunity to cast your secret vote to guarantee your rights on the job through the bargaining agency of this great labor organization.

Organizing Committee
International Electrical Workers Union, District 15
Affiliated with the AFL–CIO

Company Letter

March 11, 19XX

To Our Employees:

Within the last few days, many of our employees have asked us what the position of our company is on union membership and whether or not it is going to be necessary for them to sign up with a union for them to continue to work here. In view of these questions, we feel that our employees are entitled to know just where they stand and what our policies are. The following statement is sent to each of you to make your and our positions clear. These policies have been the same for many years, and they will continue to be our policies because they are based on sound principles.

1. Each of you is protected in your job by your ability to do your work with due consideration for your length of service. Your opportunity for advancement is based on merit.
2. It is our policy to pay wages as high as those prevailing in this locality for our industry. To ensure fairness to all in establishing wage rates, we have had in operation for several years a job-rating program under which all jobs have been carefully analyzed as to the skill, education, experience, and physical demand required. Rate ranges have been established for the various labor grades, and they are constantly monitored for fairness and equity. However, through our foresight in establishing rate ranges, we are able to make individual merit increases within the established rate ranges.
3. Our aim is to provide as steady work as possible considering the nature of our business and priorities. Our record in this speaks for itself.
4. Each of you is protected in your right to present any question directly to the management, whether personal or related to employment, and to have it carefully and thoroughly considered.
5. No employee or group of employees can or will receive any advantage or preference over any other employee or group of employees because of union membership or union activity.
6. It is our policy to operate in such a way that any employee can work as long as he or she applies himself or herself to the job and there is work to do. No individual and no organization can secure for you any right or privilege that you cannot secure for yourself.
7. We will not become a party to any arrangement whereby your right to a job with this company depends on membership in a labor union.

We stand firmly on this proposition: Every employee shall be protected in his or her right to work irrespective of membership or nonmembership in any labor organization. Our relations in the past have been pleasant and harmonious, and we will do everything in our power to keep them that way.

Sincerely,
Filmore Electric Company
C. J. Filmore
President

Union Letter

April 10, 19XX

To All Employees of the Filmore Electric Company:

On Tuesday, April 16, 19XX, you will have a choice of voting to be represented by a labor union or to continue as individual workers.

In every election, in every public question, the views of the independent voter are eagerly sought, appreciated, and respected because they represent careful thinking and consideration of the issues. To every Filmore employee, of course, it is of vital importance to his or her individual welfare to join a labor organization that will take care of your problems from time to time.

Naturally, you will and should consider the question from what it will mean to *you* and *your family*; your *future* in industry; the benefits to be obtained; the conditions and circumstances under which you will work; elements that may eventually affect your *health, happiness,* and *prosperity.*

Those elements can be swung in either direction—*for or against your best interests*—in the long run depending on your choice of continuing to work as individuals or choosing to be represented by a real organization, *remember that*!

The International Electrical Workers Union is one of the most respected units of the American labor movement, with a record of many years of experience and consistent service for the cause of the American working man and woman.

The International Electrical Workers Union pledges its platform for *your* welfare.

1. *Higher wages.*
2. *Better shop conditions.*
3. *Improved fringe benefits.*

4. *Seniority.*
5. *A fair method of time study on jobs.*
6. *A fair grievance procedure.*

Read them again, and you will realize how important it is for you to vote for a bargaining agent to represent you—*what it means to you and your family in the trying days to come.*

Assert your independence! Vote to protect *yourself, your pocketbook, your family,* and *your future.* Remember, *your* vote is of the utmost importance to *you* and *your* fellow workers. On *your* decision rests the question of what the future may hold.

Cast your vote for the *union*—April 16th.

Remember: Together we stand—divided we fall.

Organizing Committee
International Electrical Workers Union, District 15
Affiliated with the AFL–CIO

Petri Chemical Company (B): The Promotion of Kenneth Rogers

THE MAINTENANCE DEPARTMENT

The maintenance department of the Lafayette plant was made up of seven craft groups, each under the supervision of a foreman. The organization of the department at the time of this case is shown in Exhibit C–55.

The union had been placing heavy pressure on the company to eliminate the practice of having managerial personnel perform work normally performed by union members. Also, it strongly objected to the practice of having union members assume temporary supervision over people in the craft group in the absence of the foreman. The union had negotiated the following contractual clause with the company.

Article VI

No member of management shall perform nonsupervisory manual work normally performed by personnel under his or her supervision. This shall not prevent management personnel from instructing employees or from operating new or revised equipment or processes or from performing such work in an emergency or for experimental purposes.

The employer agrees to replace supervisory personnel who are absent because of vacation, illness, and so on, with other managerial personnel.

THE PROMOTION OF KENNETH ROGERS

On Friday, July 31, Jim Counce, foreman of the carpenter shop in the Lafayette plant of the Petri Chemical Company, retired. On Monday, August 3, Kenneth Rogers, foreman of the riggers, assumed supervisory responsibilities over the carpenters.

All names and places are disguised. See Case–42 for background information.

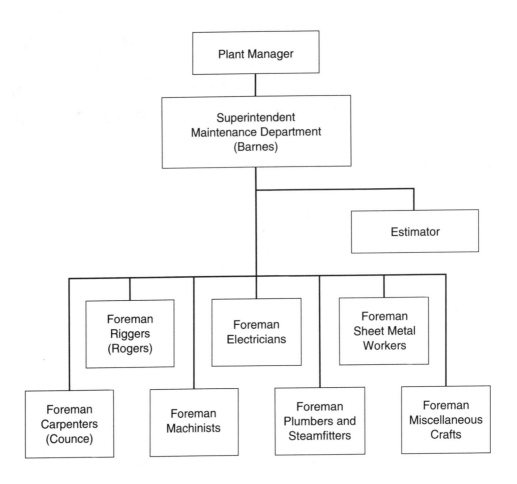

EXHIBIT C–55 Petri Chemical Company, Lafayette Plant

George Barnes, maintenance department superintendent, had been looking for a successor to Counce since the middle of July. Barnes finally had decided to place Kenneth Rogers over the carpenter shop, so on Saturday morning, August 1, Barnes posted an announcement of Rogers's appointment on the bulletin board. No one in the carpenter shop worked on Saturday. Barnes made no previous announcement of the appointment because, "I did not want to hurt Jim's feelings. I was afraid that if I asked him about his successor or announced his successor before he left, he would think that we were glad to be rid of him."

Jim Counce had worked for Petri for twenty-seven years, and he had been the foreman of the carpenter shop in the Lafayette plant for the last eleven years of that time. He supervised nine skilled carpenters. Counce, too, was a skilled craftsman who not only knew carpentry but also knew how to set up and repair the power woodworking machines, sharpen saws, and service other equipment. Because his supervisory duties did not require his full time, he spent about one-third of his time working alongside his people.

Rogers, the new foreman over the carpenters, was forty-five years old, and he had had three years of high school. Prior to coming to Petri, Rogers was a skilled bricklayer. Rogers had worked at Petri for nine years, the last five years of which he was foreman over the riggers. (Riggers at Petri did such work as move heavy machines and equipment, erect structural ironwork, and build concrete roads, floors, and walls.) Mr. Barnes expected Rogers to continue to supervise his crew of about fifteen riggers in addition to supervising the carpenter shop. The riggers were located in the same building as the carpenters, and Rogers's office adjoined the carpenter shop.

Rogers was considered one of the best maintenance foremen in the entire company. His crew was enlarged as it was discovered that he could supervise several projects simultaneously with no loss of efficiency. He was well liked by his crew, who always seemed to continue working at high efficiency even "when the boss wasn't around."

He was very quiet and seldom spoke up in the maintenance department meetings. He never raised his voice even in correcting a member of his crew.

Rogers liked to delegate responsibility to his crew; he solicited their ideas, and he often permitted them to do the job their way if he was convinced that they preferred their methods to his.

CANDIDATES FOR THE POSITION OF FOREMAN

Although Barnes had selected Rogers to be the new foreman, three other candidates considered themselves qualified. According to several carpenters, Robert Mangrum seriously considered himself a candidate for the position of foreman in the carpenter shop. Mangrum was sixty-two years of age and had worked at Petri for twenty-one years. He had more seniority than any other carpenter. About eight years ago, he was transferred to the maintenance shop of the Cartier plant, located a few blocks from the Lafayette plant, in preparation for promotion to the position of foreman of the maintenance department in the Cartier plant. Shortly after he was transferred, however, a physical examination showed that working conditions in the Cartier plant would be injurious to his health. He was then transferred back to the Lafayette plant. Mangrum expected to be promoted when Jim Counce retired.

Both Counce and a member of the plant human resources department had agreed that Mangrum was very capable. However, they also felt that he pushed the difficult and unpleasant jobs off on other carpenters whenever possible. They reported that he did not do as much of the work as he was capable of doing and that he did not work as hard as most of the other carpenters.

A member of the human resources department stated, "The other carpenters do not like Mangrum. They would not tolerate him as their foreman." One carpenter commented on Mangrum, "What do you think of a _____ like that? He spent two days cutting a hole in a roof that should have taken five hours—and then asked for a helper." Counce had stated that Mangrum was very seniority conscious.

Joe Emery also showed interest in being promoted when Jim Counce retired. In fact, when Mangrum was transferred back into the carpenter shop and announced that he expected to get the next promotion, Emery went to George Barnes to protest. Emery obtained assurance from Barnes that Mangrum was not in line for the job, and that he (Emery) was considered the most likely prospect.

Emery was forty-seven years of age and a widower. He had worked at Petri for nineteen years. Emery was considered by all his associates the best carpenter in the shop. He was regularly assigned all the cabinet work that had to be done. While the other carpenters liked cabinet work, they recognized the superior craftsmanship of Emery, and they did not resent the assignment of cabinet work to him. Emery was both respected and well liked by the other carpenters. A representative of the human resources department described him as "very neat, courteous, efficient, and businesslike. He would make a good lead man or foreman."

Although Wilbur Schuh was a third possible candidate for the foreman's job, Barnes had not seriously considered him for the position. Schuh was the union steward, forty-four years of age, and had worked for Petri for eleven years. He was liked by the other carpenters, but according to one supervisor, "Schuh is very outspoken and aggressive. At times he does not use good judgment in talking with his foreman and department head."

The other carpenters were not considered eligible for promotion at this time.

THE MONDAY MORNING MEETING

On Monday morning, the first work day following the posting of the notice of Rogers's appointment by Barnes, the carpenters congregated in the shop at the start of the shift waiting for the new foreman to appear. As Rogers and Barnes walked into the shop, Al Blount, the oldest carpenter in the shop, asked, "I want to know why a carpenter wasn't promoted to be our boss?" Before either Barnes or Rogers could reply, Mangrum exploded, "Who is going to change the jointer blades? If you think that I would run the jointer with Rogers making the setups, you're crazy! Besides, who is going to sharpen the saw blades around here?" Schuh joined in, "This is a lot of stuff. The men aren't going to stand for it. You can't treat us this way and expect us to take it. I'm filing a grievance in protest!"

Petri Chemical Company (C): Harry Thurman

THE GRIEVANCE

Robert Campbell, a foreman in the packing department at Petri Chemical Company, was walking through the department when Harry Thurman, a stock picker and department union shop steward, stopped him.

Thurman: Campbell, I'm filing a grievance today because I didn't get that promotion to stock clerk. I've been at Petri for eighteen years, and I've worked in packing for fourteen years. I can do the work in this department as well as anybody else. It's not fair to promote Bill Hendricks instead of me. Hendricks has been here only eight years. What does it take to get a promotion in this place? I think that I should get either a checker's or a stock clerk's job. Besides, the union contract says that when a man has the ability, seniority counts.

Campbell: Harry, I considered the matter carefully, and I decided that you didn't have the ability to do the stock clerk's job. Hendricks was the next highest in seniority, and he does have the ability. That's why he got the job when it came open.

Thurman: What in the hell do you mean, I don't have the ability? I've done the stock clerk's job many times in the past. You've never told me before that I couldn't handle it. It was my understanding that I'd get the next promotion in the department, since I have the highest seniority. This is a hell of a time to tell me that I don't have the ability to do what I've already done before.

Campbell: Nevertheless, that was my decision.

Thurman: You may think it's your decision now, but when the union gets through with you and your boss, you may think about it differently.

With that, Thurman walked away, and Robert Campbell wondered what his next move should be.

All names and wage data are disguised. See Cases–42 and –55 for background information.

BACKGROUND INFORMATION

The packing department of Petri Chemical Company packaged bulk chemicals into small containers, stored the packaged chemicals, and filled and shipped customer orders. Robert Campbell supervised the section that both stored the packaged items and filled and shipped customer orders.

Stock clerks were responsible for maintaining an adequate inventory of each item in stock. When a stock clerk noticed that a particular item had reached a predetermined minimum inventory, he filled out a work order that authorized the packaging sections to package more of that item. He also placed the various chemicals in their proper bins or storage areas and was further responsible for arranging stock so that the oldest stock would be shipped out first.

Stock pickers filled customer orders by passing through the aisles with a cart and placing the amount of each item listed on the invoice in the cart. Stock pickers were supposed to check each item against the invoice by both the stock number and product name.

Invoices were checked against the physical items by a *checker* to ensure accuracy of the order prior to the packing of the order by *packagers*.

Campbell insisted that orders be filled accurately. Errors in filling orders made the Petri Company liable for damage claims from customers. Petri had developed an excellent reputation for both quality and reliability. Errors would result in serious losses of good will.

Stock clerk and checker were considered the most important positions in determining the accuracy with which orders were filled. These jobs received $.62 per hour more base pay than did stock pickers and packers ($10.22 versus $9.60).

All employees in the packing department were compensated according to a task-and-bonus incentive plan. Under this plan a standard time allowance was computed for each task performed in the department. Completion of work within the standard time allowance enabled the employee to earn a 25 percent bonus. Hence, each employee had a strong incentive to complete his tasks within the time allowed.

At this time, Harry Thurman was forty-one years of age and married. He had completed high school. Robert Campbell, the foreman, had worked in the packing department for seven years. He was promoted to the position of foreman about five years ago.

Thurman had performed various duties in the packing department, including that of stock clerk when the regular clerks were on vacation. Campbell considered Thurman unsatisfactory as a stock clerk. According to Campbell, Thurman made too many errors in placing stock in the stock bins. Such errors slowed up the stock pickers and caused them to make errors in filling orders.

Also on several of these occasions, Thurman had been unable to meet the standard times allowed for shelving stock. In order not to lose his bonus, he made up several work orders authorizing the packaging sections to prepare more stock of the items indicated on the work orders. He did this even though the supply of these items had not reached the minimum established for reorder. By making up several of these work orders, Thurman was able to build up ample time credits to enable him to make his bonus. The effect of this practice was to upset production in the packaging sections and to build up excessive inventories of the items.

Harry Thurman also previously held the position of *vault man*. In this capacity, he was in charge of a locked vault containing valuable stock items. By his own admission, he was unqualified to hold this position. He made many errors in filling orders from stock, and he was unable to keep accurate control over inventories. He attributed some of his difficulties to poor vision. Robert Campbell believed that some of Thurman's difficulties in shelving and picking stock were a result of his defective vision. Campbell also felt that Thurman made more errors on his present job of stock picking than did other stock pickers. Although these errors were serious, the checkers often were able to catch them. Checkers knew that orders filled by Thurman often contained errors. As a consequence, they gave special attention to checking orders he had prepared. However, no records were kept concerning the number of errors for which Thurman was responsible.

Campbell believed that Harry Thurman lacked the ability and dependability necessary to be either a stock clerk or a checker. He further noted that Thurman was frequently absent from his work. In the previous year, he had been absent twenty days offering illness as his reason for frequent absences.

THE MEETING

Several days later, Robert Campbell was asked to meet with Rita Compton, the plant's human resources department manager, to discuss the grievance filed by the plant union on behalf of Harry Thurman.

Compton: Bob, in looking over Harry Thurman's employee record file, I noticed that his work performance has usually been rated average. I see no mention of discussions with him concerning unsatisfactory work. How was it that you passed him up for the stock clerk position?

Campbell: Look, Rita, I know and so does everybody else in the department that Thurman shouldn't get the stock clerk's job. He makes too many errors. I can't produce any records to prove it, but I know what I'm talking about. Isn't my evaluation enough when it comes to choosing the person most qualified for promotion?

Compton: It should be, Bob, but Thurman claims in his grievance that he's entitled to a chance at the stock clerk's job based on his seniority and past performance in the department. Here's what the contract says about it.

Compton showed Campbell Article V, Section 6, of the union contract, which provided that:

In filling vacancies or making promotions within a department or classification (except supervisory jobs), the Employer shall give preference to the employee having the greatest seniority in that department, provided, however, that ability and merit are equal. Any claims of personal prejudice or of discrimination may be subject to the grievance and arbitration procedure.

Campbell: Well, Rita, what do you suggest I do? I know I'm right. If I have to give Thurman the stock clerk's job, I'm going to have more trouble with departmental performance than I've ever had before.

Petri Chemical Company (D): Howard Evans

On a Tuesday afternoon during the spring busy season, Roger Lester, general production foreman of Petri's main plant, received his production schedules for the subsequent two weeks. Since the production of silver nitrate in building 11 was being increased substantially, Lester had requested five additional people who held the job-classification title of "chemical operator." Lester sought assistance from the HR department to select personnel for these jobs who had previous experience in producing silver nitrate. Among those assigned to Lester for the silver-nitrate production was Howard Evans, twenty-eight years old, a chemical operator with six years' experience at Petri.

On Thursday, Evans received a copy of the posted work schedule for the next week. The schedule indicated that he was to report to building 11 the following Monday morning to work on the silver-nitrate process. About 3:30 that afternoon, Evans walked into Roger Lester's office.

Evans: Why didn't you pick on someone else to work on silver nitrate? I want to remain on my present job. I was transferred to building 24 only a few weeks ago. I've just gotten to the point where I understand my new job. Now you are taking me away and putting me back on this job.

Lester: In other words, Howard, you feel that I am imposing on you by requesting your transfer?

Evans: I am beginning to believe that you bosses are totally inconsiderate around here. Do you realize that I have been moved six times in the past five months? I haven't been able to learn any of these jobs well. Just as I get to the point where I'm beginning to be able to do the work, one of you guys hauls me off to a different department.

Does everyone get moved around this much, or is there something wrong with me? Am I doing such a poor job that all my bosses are trying to get rid of me?

Lester: Remember, Howard, I did request that you be assigned to my department. And you do have the job title of "chemical operator," which means that we can use you as the demands of our business dictate, so long as you work in jobs that are basically similar in

---

All names are disguised. See Cases–42, –55, and –56 for background information.

nature. We've always done it this way. You've had prior experience in the silver-nitrate production process, and I felt we needed people like you to get over the spot we're in now.

Evans: Can't you guys plan your work? This is a poor way to run a department. No one shows any consideration for chemical operators. We get moved around like being on a checkerboard. And don't tell me that it's done fairly. No one ever asks us what we want to do.

Lester: I am sorry to learn that you feel this way about my department. I always thought that we clicked it off in a good manner.

Evans: Tell me, how long will I be here? Can I count on staying in this department from now on? Or am I going back to building 24 next week?

Lester: I can't promise that you will stay here. All I know is that we need production in silver nitrate for at least the next two weeks. I don't know what will happen after that.

Evans: I think I am getting a raw deal here. I'm going to see my union steward to file a grievance.

Howard Evans had worked in building 24 for five weeks before being transferred back to building 11, his former department. He had an excellent work record; in fact, most of his supervisors had given him a top rating on his semiannual employee evaluations. In recent months, however, several supervisors had commented that his previous enthusiasm and spirit on the job had diminished somewhat.

Two days following his conversation with Howard Evans, Roger Lester received a written grievance from the union steward, signed by Evans, that protested the "improper and indiscriminate transferring of chemical operators from job to job in violation of the contract." In studying Evans's grievance, Lester reviewed the union contract sections governing job transfers in the plant. The most pertinent clauses read as follows.

Section 1: Management Rights

(a) Cooperation between parties and the observance of the contract is the basis of all enduring agreements. The parties to this agreement recognize that stability in wages, working conditions, production, and competency and efficiency of workers are essential to the best interests of both employees and management and agree to strive to eliminate all factors that tend toward unstabilizing such conditions. It is understood that the administration and operation of the plant including but not limited to the

---

assignment, transfer, and disciplining of workers and the establishment of production-control procedures is the responsibility of Management …

Section 21: Transfers

The transferring of employees is the sole responsibility of Management subject to the following …
(b) It is the policy of Management to cooperate in every practical way with employees who desire transfers to new positions or vacancies in their department. Accordingly, such employees who make application to their foreman or the human resources department stating their desires, qualifications, and experience will be given preference for openings in their department provided they are capable of doing the job …

Lester decided to call the director of human resources to discuss a reply to the grievance and what courses of action might be taken.

CASE–58

The Disputed Overtime Work

Marie Caldwell worked as a production-line inspector at a bottling plant of the Sterling Brewery Company. The plant employees typically worked rotating shift schedules that were posted on a weekly basis on the plant bulletin board. They were represented by a local union of an international industrial labor organization.

Due to an error on her part in reading the posted schedule, Marie Caldwell reported for work at 11 P.M. on a Saturday night shift. Caldwell had not been scheduled to work, and she had not been called in although a small crew was scheduled to work this shift.

At about midnight, Caldwell's regular foreman, Steve Disney, entered the plant on a trouble call and questioned her regarding her presence in the plant. After some discussion, both realized that Caldwell had reported in error.

Because he had some inspection work available, Disney told Caldwell that she could finish out the shift. She worked a full eight-hour shift. Because this was her seventh consecutive day of work, by contract with the plant union, she was to be paid at the rate of double time.

Several days later, another employee, Alex Burns, filed a grievance because Caldwell had worked on a seventh day although she was junior to Burns in seniority. Burns claimed equal pay for the time Caldwell worked (eight hours at double-time pay). He claimed that in accordance with a well-established practice at the company, overtime had to be offered to employees in accordance with their seniority and their ability to perform the work involved.

At a grievance hearing a week later, the union shop steward, Bill Altobelli, argued that if Disney had sent Caldwell home after he found her working, no grievance would have been filed. However, since the company and the union both agreed that the past practice had been and still was to let the most senior employees work all overtime, the union should be upheld in this case. Burns should be paid for all time at the appropriate double-time rate that the junior seniority employee, Caldwell, had been paid.

Susan Scott, plant human resources director, replied that the company should not be obligated to pay another employee for sixteen hours. In consideration for Caldwell, who had reported by mistake at an inconvenient hour, the foreman had allowed her to work out a full shift instead of sending her

---

All names are disguised.

home with one hour's pay. Scott asserted that the grievance of the union was unjust and inequitable. No union employee had incurred any loss of work or income when the company had acted in a considerate manner. No one was scheduled to perform the extra work that evening. If Caldwell had not erroneously reported for work, no one would have performed that job that evening. In conclusion, Susan Scott stated, "Our decision in allowing her to continue to work should be commended and not condemned. I'm denying the union grievance accordingly!"

Altobelli responded, "Susan, I can't accept that decision. The union is prepared to take this case all the way to arbitration, if necessary, to maintain our rights under a long-standing plant practice!"

CASE–59

Olympic Corporation

BACKGROUND

Plant 37 of the Olympic Corporation was a large can-manufacturing plant located in a midwestern metropolitan area. The plant produced cans to serve various food, beverage, and other plants located in the same and nearby areas. Approximately six hundred workers in the plant were represented by Local 1213, United Industrial Workers Union, AFL–CIO.

The history of local union-management relationships during the plant's thirty years of operation was one that both the management and the union had described as "good." Only one strike had occurred at the plant; this was about twelve years ago during a national company contractual wage dispute. In general, local plant management felt that the local union's past leadership had been fairly reasonable in its demands and grievance processing.

Most of the jobs in the plant were classified as unskilled or semiskilled. The pay scales were considered to be above average for the type of work involved, and at the time of this case wages and fringe benefits did not constitute a major issue in union-management relationships because wages and benefits were negotiated nationally.

Local 1213 of the United Industrial Workers Union was led by its local president, Dan Maurice, who, by occupation, was a low-paid janitor in the plant. A management representative described Maurice in the following terms: "He seems driven by a desire for status. His ego was considerably inflated by his election to presidency of the union. He has a rebellious nature, having rebelled against his family, previous employers, and school. He even dropped out of school before completing the eighth grade." At the same time, however, Maurice's first two-year term of office as union president had been relatively satisfactory to plant management. Maurice had demonstrated a reasonable approach to plant problems, and he was considered by management to be "easy to talk to."

Although most workers in the plant usually appeared disinterested in union affairs, the recent election of union officers was one of the most "spirited" that management officials had observed in recent years. Dan Maurice won reelection to the union presidency for a second two-year term several months earlier in a closely contested election. His principal opposition had come from a faction of employees in the assembly department of the plant, a

---

All names are disguised.

faction that management considered to represent the most militant, anti-company element. Several preelection posters on union bulletin boards had accused Maurice of having "gone soft" with management and not "fighting hard enough for our rights." Plant management felt that Maurice's recent actions reflected a desire on his part to "prove" to the membership that he had not become "soft" as a union leader.

For several weeks immediately prior to Friday, October 6, Dan Maurice had displayed considerable impatience with management concerning a list of union grievances and complaints. Maurice insisted that he might have to "take action" for the union to "get all our problems out on the table." The union president contended that management was stalling in its handling of eight union grievances concerning disciplinary, contractual, and other matters. Tom Harper, plant personnel manager, told Maurice that management was trying to expedite the grievances as fast as possible, but several involved policy matters that had to be discussed and resolved with officials of the company at its headquarters office.

Two September incidents involving the union president also were indicative of his apparent growing resentment toward plant management at this time. In one, Maurice became involved in a loud argument with a supervisor in the quality-control department who had refused to man the department for Saturday work in accordance with the demands of Mr. Maurice. In another incident, Maurice dared a maintenance department supervisor to suspend a union shop steward who had been accused of "loafing on the job." This dare was taken up by the supervisor, who proceeded to suspend the union steward. However, the plant manager, Robert Palmer, recognized this incident to be trouble in the making, and the union steward was reinstated thirty minutes later. It was management's feeling that Dan Maurice tried to incite a walkout over this incident but was overruled by his membership.

THE WORK STOPPAGE

At 3 P.M. on Friday, October 6, Dan Maurice told Al Whitworth, press department foreman, that the press operator on presses 8A, 9A, 11A, and 12A was being subjected to a safety hazard. Presses 8A through 12A were in line with a metal platform (fourteen inches from the floor) placed in front of them to facilitate feeding operations on metal-goods parts. These presses were normally all fed by one individual, because one hopper load could run approximately thirty minutes and feeding time was approximately five minutes per machine. Press 10A had been turned around so that the platform continuity had been broken. For the operator to go from 8A and 9A to 11A and 12A, he or she had to step from the fourteen-inch platform, walk approximately ten feet, and step up on the platform again. This, Maurice said, constituted a safety hazard. Al Whitworth stated that he considered the situation somewhat inconvenient but not unsafe.

Whitworth returned to his department office and learned that his day foreman had started construction of a platform to fill the gap on the previous day, but construction had stopped because of a shortage of manpower and materials. Whitworth, therefore, told his night foreman, Sam Gore, to temporarily "double-man" the presses in question so that an operator would be on each side of the gap. Whitworth called Joe McCarthy, the union shop steward in the press department, and Bob Mueller, the union shop steward in the assembly department, to his office. He informed them that he did not think the present situation was unsafe, but that he would temporarily "double-man" the presses anyway. Both shop stewards were present when Whitworth again repeated his manning instructions to his night foreman, Sam Gore. At 4:50 P.M., Gore began an inventory check to determine which machine should be shut down to supply the extra worker. After checking the inventory, he found that the operators he wanted to contact concerning the manning procedure were absent on their scheduled rest period in the cafeteria.

About 5 P.M., Al Whitworth noticed that press lines near his office were not operating. He asked one employee why she was not working, and the employee said, "The union told me not to." Sam Gore returned from his unsuccessful manning attempt at 5:10 P.M. and found that the press department was completely shut down. In all, about fifty workers in the department had stopped working, and all equipment was turned off.

Whitworth immediately called Tom Harper, the plant personnel manager, by telephone at his home. Harper advised Whitworth to tell both union shop stewards that any employee not returning to work immediately would be suspended. This was done, and shortly after the shop stewards had returned to the plant floor, department operations resumed suddenly as though a signal had been given. The work stoppage had lasted approximately thirty-eight minutes.

Tom Harper arrived at the plant at 5:50 P.M. While he was talking to the press department foreman and the two shop stewards, Dan Maurice joined the meeting unexpectedly. Maurice had officially been off work for more than two hours. Tom Harper asked Joe McCarthy why press department operations had stopped. McCarthy said, "On orders from higher up. We're not working under unsafe conditions!" Harper then asked Bob Mueller if he had orders, and Dan Maurice immediately answered "no" for Mueller. Maurice later said, "They were my orders," but he would not say what his orders had been. The meeting was adjourned, and the two shop stewards went back to work.

At 6:30 P.M., the plant manager, Robert Palmer, arrived at the plant. Tom Harper had called Mr. Palmer earlier, but Palmer had been unable to get to the plant sooner. Harper and Palmer began an investigation of the stoppage, which included interviews with Al Whitworth and Sam Gore but not with any of the union representatives. In studying the contractual agreement between the company and union, they reread Article 15 of the contract, which stated:

The Union agrees that there will be no strikes of any type for any cause during the life of this Agreement.

The Company agrees that there will be no lockout.

If, during the life of this Agreement, any employees engage in any strike of any kind, stoppages of work or slowdowns, the International Officers, Local Officers, and paid representatives of the Union will cooperate with the Company in ending such occurrence and returning the employees to work.

Employees who engage in any of these acts may be discharged or disciplined by the Company but shall have recourse to the Grievance Procedure provided for in Article XIII of this Agreement.

"Do you know what this means, Tom?" said Palmer. "We could legally fire the whole department if we wanted to."

"The way things have been lately," replied Harper, "that's what's needed to shake things up around here. Do you know that Al and Sam estimated that with all the things going on, we lost more than an hour and a half production time? And if my figures are correct, that comes out to an operating production cost loss of $23,000."

"Well, Tom," said Palmer, "what do we do? It's 9:30 P.M. and getting late. Should we go home and sleep on it, or do you think we should take action now? Maybe we just ought to forget about the whole mess and get that platform fixed up before they decide to shut us down again. We're already way behind in production orders, and we can't afford any more lost time."

Harper replied, "I don't know, boss. It looks to me like this whole thing was all set up regardless of what we would do with the platform problem in the press department. A show of strength is involved, and I think we have to do something to show that they can't pull off stunts like this whenever they want to."

THE WALKOUT

After considerable discussion, Robert Palmer and Tom Harper finally reached a decision. They decided that the three union leaders involved—Maurice, McCarthy, and Mueller—should be suspended indefinitely.

Dan Maurice was located in the plant drinking coffee in the plant cafeteria with other union workers. Harper asked Maurice to come to the plant manager's office. About the same time, Al Whitworth informed stewards McCarthy and Mueller to leave their jobs and report to the plant manager's office.

It was 10 P.M. when Palmer informed the three men of his decision. "Boys, you're all suspended from your jobs until further notice. We'll let you know next week where we go from here." The three union men said nothing as they left Mr. Palmer's office.

At about 10:15 P.M., Palmer was preparing to go home when Tom Harper excitedly entered his office.

"Well, boss, I guess we did it now. They're shutting down the whole plant!"

Both men hurried to the plant floor, where it was apparent that a full-scale walkout was in progress. From all departments in the plant workers were shutting off their machines and leaving the plant. Palmer and Harper pleaded with several workers not to participate in an unauthorized walkout, but their pleas were unheeded. With the exception of the foremen, the management, and plant guards, the entire plant was emptied of workers in less than a half-hour.

Production had been scheduled for Saturday, October 7. However, members of the United Industrial Workers Union did not work, and pickets were patrolling the sidewalks around the plant.

Palmer contacted Felix Schulte, an International Union representative for the area, on Saturday morning. Schulte apparently had not heard all the details of the situation, but he could not understand why the three union men had been suspended, since the press department had gone back to work after the thirty-eight-minute stoppage. Schulte wanted the suspensions lifted; then he would see what he could do about getting the people back to work.

Palmer told Schulte that he could not overlook a thirty-eight-minute work stoppage, and that the employees must return to work before he would discuss the suspensions.

The walkout remained in effect on the first shift of Monday, October 9.

Palmer and Harper had arranged to meet Mr. Schulte in the latter's office to again talk over the situation. They again demanded that the employees return to work before any discussion of the suspensions could begin. At this meeting, Schulte was more cooperative and said that the employees would be ordered back to work. His order was carried out, and normal plant operations resumed on the second shift of the same day, Monday, October 9.

THE MEETING

A hearing was scheduled at the plant on Thursday, October 12, to allow management and union to present their views. The meeting was attended by Robert Palmer and Tom Harper for the company, and by Dan Maurice, Joe McCarthy, Bob Mueller, and Felix Schulte for the union. In addition, each side had an observer taking notes. At this meeting, all union representatives denied having led the walkout. Maurice denied that he gave orders for the walkout. McCarthy denied having said that he "acted on orders from higher up." They both insisted that the only orders given were the usual ones left by Maurice when he left the plant, which were, "Call me if something comes up that you can't handle." The union insisted that the walkout was a "spontaneous reaction of the workers" against management's "unfair actions" and to "protest unsafe working conditions" in the plant.

The union insisted in the meeting that a safety hazard had existed in the press department. Management responded that operators had worked off the platforms all day with no thought of safety involved. The company would admit that the situation was inconvenient but not unsafe.

At the conclusion of the hearing, Palmer said that the company felt that Dan Maurice should be fired and that the two stewards should be suspended for thirty days. However, if the International and Local union "would recognize their responsibility in preventing such occurrences in the future and not file a grievance," the punishment would be reduced to a thirty-day suspension for Maurice and a one-week suspension for each of the shop stewards. After some discussion, Maurice ceremoniously accepted this decision by tearing an already typed grievance into shreds. All parties concerned signed a statement accepting the conditions and promised to carry the matter no further.

The company later mailed a written warning to each union employee who had walked out or who had not reported to work as scheduled. A copy of the warning letter was placed in each employee's permanent record file. This letter follows.

To: All Employee Members of the United Industrial Workers
　　Union—Local 1213

I feel it necessary in view of the disruption of plant operations commencing Friday evening, October 6, to point out your responsibilities as union officers and members in participating and/or directing such demonstrations.

On Friday evening, October 6, there was an interruption of work in the press department that later led to all employees in the union local leaving the plant. No scheduled overtime was worked on Saturday, October 7, nor did employees report for work as scheduled on Monday, October 9.

Here at Plant 37, we are greatly disturbed that your local union officers would instigate and/or condone such activity in spite of the clear meaning of our contract agreement in this regard. Further, we feel each of you has a responsibility, as a union member, to respect this and all portions of the contract, and we in turn will do the utmost to administer it in like manner.

I feel we have a fine plant here, and under the right circumstances it could continue to offer full employment to many fine individuals who take pride in their work and their company. However, we cannot expect our stockholders and top management to continue to invest money in expan-

---

sion or even maintain our operation if it will be plagued by slowdowns, work stoppages, and the like in the future.

Because this recent work stoppage was in direct violation of our contract agreement and because of your obvious participation in it, we intend to make it a matter of record that will be held for review in the event you are involved in any similar act or violation in the future.

Robert Palmer,
Plant Manager

EPILOGUE

Management hoped that plant efficiency would be improved after the walkout. However, during the first month after the walkout, production was 25 percent below plant efficiency standards for the previous month of October. Management claimed that it was a "union retaliatory slowdown," but nothing conclusive could be ascertained concerning whether a deliberate slowdown was taking place.

The two suspended union shop stewards did not suffer financially from their one-week suspensions. Union members in their respective departments contributed to a union collection that paid the shop stewards equivalent weekly wages for their week of layoff.

When Dan Maurice, the local president, returned to work from his thirty-day suspension, management found that the suspension had brought little change in his approach to in-plant relationships. Several managers stated that Maurice was deliberately trying to antagonize supervisors by his activities.

Production continued to lag in November, and grievances filed by union personnel during the month were higher in number than for any previous month during the year. Management considered most of these grievances to be trivial and "harassment tactics."

Robert Palmer decided to meet with Tom Harper and other members of plant management to discuss the plant situation. At a Wednesday morning meeting, Palmer opened the meeting by stating:

The situation in this plant continues to deteriorate. Our production efficiency is about 30 percent below standard. The union is making life miserable for us. The people are openly defiant of our supervisors. We've got to do something—and fast,—to straighten this thing out.

EXERCISE–23

The Union Organizer at Morgan City Hospital

You are an organizer for a leading union in the health care field. You have been given the assignment to organize the Morgan City Hospital employees. You were told to explore the possibility of a combined bargaining unit—professional, technical, and nonprofessional employees—even though your union usually represents only technical and nonprofessional employees.

Morgan City Hospital has two hundred fifty beds and is located centrally in a semi-industrial, farm center city of sixty-eight thousand. The hospital administration and its governing body have clearly indicated to their employees that they think a union would be a serious detriment to the hospital's excellent medical and patient care record. Although typically underpaid compared to many jobs in the community—about 10 to 20 percent less than other employers pay for comparable jobs—many of the five hundred employees have been with the hospital for years. Most supervisory employees have been with the hospital for ten years or more.

At present, you have ten to twelve employees feeding you information. Perhaps one or two of these are potential union leaders, but you need more to build a core of union leadership for a successful organizing effort.

Seniority appears to play a very minor role in dealing with decisions affecting the employees, unless the "cronyism" of some of the older employees can be considered to represent the use of seniority in handing out job and shift assignments. The hospital's fringe package was slow in developing and is quite inferior to the fringes of the majority of employers in the city. There is no mechanism for professional employees to have input into the policies and procedures affecting patient care, and there have been rumors of such employees leaving for this reason alone.

Your backers in the hospital have given you information about certain situations they have observed. That information is attached. You are going to the homes of these employees with the objective of getting them to sign a card that will request a National Labor Relations Board (NLRB) election.[1] What will you say to each of these individuals? You are also interested in securing members of an organizing committee.

This exercise was prepared by Professor James A. Lee of the College of Business Administration of Ohio University at Athens. All names are disguised. Used by permission.
[1]See Appendix to this case for explanatory notes concerning the Labor Management Relations Act that could apply in this exercise and in a number of other exercises/cases in Part Six.

CAROL SIMMONS

Carol Simmons is twenty-five years old; she has been at Morgan City Hospital for one year. When she first was hired, she took a job as ward clerk because that was the only job open. She had graduated with a B.S.W. (bachelor of social work) from an accredited school a few months prior to being hired.

After she had been with the hospital for two months, a position came up in the social work department, but Carol hesitated to apply because she was fairly new and was still on her three-month new employee probation.

Recently, a third medical social worker position was created. A new graduate with no previous experience was being seriously considered. Carol filed an application with the human resources director and was told she had no relevant on-the-job experience since her internship in school.

Carol is angry and feels the main reason she was not being considered for this position was the fact that if she left her second-floor ward-clerk position, a new person would have to be found and trained and this would cost the hospital money.

TOM NELSON

Tom Nelson is an "old-timer" with the hospital. Tom is fifty-seven years old and has been with Morgan since he was thirty-three. He is employed as a boiler tender in the plant powerhouse, tending high pressure steam boilers used mainly for plant heating. As boiler tender, it is necessary that he be in the vicinity of the boilers at all times, but there is very little activity required on his part unless there is equipment failure.

During the past year, as a result of a cost-reduction program, Tom has been told by his supervisor that he would do the painting in the interior of the boiler house. This means doing a wash job and repainting the walls, machinery, floors, and so on. He feels that this is not part of his job and is also concerned that the two company painters in maintenance are going to be "down on him" for "stealing" part of their job. Tom also feels that he needs to be alert to possible equipment failures that might lead to loss of power, damage to the boilers, or even injury to patients and employees.

Tom doesn't want to be too active in his opposition in front of his supervisor, because he is getting on toward retirement. He has, however, been griping to many other workers.

LINDA COLES AND SARAH BRIGHT

Staffing of the night shift of the obstetrics (OB) ward has been a problem, especially after two full-time licensed practical nurses (LPNs) on the night shift left the hospital for higher-paying, dayshift LPN positions in a nursing home in the city. The head nurse had "strongly requested" all LPNs on the

7 A.M. to 3 P.M. and 3 P.M. to 11 P.M. shifts to take a rotation every three weeks to be "on call"—that is, to be available for the 11 P.M. to 7 A.M. shift if the patient load dictated. Linda Coles and Sarah Bright, full-time day LPNs who had been with the hospital two and three years, respectively, refused on-call status, stating that OB was too demanding physically. Also, they did not feel they could function well if they had worked 7 A.M. to 3 P.M., went home from 3:30 to 11 P.M., were called in to work 11 P.M. to 7 A.M., and then had to show up for their regularly scheduled 7 A.M. to 3 P.M. shift that morning. They felt that possibly working twenty-four out of thirty-six consecutive hours was too physically and mentally demanding, except on an occasional emergency basis. Linda and Sarah approached their head nurse and complained about being "forced" to take on-call status. When the next staffing schedule was posted, both Linda and Sarah found they were scheduled to work two weeks on the 11 P.M. to 7 A.M. shift.

SAM SPENCER

Sam Spencer had been selected among the cleanup and janitorial crews to operate the new mechanical riding sweeper, which was purchased to reduce the amount of time required to clean all of the hospital aisles. This would permit more janitorial time on off-aisle cleanup that had been done on little more than a "catch-as-catch-can" basis. Sam learned to operate the new sweeper quickly and managed to clean all the aisles in less than two hours after running it for a couple of weeks.

Only then did Sam begin to think about an increased rate of pay for running the sweeper two hours each day. At first, he told his supervisor he ought to get the next labor grade higher because he was required to do his regular janitorial work and operate the sweeper. His supervisor said he didn't see why, because operating the sweeper was easier work and less tiring than bending over and pushing a broom or running a waxer. A few weeks later, Sam came back and asked why he couldn't get a higher rate of pay for the time during which he operated the sweeper, because other employees in the area were paid higher rates for temporary higher-level work. His supervisor reminded him that this was a hospital and that the hospital couldn't afford some of the luxuries that some industrial workers enjoyed. The supervisor also mentioned that working conditions in the hospital were far superior to the cleaning work conditions in factories. Then he asked Sam if he wanted off the mechanical sweeper job. Sam said no and left.

FRANK JAZINSKI

Frank Jazinski was a "first-rate" laboratory technician, according to your sources of information. Although he had had little formal professional training, he was hired because he seemed extremely intelligent and because of a shortage of trained, experienced lab technicians. For the first six months, Frank was a diligent worker who showed his intelligence through speed, accuracy, and ingenuity.

One day, he brought the hospital employee's "handbook"—a fifteen-page booklet—to the head lab technician and announced that he wanted to ask some questions about the fringe benefits. More specifically, he told his boss that he wanted to know the exact ratio of contributions made by the hospital to the pension fund as compared with those made by employees. His supervisor took the handbook from his hand and turned to the insurance section and pointed out a statement that said the hospital contributions amounted to "more than half" of the total pension cost. Frank responded that he could read, and said that he wanted to know the exact ratio of contributions by each of the parties. His supervisor said that she didn't have those figures, but that she would see if the human resources department would release them. A few days later, she stopped by where Frank was running some tests and told him that the HR department wouldn't give him the figures because there was quite a variation in the contribution amounts, depending upon length of service, number of dependents, and the employees' ages.

SUE WEBB

Sue Webb was selected among the medical record staff typists to operate a new word processing and information system that was purchased to reduce the amount of time required to complete discharge summaries on patient charts after they were dictated by physicians. Sue learned to operate the new word processor quickly and managed to complete a day's workload in seven hours. Only then did Sue begin to think she deserved an increased rate of pay for the volume of work done. At first, she brought this to the attention of her supervisor, the head medical records librarian, and told her that using the word processor enabled her to do her normal workload plus additional microfilming. The head medical records librarian said she didn't see why a pay increase was deserved because using the new word processor was less tiring and easier to use than the old machine. Sue accepted this explanation but was very dissatisfied. A few weeks later, Sue went back to her supervisor to again make her point.

APPENDIX: AN OVERVIEW OF THE LABOR MANAGEMENT RELATIONS ACT

The Morgan City Hospital comes under the jurisdiction of the Labor Management Relations Act (LMRA) of 1947, as amended in 1974. Without becoming too technical in explaining the significance of the LMRA, it is important to understand that hospital employees have the right to bargain collectively through representatives of their own choosing, and to engage in (or refrain from) certain other concerted activities. For example, they have the right to join a union, refrain from joining a union, select a union to represent them, and negotiate with their employer in an effort to obtain improved wages, hours, or other conditions of employment.

The National Labor Relations Board (NLRB) is the federal agency that administers this law for most employers in the private sector. The NLRB will determine the appropriate bargaining unit(s). However, professional employees (such as nurses) may not be included in the same bargaining unit with nonprofessional employees, unless a majority of the professional employees agree to do so. Usually, the NLRB will conduct an election to determine whether a union will gain representation rights for employees in the appropriate bargaining unit(s). If a majority of employees votes to have the union represent them, the union becomes the exclusive representative for all of the employees in that bargaining unit.

Employers are prohibited from engaging in practices that would interfere with, restrain, or coerce employees in their right to organize, join a union, and bargain collectively. For example, employers may not threaten employees with loss of jobs or benefits if they should vote for or join a union, question employees about their union activities or membership under such circumstances as would tend to restrain or coerce the employees, spy on union gatherings, grant wage increases deliberately timed to discourage employees from forming or joining a union, or threaten to deny employees rights and privileges they currently enjoy if the union wins bargaining rights for the employees.

An employer also may not discriminate in hiring or in the tenure of employment or any term or condition of employment that tends to encourage or discourage membership in any labor organization. For example, an employer is prohibited from discharging employees because they have urged other employees to join a union and from demoting or denying transfers or promotions to employees because they circulated a petition among other employees asking the employer for an increase in pay or a change in the terms of employment.

The LMRA also makes certain acts of labor unions unfair labor practices. A union or its agents are forbidden to restrain or coerce employees in the exercise of their rights to either join or not join a labor union. For example, a union may not threaten employees that they will lose their jobs unless they support the union's activities to gain representation rights.

Employers are permitted to express their views, arguments, or opinions so long as such expression contains no threat of reprisal or force or promise of benefit. Thus, employers have rights to state their point of view and to present their case against joining a union. However, an employer may not threaten employees that they will lose their jobs if the union wins a majority vote in the hospital, plant, or office.

Finally, both parties must bargain in good faith. Section 8(d) of LMRA imposes on both parties the mutual obligation:

to meet at reasonable times and confer in good faith with respect to wages, hours, and other terms and conditions of employment or the negotiation of an agreement or any question arising thereunder and the execution of a written contract incorporating any agreement reached if requested by either party, but such obligation does not compel either party to agree to a proposal or require the making of a concession.

This duty to bargain covers all matters concerning rates of pay, hours of employment, or other conditions of employment. As determined by the NLRB, mandatory subjects of bargaining include but are not limited to such matters as pensions for present and retired employees, bonuses, group insurance, grievance procedure, safety practices, seniority, procedures for discharge, layoff, recall, or discipline, and the union shop. On nonmandatory subjects—that is, matters that are lawful but not related to "wages, hours, and other conditions of employment"—the parties are free to bargain and to agree, but neither party may insist on bargaining on such subjects over the objection of the other party.

This brief discussion about the LMRA should be helpful concerning the types of issues that may arise as you, the labor union organizer, meet with the aforementioned and other employees of the Morgan City Hospital. For further information about the LMRA, see Raymond L. Hilgert and Sterling H. Schoen, *Cases in Collective Bargaining and Industrial Relations*, 8th ed. (Chicago, IL: Richard D. Irwin, 1996), pp. 3–50.

An Organizing Question on Campus

You are Art Tipton, human resources director of Pierce University, a private university located in a large urban city.[1] Ruth Ann Zimmer, a supervisor in the maintenance and housekeeping services division of the university, has just come into your office to discuss her situation. Zimmer's division of the university is responsible for maintaining and cleaning physical facilities of the university. Zimmer is one of the departmental supervisors who supervises employees who maintain and clean on-campus dormitories.

In the next several minutes, Zimmer proceeds to express her concerns about a union-organizing campaign that has begun among her employees. According to Zimmer, a representative of the Service Workers Union has met with a number of your employees urging them to sign union authorization cards. She has observed several of her employees "cornering" other employees talking to them about joining the union and urging them to sign union authorization (or representation) cards. Zimmer even observed this during the working hours as employees were going about their normal duties in the dormitories. Zimmer reports that a number of her employees have come to her asking for her opinions about the union. They reported to her that several other supervisors in the department had told their employees not to sign any union authorization cards and not to talk about the union at any time while they were on campus. Zimmer also reports that one of her fellow-supervisors told his employees in a meeting that anyone who would be caught talking about the union or signing a union authorization card would be disciplined and perhaps terminated.

Zimmer says that the employees are very dissatisfied with their wages and many of the conditions that they have endured from students, supervisors, and other staff people. She says that several employees told her that they had signed union cards because they believed that the only way that university administration would pay attention to their concerns was if the employees had a union to represent them. Zimmer says that she made a list of employees whom she felt had joined or were interested in the union, and she could share these with you if you wanted to deal with them personally. Zimmer closes her presentation with the comment that she and other departmental supervisors need to know what they should do in order to "stamp out" the threat of unionization in their department.

---

[1] All names are disguised. See Case–43, "Salary Discrimination among the Library Staff," for a previous case involving this campus.

You (Art Tipton) have listened patiently to Zimmer's remarks, and you know that you must advise her concerning what she should and should not do. You have heard rumors about another union circulating union representational petitions at the campus library. However, you were unaware of this effort by the Service Workers Union among campus blue-collar employees. You recognize that the problem goes beyond Ruth Ann Zimmer's individual concerns. You collect your thoughts in order to respond to Ruth Ann Zimmer.

EXERCISE–25

Suspended for "Goofing Off"

Assignment: You are the impartial arbitrator selected by the company and the union to render a final and binding decision in this matter. Your decision should include a thorough presentation of the reasoning that you utilized in making your final determination.

BACKGROUND

The Margolis Machinery Company, located in a major city in a northeastern state, designed and manufactured to order various machine shop tools and production machinery. Plant and certain office employees, including the tool design group, were represented by the National Federation of Machinists Union, Local 2521.

On October 30, David Clements, the supervisor of the tool design group, noticed employee Betty Stone looking at something in the drawer of her drafting table. After a minute or two had elapsed, he walked to Stone's table. As he approached, Stone closed the drawer. The following conversation then took place.

Clements: What are you looking at?

Stone: I'm looking up information.

Clements: What kind of information?

Stone: Just information.

At this point, supervisor Clements opened the drawer of Stone's table and saw an open magazine covered with a sheet of transparent plastic. Clements accused Stone of reading a magazine and "goofing off" on company time. Stone replied, "I wasn't reading a magazine, and even if I was—so what!"

Supervisor Clements went to his office and called a company labor-relations representative, a union shop steward, and Ms. Stone to his office for a review of what happened. During the meeting, Stone was suspended for four-and-a-half days.

Stone checked out at about 11 A.M. on October 30, and on October 31 she filed the following union grievance:

All names and locations are disguised.

Management was in violation of the contract by giving me a citation and suspension, based on false accusations and not true facts, which in turn constituted unjust cause for suspension. Request to discontinue violation of contract. Restore pay for any loss of time, due to unjust suspension, and removal of citation from my record.

The matter was processed through the grievance procedure and was eventually taken to arbitration.

POSITION OF THE UNION

The position of the union was that the company had decided to "bully" the grievant and had used a "collection of trivia" as an excuse to suspend her.

Betty Stone testified that she was looking up bushing sizes in a catalog in her briefcase—which was in her drawer—and that she was also consulting a decimal conversion table pasted on the outside of the briefcase. Stone contended, in contradiction to company witnesses, that she needed these bushing sizes and decimal conversions for the job on which she was working. She accounted for some extra time she had spent on a mill fixture design on which she was working by stating that she prepared an additional sheet, which she had shown her supervisor, but which he refused to accept or believe. Stone denied that she was reading a magazine.

Stone and the union did not deny that when Clements opened the drawer (which Stone had closed on the supervisor's approach), he saw a magazine covered with a piece of transparent plastic material. Supervisor Clements had said the plastic was clear, but Stone said it was dark and that she kept it to put over glossy surfaces to reduce the glare. Stone claimed that she could not have been reading because of the dark plastic that was covering the magazine.

In closing arguments, the union's business representative claimed that the company had overreacted in this matter, and that the company had failed to prove anything. The company had simply relied upon Clements' opinion, not objective proof about what really happened. Even if the arbitrator would rule that Stone did violate a company rule by reading a magazine during business hours, the punishment imposed by the company was far too severe for such a minor infraction. The four-and-one-half-day suspension should be reduced to a written warning at most, and Stone should be reimbursed for the pay she lost while she was serving her unjust suspension.

POSITION OF THE COMPANY

The company strongly contended that Betty Stone was reading private material—that is, a magazine—during working hours, even though the evidence in part was circumstantial.

The position of the company was that Stone gave every appearance of reading a magazine lying open in her drawer and covered with a piece of transparent plastic. As for Stone's explanation that she was looking up bushing sizes and consulting a decimal conversion table, supervisor Clements testified that when he first looked into the drawer he saw, in addition to the plastic-covered magazine, several catalogs but no briefcase. He testified that after Stone checked out, he again looked into the drawer and this time saw a briefcase with a decimal conversion table fastened to the outside cover with "what appeared to be freshly applied masking tape."

Several company witnesses offered their opinions that it was not necessary for Stone either to look up bushing sizes in a catalog or to consult a conversion table because bushings should not be used for the job Stone was doing. Further, they claimed that on this particular job, the dimensions "from the screw to each of the dowels" were not fixed on the blueprint but were discretionary with the toolmaker. So, even if Stone needed any dimensions (which was denied by the company witnesses), Stone would not get them from the blueprint but from the toolmaker after the part was made in the shop. Hence, the reason Stone gave for looking into her drawer was "doubly spurious."

The company's director of labor relations summarized the company's position by referring to the current labor management agreement, which included the following provision:

Article II, Section 1

The Company has and will retain the right and power to manage the plant and direct the working forces, including the right to suspend or discharge for just cause.

All company witnesses maintained that, in their judgment, employee Stone must have been reading a magazine during working hours. In the absence of any proof to the contrary, management's judgment in this matter should be considered valid. Therefore, the disciplinary suspension met the just-cause standard. The company urged the arbitrator not to disturb the disciplinary suspension given to Betty Stone and to deny the union grievance.

EXERCISE–26

The Disorderly Refrigerator

Assignment: You are the impartial arbitrator selected by the company and the union to render a final and binding decision in this matter. Your decision should include a thorough presentation of the reasoning that you used in making your final determination.

BACKGROUND

Value Brands Corporation was a large distributor and retailer of several brand names of breads and cakes. The Hoover, Michigan, branch employed eight driver-salespersons and five sales clerks who were members of a local of the Teamsters Union. The company had outgrown its former building and decided to move to a new location which would house the branch office, a garage for delivery trucks, a storage area, and a thrift store.

The new distribution facilities and thrift store were located about three blocks from the previous facility. Shortly after the move, Tina Heuser, the branch manager, noticed that the employees had moved their old refrigerator to a space in the garage of the new building. She immediately discussed the matter with supervisor Bill Murata. Murata subsequently informed the employees that the old refrigerator constituted a health and safety hazard and that the refrigerator would have to be removed from the new building within twenty-four hours. The employees protested his directive, and through their union they filed the following grievance:

> No refrigerator in new depot for cooling of perishable lunch items. There was one in the old depot, which was past practice. This is a violation, we feel, of Article VII, Maintenance of Standards.

The disputed refrigerator dated back to about ten years previously when the employees had gotten together and purchased an old refrigerator. They had used it to store soft drinks, cold cuts, cheese, and other snack and lunch foods. The refrigerator was placed in the garage near the rear entrance to the store. It was the type that required defrosting, especially during the summer months when it received heavy use. The refrigerator enabled the employees to bring

---

All names and locations are disguised.

their lunch from home or prepare it at work, thus saving the costs of gasoline for travel and the cost of eating out. This also gave them time and opportunity for socializing and relaxation.

The grievance was not settled during steps of the grievance procedure, and the parties submitted the following issue to the arbitrator:

> Did the company violate the collective bargaining agreement when it refused to permit employees to keep a refrigerator in the new depot for the same purposes as the refrigerator was kept in the old depot prior to the physical relocation of operations? If so, what should be the remedy?

POSITION OF THE UNION

The union maintained that the company's action violated Article VII of the parties' collective bargaining agreement by unilaterally changing the employees' working conditions without negotiating the matter with the union. This article read as follows:

Article VII—*Maintenance of Standards*

The employer agrees that all conditions of employment relating to wages, hours of work, and general working conditions shall be maintained in no less than the highest minimum standards in effect at the time of the signing of this Agreement, and the conditions of employment shall be improved whenever specific provisions for improvement are made elsewhere in this Agreement.

The union pointed out that employees had used the refrigerator for some ten years without prior objection by management. No one in the company had complained about the alleged unsanitary conditions or any safety problems created by the refrigerator until after the move to the new facility.

The union also argued that in the absence of a refrigerator, some employees would have to buy their lunch and incur the expense of driving to a fast-food diner. Some employees earned low wages, and this would constitute a financial burden for them. Further, the union pointed out that sales clerks had only one half-hour for lunch on a variable schedule, and the absence of a refrigerator on company premises imposed a hardship on them if they had to go out for lunch.

The union contended that as a well-understood past practice, employees should have the right to keep a refrigerator in the new building. This was an important working condition that could not be changed unilaterally by management. The remedy sought by the union was that employees should be permitted to keep a refrigerator in the new building as they had in the old facility prior to the move.

POSITION OF THE COMPANY

The company argued that the presence of a refrigerator in the building did not constitute a "general working condition," as that term was used in Article VII of the agreement. The company contended that the refrigerator had not been maintained in a sanitary condition, and that it constituted a safety hazard because of water collecting on the floor during defrosting. Management's responsibility was to maintain its new facility in a sanitary and safe condition, and management was responsible for violations of sanitation and safety standards under federal and state laws. This had become more serious under regulations of the Food and Drug Administration (FDA) and the Occupational Safety and Health Act (OSHA). The company claimed that each time the refrigerator was defrosted, water accumulated on the floor and was tracked into the store where it created a safety hazard. Since the employees owned and used the refrigerator, in the past the company felt that it was not possible for management to force them to maintain it in a sanitary and safe manner.

Experience over the years had demonstrated that the employees would not maintain the refrigerator in a sanitary and safe condition. The company had tolerated this in the old building, but the company was not willing to tolerate this in its brand new facility. The company cited Article XXV of the parties' collective bargaining agreement, which stated:

Article XXV—*Management Control*

The control, operation and direction of the Company and all aspects of the business is the exclusive right of management, and such rights shall not be limited unless specifically restricted by a provision within this Agreement.

The Company's failure to exercise any function or rights reserved to it, or its exercise of any function or right in a particular way, shall not be deemed a waiver of its authority to exercise such right or function in a particular way, nor preclude the Company from exercising the same in some other way not in conflict with the express provisions of this Agreement.

The company argued that it had acted within its reserved management rights under Article XXV in denying employees the use of the refrigerator in the new facility. The company requested that the grievance be denied.